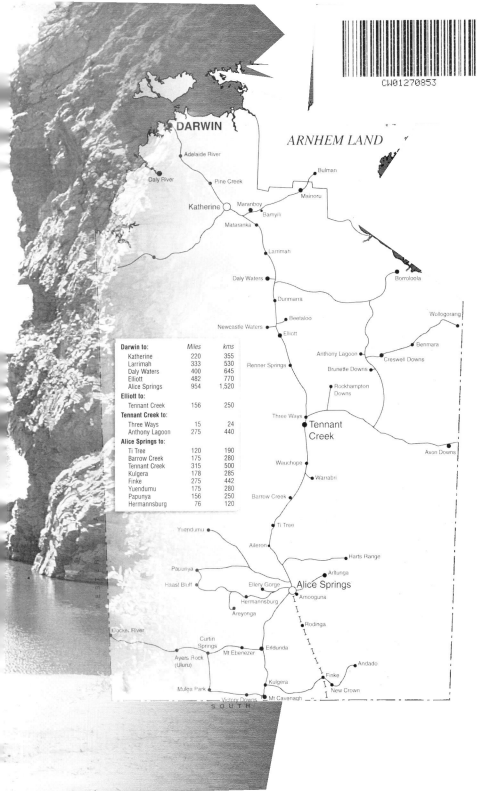

CW01270853

DARWIN

ARNHEM LAND

Adelaide River

Daly River

Pine Creek

Bulman

Katherine

Maranboy

Mainoru

Bamyili

Mataranka

Larrimah

Borroloola

Daly Waters

Dunmarra

Beetaloo

Newcastle Waters

Elliott

Wollogorang

Anthony Lagoon

Benmara

Renner Springs

Creswell Downs

Brunette Downs

Rockhampton
Downs

Three Ways

**Tennant
Creek**

Avon Downs

Wauchope

Warrabri

Barrow Creek

Ti Tree

Yuendumu

Aileron

Harts Range

Papunya

Arltunga

Haast Bluff

Ellery Gorge

Alice Springs

Hermannsburg

Amooguna

Areyonga

Rodinga

Docker River

Curtin
Springs

Erldunda

Ayers Rock
(Uluru)

Mt Ebenezer

Andado

Mulga Park

Kulgera

Finke

New Crown

Victory Downs

Mt Cavenagh

S O U T H

Darwin to:	Miles	kms
Katherine	220	355
Larrimah	333	530
Daly Waters	400	645
Elliott	482	770
Alice Springs	954	1,520
Elliott to:		
Tennant Creek	156	250
Tennant Creek to:		
Three Ways	15	24
Anthony Lagoon	275	440
Alice Springs to:		
Ti Tree	120	190
Barrow Creek	175	280
Tennant Creek	315	500
Kulgera	178	285
Finke	275	442
Yuendumu	175	280
Papunya	156	250
Hermannsburg	76	120

OUTBACK IN UNIFORM

I took adventure

OUTBACK IN
UNIFORM

by David Pollock

ISBN 0-646-37617-9

Published by
David L. Pollock, PO Box 517, Malvern, Victoria, 3144, Australia
e-mail: outbackinuniform@yahoo.com

Proudly designed, typeset, printed & bound in Australia
Fast Impressions Pty Ltd, 2 Kembla Street, Cheltenham, Victoria

Cover design by Craig Stephens

DEDICATED
TO

MUM AND DAD

FOR THEIR LOVE AND SUPPORT
ALL MY LIFE

Acknowledgements

First, I must thank Mum for the foresight of keeping all my letters which have been invaluable in recording when and where, jogging my memory, the closest thing to having kept a diary. While writing the book I've been able to speak to several former colleagues to confirm a point or remember a name. I thank them all. I am grateful to Mick Palmer who readily agreed to write the foreword.

My mate from football administration days Dean Newman not only picked up on my spelling (computers haven't improved it) but also made a suggestion or two to reduce the "police speak". Thanks Dean.

The enthusiasm of Garry Sidwell and his team at Fast Impressions to print and help me publish the book is much appreciated. Their pride in their work is exhibited by what you hold in your hand.

I thank the Northern Territory Police Association and the Retired Police Association of the Northern Territory for their help in launching the book during the 60th Anniversary of the Establishment of the Northern Territory Police Association Police Re-Union, Darwin, September, 1999.

Above all, I thank those responsible for giving me the opportunity to serve in the Northern Territory Police, the men and women I had the great pleasure to work with and no less the people of the Northern Territory who I had the honour to serve while at the same time providing me with some of the best years of my life.

Contents

Illustrations

Foreword

By Commissioner Mick Palmer,
Australian Federal Police and former Commissioner,
Northern Territory Police

Occasionally an opportunity arises to be involved in something both refreshing and pleasurable. Such an opportunity arose when David Pollock invited me to write the Foreword for his book "Outback in Uniform".

"Outback in Uniform" is a reflective, personal account of a young man's experience as a police officer in the remoteness of Australia's Northern Territory in the 1960's. Whilst clearly it is simply one person's perspective and memory, it offers an illustrative and educational window into the people and events of the time. In many ways it is a typical story of those times and David, like so many others, being recruited into the Northern Territory Police from southern parts of Australia, having no real perception of the environment to which he was moving nor any real understanding of the social structure he was likely to encounter.

David, an ex-journalist, has an easy free-flowing writing style coupled with a memory for detail and accuracy which reflect long years of careful record keeping. These attributes combine to deliver not only an enjoyable read but an informative insight into the real world and real people of outback Australia in the 1960's.

His story, which in many ways is written in the style of the times, combines refreshing ***honesty and personal candour:***

"It was three weeks, nearly four, before advice came thanking me for '*... your interest in submitting an application but after careful consideration of the claims of all applicants, I regret to advise you that you were not successful in securing an appointment...*'"

with humour:

"I wrote a story home to both the *'Free Press'* and to Tom Gannon at *'The Express'.* In typical form, Jack Bennett printed the report word-for-word; Tom edited it to half what I'd written, and then sent a note of thanks plus a postal note for $3, the envelope addressed *'Dave Pollock, An otherwise intelligent young man who forsook newspaper work to join the police force...'*"

and colourful word pictures:

Mainoru Station was a picturesque spot, the homestead on a rise overlooking a river flat, with a meandering spread of river lagoons with masses of pandanus palm along the bank. The cattle station aboriginal camp was on the edge of the river, an idyllic place for their pace and style of life. There was plenty of wildlife – duck, geese, and fish – right at the lagoon while they had station rations of beef as well"

Perhaps it is simply because I am a 25 year veteran of the Northern Territory and a colleague and contemporary of David Pollock that I found his story so readable and enjoyable, but I suspect not. I suspect his story will appeal to anyone with an interest in the history and development of Australia and in the difficulties, challenges and the many "larger than life" characters that formed (and probably still form) life in outback Australia.

Sadly Australia has too shallow a "record reservoir" of its social development and the real experiences of ordinary people associated with it. David's story adds significantly to this reservoir and I sincerely commend it.

M. J. Palmer

Constable David Pollock, 22 April, 1966 – Darwin

Melbourne Herald
Tuesday, 27 March, 1962

ADVENTURE IN NORTH — BUT FEW TAKERS

From DOUGLAS LOCKWOOD

DARWIN, Today.—Are Australia's young men losing their spirit of adventure?

The response to recent advertisements throughout Australia for police recruits in the Northern Territory has been disappointing, the Deputy Commissioner, Mr Clive Graham, said today.

The force is now 159 strong, but it has vacancies for 30 men and five women.

Most of the men would get a chance to serve on one of the 23 remote stations — places like Wave Hill and Timber Creek in the far north-west, and Anthony Lagoon, Rankine River and Lake Nash on the Barkly Tableland.

All these stations have radio-equipped vehicles. Six of them still use horses for long patrols.

QUICK RISES

Promotion is quicker than in any other Australian police force.

There are 29 sergeants. One of them, First-class Sergt. Charles Porter, now in charge of Alice Springs police district, has reached this rank only 5½ years after joining.

Second-class Det.-Sergt. Phil McLoughlin joined in 1957. Second-class Sergts. Roger Textor and Pat Grant have been in the force for less than six years.

The average period before a man reaches sergeant's rank in southern forces is about 20 years.

FREE QUARTERS

Here they are eligible to sit for sergeants' examinations after only three years' service and can be promoted to senior constable on completing four years.

The pay is better, too.

A single constable starts on £1368 a year. He gets free quarters, and a married man gets a free house. He also gets six weeks' holiday a year, with his fares paid to the south every second year.

Despite all this, fewer young men appear to be keen to "go bush."

CHAPTER 1

The thought of adventure

"Adventure in North – but few takers" read the headline of a two-column story from Darwin correspondent Douglas Lockwood, in a March, 1962 edition of the Melbourne "Herald".

Douglas Lockwood, was a household name for *"The Herald"* and *"The Sun News-Pictorial"* readers. He had become synonymous with Darwin and the "Top End" of Australia, not only from his days as a war correspondent, on the spot at the time of the Darwin bombings, but also for his coverage of the Petrov affair, his "Top End" books and the "it could only happen in the Territory" stories.

DARWIN, Today. – Are Australia's young men losing their spirit of adventure? he asked.

*"The response to recent advertisements throughout Australia for police recruits in the Northern Territory has been disappointing...*he continued.

That was back in the early 1960's when I was still an apprentice printer working in Belgrave, Victoria, for Norm Gill, the local job printer. Two doors away was the local newspaper, the *"Mountain District Free Press"*. Its editor was John Bennett. Although everybody knew him as Jack, he always signed his editorials John Bennett. To me he was always Mr Bennett. His son, John, was in my form at high school; his wife wrote the social columns for the paper – weddings, the various local belle of belles balls, the Masonic debutante ball, hospital auxiliary events and so on. The local paper reported the fine details of these social events; the dress the wife of a local councillor wore to the ball, the bride's dress details down to who sewed the last stitch.

I'd got to know Mr Bennett pretty well, not just because of the work association but also through my involvement with the local amateur athletic club and the local Australian Rules football scene. I began writing the local Australian Rules football reports for the *Free Press* – match reports – my own column *"Around the Packs with David Pollock"*, match tipping, reports on club events as well as Mountain District Football Association news. I just happened to end up assistant secretary and treasurer, thus an executive committee member of the association. Ironically, I scored the job of reporting on the various football club presentation balls and the "Belle of Belles".

At work at "The Express", Wonthaggi, 1965

Members of the Mountain District Amateur Athletic Club gather around to farewell me as the new Club President, Earl Cook, presents me with a trophy to remember my days with the club

Jack Bennett was an active supporter of the Australian Labour Party (ALP) and through this connection he became involved with the *"Centralian Advocate"*, the Alice Springs local newspaper which at the time was owned by the ALP and its supporters. To boost the paper's operation, perhaps even save it financially, Mr Bennett had been seconded to provide professional newspaper advice. Today he would be called a consultant.

Consequently, copies of each edition, published twice-weekly at the time were airmailed to him, the Thursday issue usually arriving in the Saturday morning's mail. It would be on his desk when I called, either to head off together to amateur athletics, or to talk over my plans for coverage of the local football. While I waited to speak with Mr Bennett, I'd often pick up *"The Advocate"* as it was known, and have a read.

It had heightened my interest in the Territory, then Douglas Lockwood's article really got my interest moving and off I wrote to find out details of how I might join the Northern Territory Police.

This brought my first set-back – I needed to be 21 years old, worse still, I needed to be five feet nine inches tall, in bare feet. While I could make it to 21 in time, I wondered if I could reach the height requirement. Under the house, from the concrete slab to the floor beam was five feet ten inches; for the next couple of years I think I tested myself daily to see if I could touch the beam with my head, with my shoes on, hoping the sole wouldn't be thicker than an inch. Other requirements included being unmarried.

I looked over maps of the Territory. Shell published great Australian State/Territory road maps which you used to be able to get for free. I guess it was through people like me writing in wanting so many maps that they started to charge. I saw police stations such as Wave Hill, Roper Bar, Harts Range marked on the maps. I even wrote to some of them asking for information about life in the police force, but none of them replied. Then I was given the name of a police clerk in Alice Springs, Tim Egan, and wrote to him. He did reply and further built my interest.

I read a couple of Douglas Lockwood's books on Darwin and the Territory – *"Up the Track"* and *"Fair Dinkum"*. The vivid stories along with pictures of the Darwin involvement in the 'Petrov Affair' characterised the Territory. Even today when I pick up *"Fair Dinkum"* I immediately turn to the photograph of then Sergeant Greg Ryall with a stranglehold headlock on one of the Russian couriers who was attempting to escort Mrs Petrov out of Australia.

In 1963 I also came across the newly published book *"Patrol Indefinite"* by Sidney Downer, full of encounters of the Northern Territory police from its formation in 1870 through to the present time. I read it intensely, and read it again and again.

Then in 1963, as my 21st birthday got a little closer I saw an advertisement calling for applications for Constables for the Northern Territory Police. I wrote asking if I could apply and be considered for appointment when I turned 21 in mid-November, 1963. I was on top of the world when the response came – *"yes"*.

Other things appealed too. For example, the wages . . . an annual salary of £965 ($1930), plus a basic wage adjustment of £133 ($266) and a compensation allowance of £80 ($160). There was also a district allowance of £150 ($300) for single officers, a total of £1328 ($2656) a year, or £25/10/– ($51) a week. That was £5/10/– ($11) or 25% a week more than I was earning now. But there were also free uniforms, free accommodation, six weeks annual leave with a return airfare to your leave destination within the Commonwealth, the first after the first year of service and then every subsequent two years. There was a tax allowance and there was paid overtime for work over 80 hours a fortnight.

My mind ticked with the thoughts of adventure, the Outback, the dust and heat, not so much of the tropics, but of the red heart of The Centre. There was a sense of responsibility and the feeling of doing something different in my life to date, of chasing that crook through the Outback, of searching for lost tourists, a feeling of doing something different for myself.

So what did I have to lose?

Off went my application. Next came my notice to appear for an interview, on Friday, 20 September, 1963, at 10am at the office of the Commonwealth Public Service Inspector, 10th Floor, Commonwealth Centre, corner Spring and Latrobe Streets, Melbourne, reporting to Chief Inspector S. J. Bowie.

It meant a day off work. Just plucking the courage to tell a lie that I wouldn't be in on the Friday was hard enough, let alone having to 'front' for the interview; still I did. And so for the first time I met Chief Inspector Bowie, in his 40's, wiry, thinning hair, in plain clothes. He was accompanied by a member of the Victoria Police recruitment unit. I don't remember much of the interview, I guess it took some 20 minutes or so after which I was asked to wait outside a few minutes. Recalled to the interview room I was given the papers to go to the Commonwealth Medical Centre for a TB chest X-ray and as I lived in Belgrave at the time, to report to the local Commonwealth medical officer for a medical examination. That just happened to be my family doctor, Dr Elef Jorgensen. I'd cleared the first hurdle, I was on top of the world.

My main medical fear was my height and my weight...I got over the first by "Doc Jorgy", as we all knew him, asking *"how tall are you young Dave?"* – *"Ah, five feet nine"* I nervously answered; *"Hop on these scales"* he asked; I was 9 stone 9 lbs (61kgs). *"You've got no problems young Dave"* Doc Jorgy re-assured.

It was three weeks, nearly four before advice came thanking me for *" ... your interest in submitting an application but after careful consideration of the claims of all applicants, I regret to advise that you were not successful in securing an appointment".* While there might have been a deep sigh of relief in other parts of the household, I was very disappointed. But I wasn't going to give up. I wasn't even 21 yet.

⎯⎯❖⎯⎯

Two months after my 21st birthday I again wrote to the Deputy Commissioner asking when the next recruitment campaign would take place. Chief Inspector Bowie, as Acting Deputy Commissioner, responded to say the campaign would be later in the year; that my previous application would be further reviewed and I'd be advised should it be more successful this time around.

Then in July, 1964, I received a letter from Chief Inspector Bowie reminding me that my medical examination had revealed the weight of only 9 stone 9 lbs. (61kgs) *"After giving your application quite a lot of thought, I decided I had to reject it on the grounds that you were not robust enough for the job."* He continued *"It seems probable that you may have put on some weight since last year and that you will continue to do so as you get older. It will not be possible, however, to recommend your appointment unless you can increase your weight to 10 and a half stone (67kgs). If you have reached this weight or do so in the future, I suggest you contact me. I will then arrange for your appointment to receive further consideration."* As I recall, I hadn't put on any weight really but the campaign began in earnest.

It was only a month later that the time had come for me to move on from working for Norm Gill. The new apprentice was well established, there wasn't really enough work for the three of us, so just as it had happened with the three apprentices before me, I had to find another job.

Again Jack Bennett had an influence. Through his connections with the Country Press Association, he was able to tell me of a position at Wonthaggi, with the *"Wonthaggi Express"*. They needed someone who could turn his hand to reporting for a couple of days a week and to the printing press the other days.

As well as writing the sport for the *"Free Press"*, for the past 18 months I'd been the district correspondent for *'The Age"*, a Melbourne morning daily. I covered the events of the lively Shire of Fern Tree Gully, the establishment of the Shire (now City) of Knox and other local incidents. In all, I was pretty well suited for the position.

So one Sunday in August, 1964, in Dad's car, I drove the 80 miles (130kms) to Wonthaggi and met *"The Express"* editor, Tom Gannon, a man unique in country newspaper journalism and someone I grew to admire as a person who taught me so much about reporting facts, being concise, saying what had to be said in as few words as possible. In the week or so that followed, I bought my first car, a new Holden sedan, an EH, dark blue with a white roof, and 179 engine. As with all first cars, and a new one at that, it was my pride and joy. Another big move was to leave home and to board during the week at Wonthaggi.

The first jobs were the police rounds and I remember on the Tuesday, the Wonthaggi Court of Petty Sessions, with Magistrate T. J. (Tom) Mayberry S.M. on the Bench. The Wonthaggi court house was unique for a town its size. A high bench and a jury box, used in the days of inquests into tragedies at the local coal mines became the Press box – there usually would be two of us, Warrick McCrimmon from *"The Sentinel"*, the second local weekly newspaper – and myself.

As editor Tom had certain standards he required with every story. It was mandatory to have the full name of all persons, their age, their occupation, their street address, but for reasons best known to himself, never the street number. It was something that stood me in good stead later with an eye for detail. He always needed reassurance that a name was Graham or Graeme, Geoffrey of Jeffrey, Garry or Gary, Jean or Gene. What made it so frustrating was that he had grown up with most of these people, and he knew, or thought he knew, the correct spelling of many of the names and other details. Details just had to be right. In reporting the local news, in particular the local courts, Tom gave no favour, and had no fear.

I don't know if it was the change of job, more likely a more relaxed life style with less athletic or football meetings and activities, but soon I began to put on weight ... 10 stone ... 10 stone 4 lbs ... it was almost *"eureka"* when I hit 10 and a half stone, (67kgs) even if it was with my clothes on; a couple of bananas and a good drink of water would fix that I'd been told.

So in August, 1965, I again wrote to Darwin, this time jubilant in the knowledge I had reached the weight requirement set out in Chief Inspector Bowie's letter a year earlier.

But it wasn't to be that simple. Now they wanted a new application and personal particulars form completed; they considered the previous forms *"antiquated"*. Then came the advice for a new interview, on a Wednesday, 10 November, 1965, in the morning and again in Melbourne. That couldn't have been a worse day or time for me, as there was no way I would be able to get a Wednesday off work with the paper being "put to bed" Wednesday afternoons. The original idea of me working for a couple of days on reporting and the rest of the week in the print room had lasted about a week, now 12 months after I'd started at *"The Express"* I was virtually full-time reporting. Was there the chance of an alternative time later in the week I asked. The response was *"yes, but in Sydney, between 2.30pm and 3.45pm on Friday, 12 November, 1965 ... but travel expenses would be my own responsibility"* There was no way I was going to miss this opportunity for an interview, even if it meant a week's wages spent on an airfare to Sydney. It really seemed bizarre at the time, flying to and from Sydney on the same day but I was determined to do it. And I did!

The interview this time was in the Department of Territories offices, at West Circular Quay, a building that today houses the Museum of Contemporary Art. This time a member of the New South Wales Police accompanied Chief Inspector Bowie at the interview. It was fairly straight forward. Again I don't remember much apart from Chief Inspector Bowie asking me more than once why I didn't drink liquor, something he seemed a little amazed about, something he felt sure would change if I went to the Territory.

I was again sent for a chest x-ray and given the medical examination papers and it was back to Dr Jorgensen again. I felt confident that it was a matter of just waiting. The next intake of recruits was to be mid to late February, 1966, so each Friday night when I got home to my parents, the first thing was to see if there was "that letter".

Then it was the week before Christmas and I came home to my parents a little early. One thing I'd found working for Tom Gannon was that holidays did not come easy, so the chance to have the week off between Christmas and New Year was quickly accepted. I arrived home and "that letter" was waiting ... *"Dear Sir ... your application was carefully considered but you were not successful in obtaining an immediate appointment. Your name however has been placed on a wait list. Further consideration could be given to your application if a selected applicant does not take up duty. I will write to you again should a vacancy occur. Yours faithfully, C.A.J.McRae for Secretary, Department of Territories".*

I was bitterly disappointed, it was the worst Christmas present I could have received. I didn't believe I had any hope of gaining an appointment and I was ready to look for some other adventure. I knew I couldn't stand it much longer at Wonthaggi, and thought I'd wait until New Year and decide. At home there was another silent sigh of relief and a hope too that *"David would give up this fantasy of joining the NT Police".*

Christmas passed, it was back to work at Wonthaggi. Of course nobody there knew anything of my dreams, only a handful of people knew of my application – immediate family, the people I'd listed as personal references and a couple I had asked for a reference to take to the second interview in Sydney.

I really thought nothing more of it for the next couple of weeks so it was with considerable surprise when I got home in the second week of January, 1966, to find a familiar brown Department of Territories envelope waiting ... *"Dear Sir, Enclosed herewith are letters of appointment for the position of Constable in the Northern Territory Police Force. You are required to attend a training course in Darwin commencing Monday, 28 February, 1966. Your travel arrangements should be made accordingly. Yours faithfully ... "*

Attached was a two-page foolscap letter addressed to me. It spelt out the conditions of appointment. The salary was now an all-up £1513 p.a. . . . in a few weeks after decimal currency day that would be known as $3026. Then there was the uniforms, the quarters, the leave and paid fares. It didn't take me any time to sign the letter of appointment, it was something I wanted to do ... after all, I had been trying to join for years! Even if it did not work out, what did I have to lose? ... I'd give it 12 months and if it didn't work out, then I'd come home on leave and stay – but that wasn't really in my mind at all.

On the Saturday morning I just had to tell Jack Bennett; I went to amateur athletics that day, as I did every Saturday during summer, and let it be known I was off to the Territory. I expected a few expressions of surprise and I wasn't wrong!

I immediately started to plan ... I'd give Tom Gannon four weeks notice ... that would give me two weeks to get to Darwin, I'd drive to Port Augusta, put the car on The Ghan to Alice Springs and drive on from there. I wouldn't rush it but there wasn't a lot of spare time.

No one got a bigger surprise than Tom Gannon. Mid morning I told him I would be leaving in four weeks, I was going to Darwin. *"Write a story about it, say we are looking for a new journalist ... "* he told me. I wrote the story and he nearly fell out of his chair when he went to edit it to find I was joining the Northern Territory Police. He thought I was off to work on the Darwin newspaper!

A travel warrant came for the rail travel and I got booked on The Ghan OK. I wrote to friends in Adelaide and arranged an overnight stop on the way. I had a busy time getting my personal affairs in order ... I was still assistant secretary/treasurer of the Mountain District Football Association, I was president of the Mountain District Amateur Athletic Club; there were bank accounts and signatures to arrange, a sun visor and protectors for the car and a spares kit – radiator hose, fan belt etc. A visiting army disposals store had some cheap good binoculars and I bought a pair – they are in the boot of my car still today, I've taken them to the football at the MCG more times than I used them in the Territory.

I said my farewells at Wonthaggi and drove home on the Friday evening for the last time to find that my mother was in hospital. She had been in a car accident a couple of days earlier and received some severe lacerations to the bridge of her nose. At first I thought this was going to delay my departure but on checking I found that her injuries were by no means life threatening and decided to leave as planned.

It was a hurried trip to hospital to see her before going to the athletic club's farewell evening they had arranged in the club rooms at Kings Park, Upper Fern Tree Gully. First there was a meeting to elect a new president, then a social evening and the presentation of a trophy to me in appreciation of my work for the club. It was a piece of polished wood with a running athlete mounted on top with a large inscription plaque reading *"To David Lloyd Pollock. In appreciation of the valuable services rendered to this Club during the past 9 years from The Committee and Members of The Mountain District Amateur Athletic Club, February 11, 1966"*.

Next day was my last as the club's official at Olympic Park. It was a touching moment when I was called up to receive an engraved pewter mug *"David ... from fellow Officials and athletes, Olympic Park Track & Field Group, February, 1966"* with a Victorian Amateur Athletic Association laurel wreath badge mounted on the side.

My mother remained in hospital over the weekend which was a bit of blow in trying to get things at home organised, and packed. It was also decimal currency day on Monday, 14 February, 1966, so before leaving I had to have my passbooks converted, and of course have in hand money for the trip, which was all in brand spanking new decimal currency notes.

I was organised to leave on the Tuesday morning; I had the car packed, I had to call at the William Angliss Hospital in Upper Fern Tree Gully and see my mother, then I was off on my *adventure!*

CHAPTER 2

The first journey North

I'd never driven to Adelaide before, I'd been as far west as Stawell a few times, so the thought of a day's drive west was a little daunting, but still it was only the first stage in what was planned to be about a week's travel to Darwin.

Six months earlier I'd changed my car. The first of the Holden HD models had come out and I was pretty taken by the X2 Premier sedan in maroon and white which was on display at the Holden dealer's showroom at Wonthaggi. I liked it and although I had bought my first car only a year earlier, I succumbed to the car salesman and changed over to the latest model. It was a very comfortable car to travel in, ideal for the trip ahead of me, even with the reasonable load I had on board..

The drive through Melbourne city, virtually in peak period, was nerve-racking. I wasn't used to city peak-hour driving. I remember on every later trip across to Adelaide it seemed to take forever to get through the city, out to Bacchus Marsh and the Avenue of Elms and on to Ballarat. At that time there was very little duplicated highway, some passing lanes but no freeway.

I stopped at Dimboola for lunch, at the trusty Golden Fleece service station. The petrol bowser was still in shillings and pence but I paid in dollars and cents using nice new crisp notes. Nhill, then Kaniva, eventually Bordertown, there was no by-pass then. Across the plains to Tailem Bend, Murray Bridge and the Hills towns of Hahndorf, Aldgate and Mt. Lofty; again no by-pass but a winding two lane highway before the descent into Adelaide.

I had to find my way through Adelaide and down to Port Adelaide where I was staying the night with Jim and Pearl Revell. They were brother and sister and had lived all their adult life in a house in Dale Street. I'd met Jim back in November, 1962 on the Trans Australia Railway, crossing the Nullarbor to attend the Commonwealth Games in Perth. In fact we shared a compartment on the Kalgoorlie–Perth leg of the trip. At that time it was three separate trains from Adelaide, (four from Melbourne), to get to Perth, with plenty of time to get to know fellow passengers.

Jim and Pearl were to be a great Adelaide base for me on my trips to and from the Territory. I'd get there for dinner, we would spend the evening talking and then next morning I'd head off. Neither Jim nor Pearl had ever

My car, second from left, loaded on the flat-top, Port Augusta, ready for the first stage of its Ghan trip

The Ghan passes through The Gap, Alice Springs, on its return trip to Marree

married, they were part of quite a large family. I heard about most members of their family each visit, and being in their senior years, there was usually plenty of 'ills' associated with what they had to tell me. Jim was a bookmaker and fielded at the Adelaide races. He usually had members of his family clerk for him, his brother-in-law Harold and nephew John in particular who were with him on the trip to Perth when I first met him. He was a keen fisherman too and had his own boat which he would slip at Port Adelaide and go out on to the Gulf for a day's fishing. I never seemed to coincide my visits with a fishing trip, or after a good catch, but I heard plenty about race days and fishing.

The second day of my trip north was an easy one, just the 200 miles (320kms) from Adelaide to Port Augusta where I would overnight and be ready to load the car the following morning. This was one of the big frustrations of taking your car on the train trip north; you had to have it ready to load at Port Augusta station at 9 o'clock on the morning of the day of travel but the passenger section of the train did not leave Port Augusta until 5 o'clock in the afternoon. Fortunately, on later trips north, the loading time was 2 o'clock in the afternoon which meant you could drive up from Adelaide in the morning, even have some lunch, before loading, and then only have to wait around a couple of hours before the passenger train departure.

One thing about the early departure was that the vehicles travelled to Marree in advance and were trans-shipped ready to be part of the "The Ghan" for the narrow-gauge section trip on to Alice Springs. With the later loading time, the vehicles travelled with the passengers to Marree and were trans-shipped and followed on "the chaser" and were then available to collect in Alice Springs early on the morning after arrival.

At the railway station the cars were loaded on to flat-top wagons. You had to drive your car over a ramp connected to the first flat-top and then drive along a number of flat tops, over joining ramps until your car was the next in position. Depending on the car sizes, whether there were trailers or caravans, there could be two or three cars on a flat-top. This time there were not many vehicles to be loaded as February wasn't a peak time for travel to the Territory. The frustration was that there was absolutely nothing to see in Port Augusta, and in the near 100F (37.7C) heat, the day was one of total boredom.

Those passengers who had loaded their vehicles at Port Augusta then travelled on a two-carriage train a few miles out of town, to Stirling North meeting the main Ghan, which had originated in Port Pirie, with an Adelaide connection. The two sections would be joined, then head off swiftly north-wards along the western edge of the Flinders Ranges. It was normally a sit-up section of the trip, as far as Marree.

The season had been good and I remember as dusk fell, wildlife abound-ed; several large mobs of kangaroos bounding away from the tracks. It also came time for the conductors to check tickets and issue passes for the vari-ous meal sittings. There were always at least two sittings for lunch and din-ner, sometimes three. The seasoned traveller learnt to try to get in the second sitting for meals, it helped pass the time.

To our surprise, the conductors not only issued meal sitting passes but were allocating sleeping berths for the night . . . *"there'll be a slight delay in the arrival of the southbound Ghan into Marree so you will be sleeping on this train overnight sir"!* Normal routine was for the Port Pirie/Port Augusta stage of the train to arrive in Marree around 10pm, then after trans-shipping, the real *Ghan* would leave Marree for a 24 hour journey on to Alice Springs, arriving late on the Friday night.

It reminded me a lot of the days before the standard gauge between Melbourne and Sydney when everybody making the trip had to change trains at Albury ... not just the passengers, but the mail and parcels too. With the *Ghan,* the train staff also had to move over all the fresh provisions for the trip, the table linen, the bed linen – everything that would be needed for the next section of the journey. It was usually a hectic half hour, one difference between Marree and Albury was not the length of the platform, but the open-ness and no cover, a job done in either blazing heat, rain or the warmth of the evening on normal northbound journeys. The need for the change was that the Central Australian Railway, from Marree on to Alice Springs was only a 3ft 6in gauge line which in its early days had run south through the Flinders Ranges and towns like Hawker to Port Augusta.

However, with the development of the Leigh Creek open cut brown coal mine to power the Port Augusta power station, South Australia's main elec-tricity source, a new standard gauge line had been built further west to avoid the undulations of the Flinders Ranges. The line extended some 60 mile (100kms) north of Leigh Creek to Marree, the head of not only the Central Australian Railway, but also the Birdsville Track. Significant cattle move-ments by rail were coordinated out of Marree from not only northern South Australia and the Northern Territory but also the north east corner of South Australia bordering on to Queensland.

So after dinner, I found the sleeping compartment I'd been allocated and settled down for the night. It was a second class roomette but with sole occupancy, a little more cramped than a first class roomette, but a bed for the night. I was too excited to sleep and we were in Marree some time before I went to bed. The train was stationary all night at the platform.

Next morning we were told that due to flooding north of Marree it would be at least another 12 hours before the southbound *Ghan* would arrive and we could change trains to head north.

The then Commonwealth Railways ran the Central Australian Railway system and tended to have the older rolling-stock of the system in use to Marree. Not only that, they only had enough rolling stock for one *Ghan*, there wasn't a back-up set of sleepers, dining and lounge car for us to head north in. The *Ghan* rolling stock was actually the first of the air-conditioned cars which had been in use years earlier on the Trans-Australia Railway. The lounge car had been German built with magnificent inlay veneer designs on the walls, a rail car of real character.

I hadn't heard of the rain in the north of South Australia during my trip from Adelaide up to Port Augusta – probably just as well as I had nothing to panic about. But it had clearly rained quite significantly in Marree; the surrounds of the station, the main street of Marree was a quagmire of mud, only too eager to stick to your shoes. So there was no fun, or relief from the rail cars by going for a walk around Marree, although I did walk across to my car sitting on a rail flat top and get a hat. I'd left it in the car the previous day in Port Augusta and once again I had got a very burnt nose in the sun.

There was even less to see in Marree than in Port Augusta; there was a hotel, post office, a general store and butcher shop and the school. One prominent feature of the town was the 35 mph (60kms) speed restriction signs, I guess that helped keep the dust down most of the time.

The day did provide time for those travelling (about 24 of us in first class) to get to know a little about each other and why we were travelling north at this time of year. I kept quiet about my reason for being there until I got to know a few of the fellow passengers. It turned out that five women amongst us were five policewomen recruits on their way to Darwin for the same recruit intake as myself. Police headquarters had arranged their travel as a party; two had cars and they had all originated from in and around Sydney and had driven together to Port Augusta, and then would drive on from Alice Springs to Darwin together.

There was also 'Kil' Webb, his wife, son Thomas and daughter, Jane, from Mt Riddock Station, about 145 miles (230kms) north east of Alice Springs. They were returning from their Christmas holidays, in their 4-wheel drive. They had driven part of the way north from Port Augusta towards Alice Springs but ran into the wet conditions so had back-tracked to Port Augusta in time to get their vehicle on the train and head north. In the 1960's the 1,000 mile (1,600kms) stretch from Port Augusta to Alice Springs was an all dirt and gravel road and very susceptible to flooding, bogging and being totally impassable for days, even weeks.

There was also Mrs Edna Watt, and her young daughter, Shirley. Her husband, Ossie Watt, a former Air Force man, had recently taken the job of chief instructor of the Alice Springs Aero Club. He'd been living in Alice Springs six months, waiting for allocation of a Housing Commission house. Now Edna and Shirley were joining him. There were a couple of other station folk and their children from near Katherine, but not many others.

Some of the day was spent playing cards, eating (morning tea, lunch and afternoon tea) before dinner came – and still there was no definite time to expect to be leaving for the north. Expectations were raised when we were all taken on a four mile trip around the rail yards of Marree as they re-watered the carriage and in general got things serviced for the return trip with passengers off the southbound *Ghan*.

Fortunately, the railways theatrette car was in Marree. It was a rail carriage set up as a theatre which travelled the Commonwealth Railways system stopping off at the various railways fettler camps and communities and screening a couple of movies, a recent newsreel and a couple of cartoons – *Mr Magoo* and *Donald Duck*. This filled in the evening nicely and by the time the movies had finished the *Ghan* had arrived, it was serviced and we boarded, and went to bed, moving off during the night northward – 27 hours late.

———⇒◦⇐———

Washaway repairs, then a locomotive breakdown further slowed the trip. To keep the train moving on one engine, the freight section, but fortunately not the motor vehicles, was left behind. I recall at one stage we stopped at a stark, outback, barren spot, it could have been the end of the earth. The excited chef ran to the driver asking how long we will be stationary. *"Why?"* asked the driver. *"Well if you stop for one hour, I cook custard for dinner!"*. We didn't have custard, but provisions did start to run a little short. I remember on the Saturday evening as we had our third dinner on the train, the main course menu choice had gone. *"Would you like ham with roast turkey sir?"*, *"That will be fine"*. *"Just as well, as there is nothing else!"* the waiter jokingly replied.

As we travelled north we saw no real sign of the rain of a couple of days earlier. It had quickly cleared and the weather returned to the searing Central Australia heat of summer. It was Saturday afternoon, instead of Friday morning, when we passed through Oodnadatta. The heat and the boredom had had its effects on some aboriginal women beside the railway line. Several were in an obvious intoxicated and agitated state over some matter. One wielding a half railway sleeper to try to settle the situation ... *"Go on girls, get out and sort them out"* remarked someone to the police women recruits, who all with a cringe of horror retorted *"oh no!"*. *"Well you had better start to get used to it"* came the response.

We ended up on the train from Port Augusta for three nights, instead of the scheduled one night, arriving at Alice Springs late on the Sunday morning. We were scheduled to arrive 10pm on the Friday evening, so in all we arrived 37 hours late, or three or four hours after the return Ghan would have normally left for the south on a Sunday morning.

Delivery of the car didn't take long; the Midland Motel had been recommended, it was new, air conditioned and central. Well, everything in Alice Springs was pretty central. It was a town of little more than 5,000 but with evidence of growth. I took a drive around The Alice, to the Telegraph Station, "The Gap" and to Anzac Hill where I again met Edna Watt and for the first time, her husband, Ozzie. I also took the drive out to Simpson's Gap, 15 miles (24kms) to the west, out past Mt Gillen, and for the first time, saw the *"Twin Gums"*, a legendary site of The Centre.

I also checked-out the police station, but not the police barracks. I didn't make myself known, just drove past and later went for a walk past the Parsons Street building of the 1930's, plastered brick with obvious extensions, with fly-wired covered louvre windows featuring.

Next morning, vehicle fuelled, I headed north the 315 miles (500kms) to Tennant Creek along the Stuart Highway, or perhaps better known as "The

Flynn's grave in the shadow of Mt Gillen, 5 miles west of Alice Springs

Roadside Territory humour on the Stuart Highway south of Darwin

Track". It was bitumen all the way, the original bitumen being laid by the Allied works force during World War II. The road was actually constructed by a work force headed up by engineers from organisations such as the Victorian Country Roads Board, but is now maintained by the Commonwealth Department of Works.

Just out of Alice Springs the highway had a 12 miles (19kms) run of hills, twisting and turning until hitting the first of the plains, and the highest altitude point on the highway between Adelaide and Darwin, 2,387 feet (727.5m) above sea level. It was only a few miles further to the crossing of the Tropic of Capricorn. It surprised me, in fact it surprises most, that the tropic is only a few miles north of Alice Springs, not giving any thought that The Alice is inland almost parallel to Rockhampton in the east and North West Cape in the west.

It wasn't long before I experienced my first road train – usually a prime mover with three trailers, each laden with two containers. They thundered along the highway at 60mph (100kmh) plus, on a highway with no speed limits. It was a matter of drive as conditions allow, just slow down for the towns, the river crossings and some bends!

While severe droughts of recent years had been broken, there was still plenty of dead mulga and sparse growth but not the desert-like country I had built up in my mind to expect. In fact, the whole trip to Darwin was one of ever changing geographics, plains, hills, scrub, bush and timbered land.

The first town north of Alice Springs was Aileron, but the highway bypassed the roadside inn/garage anyway. Then 120 miles (190km) north of The Alice was Ti Tree Well, another roadside-inn, cum general store and a police station. A little further north Central Mt Stuart, 2,769 feet. (844m) came into view, the geographical centre of Australia, a compulsory road-side photo stop.

Next came Barrow Creek, still a telegraph repeater station site and also an establishment which called itself a hotel where petrol was available as well as a sandwich for lunch. Little did I know the man perched in the bar was Tom Roberts, the "Mayor" of Barrow Creek, in real-life the long term resident PMG technician who maintained the repeater station. Then Wauchope and a little to the north of Wauchope, the Devil's Marbles, a unique rock formation of dozens of cylindrical rocks, as big or bigger than houses, some perched on top of each other, others side by side, covering an area of several hundred square yards. Their ochre red colours stood out against the general sandy area with gums and other vegetation intermingled.

Then it was on to Tennant Creek. There were only two hotels in Tennant Creek and I stopped at the first coming into town, The Goldfields, a fact I never admitted to anyone on my subsequent periods of duty in Tennant Creek. It was a bed for the night, and the cheapest in town. If I had known I would be recompensed in the form of a government travelling allowance, I'd have probably stayed at the Tennant Creek Hotel, a Swan Brewery owned establishment. But I was starting to watch my pennies, or dollars and cents as it was now, as I was not expecting a pay for another week or two.

Katherine was my goal for next day, on some 400 odd miles (645kms). Just 15 miles (24kms) north of Tennant Creek was Threeways, where the Barkly Highway branched off at a right angle to head east for Queensland. It was the site of a Memorial to Rev. Dr John Flynn, founder of the Royal Flying Doctor Service, an impressive rectangular stone pillar surmounted by a concrete white cross.

Then there was Banka Banka, Churchill's Head, a rock formation in the side of a cutting complete with mulga stick simulating a cigar which certainly gave the formation an accurate name. Renner Springs, Elliott, Newcastle Waters (actually off the main Highway), the Newcastle Waters causeway and on to Dunmarra and my first so innocent experience with "Ma" Healey. Daly Waters (again off the highway), Larrimah, Mataranka and Katherine.

Now more than 700 miles (1,125kms) north of Alice Springs the weather had changed to a more tropical nature as had the countryside. It was muggy, it was greener, and there were mosquitoes. I also had my only vehicle problem for the trip, the regulator from the generator to the battery had defaulted resulting in a high charge continuously to the car battery, boiling it, needing water to be added frequently.

While there was a Holden dealer in Katherine, March Motors, they seemed to have an interest in only selling new cars. If there was a fault like I had, it was a bit much to expect a repair, rather the attitude was *"Go on to Darwin and get it fixed mate"*.

It was a further 220 miles (355kms) on to Darwin. Access to the highway north was via the high level railway bridge. The low level highway bridge was under water from the Katherine River, as it was for much of all wet seasons. The high level was a one-way bridge, about 150 yards (140m) in length. The bridge was planked with timber between the rail tracks to allow vehicle traffic. The North Australia Railway, which ran from Darwin down to

Larrimah, 110 miles (177kms) south of Katherine, was a 3ft 6in gauge line. The line was mainly used for freight from Adelaide or some Queensland-eastern sea-board destinations, trucked to Larrimah and moved on to Darwin. Through what was known as the "coordinated service", freight was brought by rail to Alice Springs, then trans-shipped on to road trains and rushed to Larrimah to be again trans-shipped and put on rail into Darwin.

It would have been much quicker to road transport the containers right through from Alice Springs to Darwin, but that would have put the loss-making railway out of business. It would have also needed much greater up-keep on the highway sections on to Darwin, particularly in the wet season. So while it would be logical to close the railway and truck the goods straight through to Darwin, other logic prevailed.

I passed Pine Creek, then Adelaide River, towns of little more size than those south of Katherine. At several locations there was water across the road. Fresh clear water through the pandanus palms. There was also increased evidence of the war time years with disused airstrips regularly appearing beside the highway and others sign-posted off the highway. I kept a look-out for buffaloes but saw none but I did see a few feral donkeys and brumbies and a few head of cattle.

One thing that had been consistent along the whole length of the highway was the telegraph – steel poles of consistent design, a single cross arm and a double pair of wires. There were sections where added wires ran between communities but the telegraph was a dominant feature of the skyline the whole trip. It only disappeared as I approached Darwin, within 15 miles (24kms) of the city.

My instructions were that on arrival in Darwin I was to report to the officer-in-charge of the Darwin police station. It was located in Bennett Street, a double story uninspiring aged building, with the front office to the left, the traffic section office to the right with a centre stairway that led up to the CIB and information sections. I walked in, introduced myself and asked for the officer in charge, a Sergeant First Class Noel Owens. First impressions were of a soulless man. *"Oh, you are here, I wasn't expecting anybody to arrive this soon"* was his response. *"Well, the Barracks Master, Sergeant McMahon, is around at the barracks now organising things, so go and report to him".*

So off I went to find Sergeant McMahon.

The Darwin police barracks, Marrenah House, were situated on The

Esplanade, the best part of a mile from the Darwin Bennett Street police station, but commanding a magnificent view across a grass covered clifftop and the bay. The building was a war-time women's officers quarters, elevated seven or eight feet off the ground allowing vehicle parking underneath, with two F shaped corridors with adjacent rooms running from a disused kitchen area and a large empty hall or lounge area.

It had concrete piers but generally was of timber and fibro construction with a corrugated iron roof. It had actually been condemned for six or seven years and there were plans for a new police barracks.

Ironically, the next door neighbour of the barracks was Douglas Lockwood, who lived in a well presented, heavily timber louvred Territory home. However, there wasn't a friendly neighbour relationship between him and the members of barracks. I guess that had something to do with noise which no doubt came at unusual hours, or the reputed shooting of his cat when it ventured through the back yard of the barracks. He was regarded as a good mate of the Commissioner, or at least having a direct line to the Commissioner, at home as well as at the office, if there was any disturbance at the barracks which he might take offence to. I thought it best not to mention his articles in the southern papers, or his books, but just be aware that he lived next door.

All the male single officers stationed in Darwin were required to live in the barracks. The first person I met at the barracks was a young Constable John Woodcock. John had been in the previous recruit intake some 9 – 10 months earlier. He was a "Darwin boy", he'd grown up and been educated in Darwin, done his apprenticeship as a motor mechanic at the government garage where he had worked until joining the force.

Even though his family lived in Darwin, because he was single, he was required to live in the police barracks. He couldn't sleep a night at home without approval of the Divisional Inspector; unless he was on duty, he had to be in barracks every night between 2am and 6am. You were not even allowed to leave your police district at any time without Divisional Inspector approval, so to make a day trip to Adelaide River War Cemetery, approval to leave the Darwin police district was required.

I found Sergeant McMahon. He had the aboriginal police trackers attached to Darwin station organising beds, wardrobes, chairs and the likes for the rooms necessary for the 12 new recruits. Without any hassle I was allocated a room, next to John Woodcock's, which, for the first couple of days

Alice Springs from Anzac Hill, looking south to the Gap, February, 1966

Alice Springs, March, 1971

I had to myself. There was a standard issue of white sheets, a blanket, pillow and new pillow cases. The bare boarded room had a floor mat and there was a standard 15 inch (38cm) fan. The next day an overhead fan was installed in the room – *"like the ones in fish shops"* I wrote home.

My first set-back was to find that while accommodation was provided for single officers, accommodation was a room, not board, no meals; that was something to find yourself. Regulations prohibited the preparation of a meal in barracks, although you could prepare a snack. Some members had various arrangements at hotels and other eating houses, and then there was also the Commonwealth Hostel at which arrangements could be made. All the recruits ended up eating at the Commonwealth Hostel for the time of the recruit school.

Later, at barracks at Alice Springs and Tennant Creek, the same food preparation restictions applied. However, both barracks had full cooking facilities including an electric stove and oven. I saw some mighty snacks prepared – roast lamb with all the trimmings was a classic. Female company, for that matter, any form of pets, in the barracks was also absolutely prohibited!

A strict requirement of all single officers in barracks was to have a current radio licence – $2.80 for the Northern Territory.

One of the first things that was drilled into me was the need to immediately change the registration of my vehicle – the quirk of the law deemed a worker in the Northern Territory to be a resident and interstate registered cars of residents were thus unregistered, and drivers unlicensed. So I took the time to change the registration. Another quirk of the law was that Compulsory Third Party insurance was not something that was done as part and parcel of registering a car in the Northern Territory. Instead, before attending the Motor Registry, you went to an insurance office and bought a Third Party policy, then took it to the registry where your registration was fixed. All motor vehicles were inspected annually, a form of annual road worthiness inspection. Fortunately, my vehicle passed, well, it was less than 12 months old. It soon wore new Territory plates – NT 32 125. I didn't arrange a new driver's licence, that would come after I'd been sworn-in, for free.

Shorts and white long socks were the order of the day; I started to get a collection together the day after arrival. It was hot, it was humid, but to my relief, in the barracks there was a Coca Cola bottle dispenser, run by the Police Rugby Football Club – 10c a bottle. I don't know what it was about Darwin-bottled Coke, I'd never been a Coke man, but it was my life blood in the stifling wet season tropical weather.

While cricket and athletics were the dominant summer sport "Down South", the Australian Rules football season was coming to a close in Darwin and training was under way for the dry season sports of Rugby League and cricket. Police had a team in the N.T. rugby competition. After my name, the first thing members would ask was *"do you play football?"* – rugby league they meant. With only two Victorians, and a Tasmanian, amongst the recruits, the rugby supporters hoped for some new talent. I don't think they found any. I never took to rugby the whole time I was in the Territory. I recall, eager to be seen to at least morally support the police team, I went to a practice game one afternoon at the RAAF base, the first time I had actually seen the game played. I was naive enough to ask some questions about the rules, how the game was played. The responses put me off the game for ever.

The first Saturday I was in Darwin I went to the second semi final of the Northern Territory Football League, at the Gardens Oval. It was played in 90F (32C) degree heat and the trainers, in shorts, fielded buckets of iced water to cool players. Even I went to the football in shorts and thongs, in total contrast to overcoat and hat at home.

The goal umpires wore tropical dress – white hat, white open neck shirt, white shorts and long white socks. In the eyes of the spectators, the field umpire was just as big a mug as he was at home.

Despite the hot and humid conditions, the standard of play was outstanding, in particular the major game, Nightcliff and St Mary's, who again featured in the grand final a fortnight later. St Mary's was predominantly made up of aboriginal players, many from the Tiwi islands while Nightcliff was predominantly a team of Europeans.

The games were fascinating to watch, many of the players in the junior grades not wearing boots. Nearly all had a headband, and many a handkerchief to wipe away the sweat. On many an occasion I saw the handkerchief disappear into the mouth as the ball approached. Tricky marks, a kiss for the ball, and goals from the oddest angle highlighted the games.

I wrote a story home to both the *"Free Press"* and to Tom Gannon at *"The Express"*. In typical form, Jack Bennett printed the report word-for-word; Tom edited it to half what I'd written, and then sent a note of thanks plus a postal note for $3, the envelope addressed *"Dave Pollock, An otherwise intelligent young man who forsook newspaper work to join a police force, PO Box . . ."*

It was 21 years before I attended another Northern Territory Football

League grand final. Again a St Mary's win. Perhaps this time the players had been spurred on by a visit from Her Majesty, the Queen, who as part of her 25th Silver Jubilee Anniversary Australian tour, was driven on a lap of honour at Garden's Oval, before the game. She was dressed in red and white, St Mary's colours. I'd been at the City Council Chambers to meet the Queen as had the Catholic Bishop of Darwin, Bishop O'Loughlin. After the Queen left the reception, he and I went to the game ... more people, better facilities ... but still the same canny play.

CHAPTER 3

Monday, 28 February, 1966

"I was sworn-in this morning and now have all the powers of any other Constable of the Force, even though I don't yet know the law ... I've been issued with copies of some Ordinances, my notebook, handcuffs, baton, metal buttons for the uniform etc. and my uniform collar numbers; mine is 204. The uniform shirt is an open neck shirt, you only wear a tie when you go to Court.

"We had our photographs taken for the identification cards which will be issued when we finish recruit school, that will have my official number, around 250–267. There are 12 men and five women in the recruit school"

I just had to write home the first night of the recruit school and tell my folks that finally I was a sworn member of the Northern Territory police.

As I understand it, in most State recruit intakes, the members are not sworn until their completion of training, at their graduation. But with as small a force as the Territory's was, having us as sworn members meant we could be called on to assist at any time, not that we would be encouraged to, in fact, it was stressed that we should avoid involvement in matters while in recruit school.

This was a little harder for two of the recruits who being locally recruited had been sworn some weeks before-hand, and in plain clothes assisted with general duties around the Darwin police station until the actual recruit school.

Sergeant Second Class Frank Cronshaw was in charge of recruit training. Sergeant Second Class was the middle non-commissioned officer rank and generally occupied the middle tier of positions. The structure of the force was the Commissioner, answerable to the Administrator, (who in fact had been the Commissioner until a year or so earlier when the highest ranked officer was the Assistant Commissioner). Then there was the Chief Inspector, three Divisional Inspectors, a number of Sergeant First Class positions, men who generally acted as officer-in-charge of a station such as Darwin, Katherine, Tennant Creek or Alice Springs and the Darwin CIB.

The Sergeant Second Class officers were generally in charge of the likes of Darwin Traffic Section, Prosecuting, Liquor Licensing, Special Branch, Fingerprints, the Alice Springs CIB. Sergeants Third Class acted as shift or operational supervisors and were the first reference point for advice from the general rank of Constable. There were only a smattering of Constables First Class or Senior Constables, men with years of service who had not success-

"Marrenah House" Police Barracks, The Esplanade, Darwin, 1960's

The Centra Hotel, 1999, now on the site of the former police barracks

In uniform for the first time on the day of the Recruit School Passing Out Parade

fully sought promotion or really didn't want it although many Senior Constables were qualified for promotion to Sergeant Third Class when a vacancy occurred.

Sergeant Cronshaw (all Sergeants regardless of rank were referred to as Sergeant, only their signature title making reference to the level of rank) told us that when he joined the force nearly 15 years earlier, his experience was to be recruited from his home town of Sydney, flown to Darwin on a Saturday, taken to the Chinese tailor on the Sunday to be measured for his uniform which was virtually made up on the spot, before commencing duty on the Monday. Real on-the-job training. More recently recruit school had been of six weeks duration but our recruit school was another milestone – it was to be eight weeks.

The 17 recruits – including the five women – could not have been more diverse. This diversity extended right through the force and probably made it not only unique but gave it a special group of people with extremely varied talents. This worked well not only in gaining community respect but achieving a high degree of success in policing.

Policewomen had been a relatively new addition to the force and retention had been a great difficulty. Of the eight positions – six stationed in Darwin and two in Alice Springs – there were only three filled until the new recruits joined. Apart from being single, the women were required to be 25 years-old. While all the women had been recruited in Sydney, Jean Lilley was an English migrant, Angelina Butta had travelled overseas before deciding to try N.T., Marie Christopherson and Diana Tracey had worked in Sydney while Patricia Keaton had grown up in Camden, NSW, and worked 10 years as a PMG telephonist. At least she was a 'rural girl'.

Brian Craig had worked around Darwin as had Doug Vallance, who had come to Darwin with the PMG some years earlier. Jim Carstairs was from Scotland and had been a member of the Edinburgh City Police before migrating to Australia six months earlier. Bob Haydon was another ex-PMG guy who had been working at Bourke in New South Wales while Bob O'Keefe had been with the postal side of the PMG's department in Sydney. Another New South Wales recruit was Dave Dunstan.

Ray Weir had only 10 days notice of his appointment. A carpenter and joiner, he'd been working as an overseer at Long Bay gaol. Then there was also Ray Wein, another Sydney guy with experience in the Commonwealth Police as I recall. The only other Victorian was Chris Crellin who'd been working in insurance. His claim to fame during the recruit school was, as a dare, eating a live green frog, whole, while out with the boys one evening. Queensland was represented by Frank Aitchson who'd been working as a radio announcer at Mt Isa while Tasmania's contribution to the recruit school was my room-mate, Doug Trenhan, who had five years in the Tasmania Police before coming to Darwin.

To me, the most consoling feature of my fellow recruits was that at least two if not three appeared to be shorter than me, although I was equal to the lightest framed amongst the guys.

The recruit school was conducted in a room of a wing of the old Darwin primary school, now used as the Adult Education College. It was an 8am start with I think an hour for lunch. We finished at 4pm, much the same routine as a day shift although we did have a mid-morning break providing an opportunity for those who wanted a smoke, and a relief for the rest of us from the unpadded, desk type seats.

The days started about 6.50am when someone from night shift at Darwin station would call by the barracks and wake those working day shift, and the recruits. A shower, then to the Commonwealth Hostel a few hundred yards along The Esplanade for a quick breakfast and on to recruit school.

The recruits were "encouraged" (instructed would probably be a more appropriate word) to eat at the Hostel for the duration of the recruit school. This had a couple of aims, to try to ensure everyone ate reasonably well, got settled into a routine, got to know each other out of the class room and kept meals to a timetable to work in with the recruit school.

We got the meals at Government rates which made it fairly attractive cost wise. We paid in advance each pay-day, the figure $28 a fortnight comes to mind but it could have been less. There was always plenty to eat, and as much to eat as you liked, as long as you liked what they had to eat. Some people said breakfast was the best meal of the day, well, there is little than can go wrong with cereal, toast and tea ... tea, well being someone who really likes a good cup of tea, the tea was probably the worst part of the meal. Then there was always bacon, eggs, baked beans, or something else hot.

At lunch time it was to-and-from the hostel pretty quickly, usually trying to find some time to get to a bank, or a shop or two, for something. Government offices in Darwin closed at 4.21pm sharp; they opened at 8am and also had an hour for lunch, nearly all 12noon to 1pm. The business area closed at 5 o'clock except Fridays which was late night shopping night, through until 9pm.

One draw-back with the hostel meals was the early hour of dinner, which made it a long time between dinner and breakfast, remembering that there were no facilities for food at the barracks.

One of the first things I noticed about Darwin was the milk "Pasteurised, Homogenised, Reconstituted Milk" read the Paul's carton. There was virtually no fresh milk in Darwin, the little that was around went to the hospital. However, the Perth based company "Paul's" provided the general supply of "fresh" cartoned milk around Darwin. I never drank plain milk anyway, the real taste difference in tea or flavoured milk wasn't noticeable, in fact, I quite liked the taste of the flavoured milk.

The other thing I really noticed in shops was the smaller range and supply of fresh fruit and vegetables. I wrote home *"fresh fruit is dear, an orange is 10c. Tonight at the hostel there was fresh fruit so everyone took two apples, one for themselves and one for "Ron" – later-on!"*

During recruit school "Tom the Cheap" grocers, another Perth based company, opened a Darwin store with a great fan-fare of advertising in the *"News"* and a saturation campaign on the local commercial radio station. The day the store opened, I passed by at 5 o'clock and they wouldn't let any more people into the store ... it was just so crowded ... I think I was after the razor blades *"8 for 9c, guaranteed three shaves each"*. Woolworths was deserted ... but it was easy shopping especially when they reduced most of their store prices to the same at "Tom's"! It really gave the town something to talk about.

We were "encouraged" – again, everybody complied – to have a cheque account for direct payment of our wages. I'd never had a cheque account before but opened one at the Commonwealth Bank where I had a savings account I could also use. Stamp duty in the Territory was 1c a cheque but that was of no use for cheques I had to send home so I arranged with Mum to send up some 5c Victorian Duty Stamps which I'd put on any cheque I was sending down for something I needed.

A pleasant surprise was my first pay. Unexpectedly, I was paid from the day I left home. I was also paid Commonwealth travelling allowance (T/A) from when I left home to when I arrived in Darwin which well covered my travelling costs for petrol, accommodation, meals and vehicle repairs, plus the cost of putting the car on the train between Port Augusta and Alice Springs.

At the time, a cheque was a very negotiable bit of paper for someone known to be in the police force. It wouldn't "bounce" – to "bounce" a cheque was a breach of police regulations; a real "no, no". Amongst the general population, false pretence offences involving cheques were all too frequent.

In the time between when I'd received my letter on Christmas Eve advising of my unsuccessful application for the force, and the letter of appointment three weeks later, I'd bought a block of land at Wonthaggi, well, not quite Wonthaggi but at an ocean front estate at Cape Paterson, 10 miles (16kms) out of Wonthaggi. I bought it for £440 ($880) through Jack Elkin, the local real estate agent. As well as the estate agent, Jack was one of Wonthaggi's two undertakers. One thing Tom Gannon and *"The Express"* did was record an obituary on every local person who died. Everybody got an acknowledgment, sometimes half a page, other times only half a dozen paragraphs with the concluding lines always *"Funeral arrangements were in the hands of ..."*

Jack was also a councillor of the Borough of Wonthaggi, so I was constantly at his office. I saw this block for sale, went and had a look at it and bought it, on terms. I was no sooner in Darwin when I received a letter from the vendor, an Italian migrant chap, saying he really was selling the block to finance a trip home to Italy and if I could manage to pay off the balance immediately, he would give me a 10% discount. I thought this was too good an offer to miss so I decided to speak to the manager of the Commonwealth Bank in Darwin to see if he could assist.

To my amazement, he authorised a $500 overdraft, for six months, on my new cheque account, he'd hold the title in his safe until that was cleared. It was all fixed in minutes. Nobody could speak ill to me of the Commonwealth Bank for the next 20 years.

Recruit school was not all law, either theory or practical application. There were sessions a couple of time a week for typing carried out in another part of the complex conducted by Mrs Garner, wife of the principal of the college. From my journalistic work, I was probably the best typist amongst the recruits, not that I could touch type or anything like it, but many, including most of the women, had never typed a word in their life, and if there is one main chore of a police officer, it is typing – all sorts of reports, briefs, witness statements, interviews, traffic accident reports ... and never a single copy, at least in duplicate and up to seven copies of some forms in a death file.

There was an afternoon a week set aside for swimming. What a disaster. I couldn't claim to be a swimmer, I was the poorest swimmer of the lot but as eager as I was to learn, it seemed there was a jinx on us taking advantage of the weather to swim.

Pistol Practice, under instruction from Sergeant Barry "Tubby" Tiernan, I have my first shots on the range. From right: Bob Haydon. myself and Doug Vallance. (Sergeant Tiernan was a Special Branch Officer who instructed colleges to ignore him at official functions and "just think of me as a refrigerator")

The Administrator, Roger Dean, presents me with the prize for Dux of the Recruit School – a copy of "Patrol Indefinite"

First attempt at swimming was to be at the Larrakeyah Army Barracks where the army had a salt water pool. We arrived to find the water being changed, and the pool less than half full. At an alternative pool the cyclone fence and gates were secured so the lesson was abandoned. We did get to other pools and over the next few weeks I got to swim to at least save myself, something I doubt I could do today.

As hot as the weather was in the Top End at the time, it was impossible to swim in the sea ... box jellyfish, blue stingers were abundant in the months October to April so pool and inland streams were the only swimming resorts during the hottest part of the year.

There was a visit to the government garage to learn basic vehicle maintenance; how to start a vehicle without keys and other vehicle formalities. Apart from visiting Court as part of the recruit school schedule, any other spare time, such as a failed swimming outing, would be at Court. There were also self-defence sessions but above all, civil defence exercises.

In hindsight, it could be said Darwin was in a state of phobia, for fear of attack; from whom I am not sure, but at the time the greatest fear was of Indonesia. Not only did the city have a full civil defence service, which would have been great in the event of a cyclone or some natural disaster, but the emphasis appeared to be on attack from outside, and a nuclear one at that.

There were air raid sirens set up over the entire city, and at 9am on the first Monday of each month there was a full siren test – sirens wailing away. What it all achieved, I will never know – nor it appeared did many other people in Darwin know either.

With a large RAAF base in Darwin – the airport was actually the RAAF base but used for domestic services also – there were military planes around constantly with air exercises always coming up. These included RAF aircraft, one of which was a massive RAF V-Bomber, a jet with a delta wing which had the capacity to also fly low, the theory being to avoid radar. It would approach Darwin from the sea and come in over the city barely above the tree tops with a thunderous roar that shook the whole city.

The chap in charge of civil defence was an Englishman, Dick Webber, known to all and sundry as "Disaster Dick". He conducted the civil defence sessions of recruit school, some in the class room, others at civil defence headquarters at Parap, the sit of a former police station, and others at the civil defence training range.

For me the excitement of civil defence training was being "rescued" from the second storey of a disused municipal incinerator, a concrete structure at the range. I was supposed to be "injured" and ended up, dressed in my boiler suit, steel-toe-capped boots, gaiters and red safety helmet, lashed to a stretcher and by the control of ropes, slid down an extension ladder. I was selected as the real-life dummy because I was the lightest to lift. When I safely reached ground level Sergeant Cronshaw remarked he had never seen anyone looking so white-faced. I felt very relieved.

We also had regular first aid sessions conducted by the St John Ambulance Brigade, which operated the civil ambulance service within the Darwin city area and immediate surrounds although we did not proceed to formal first aid exams and a certificate.

There were talks from the fire brigade and the prison service. We were all a little astonished to learn that prisoners in the Territory, if they behaved themselves, earned 9 cents a day.

Other time was spent with lectures on criminal investigation, fingerprints, preparation of court briefs, questioning and other general police procedures. Apart from being police officers we got to learn that we had *"ex-officio"* powers in respect of a great number of other positions like Deputy Inspector of Brands (livestock) with the powers to enter lands, round up cattle and inspect their brands, Dog Registrars, Wildlife Rangers, auxiliary firemen (an even greater list when you are officer-in-charge of a one-man police station).

We seemed to be always filling out forms for one thing or another, being asked to join in this or that, one becoming blood donors. The Blood Bank while run by Red Cross, was very closely linked to the Darwin hospital. There was no true blood bank in Darwin, donors were generally called on as blood was needed and could be used in a fresh condition. We were all asked to become blood donors and all did. Later we learnt that the hospital declined to pass on to the Red Cross our blood-type results because somehow, someone at the hospital was "told" that we had not voluntarily agreed to become donors; that there was a sense of compulsion and as such this conflicted with the voluntary principles of the service. Sergeant Cronshaw was furious. Most of the recruits were quite upset too, to the degree that on-our-own-bat, we arranged for the bulk of us to again report for blood-typing, even though we knew some of us were being transferred to Alice Springs or Tennant Creek at the completion of the recruit school.

We had been told the first day of recruit school that at the end of the school one or two of us would be transferred to Tennant Creek and probably

1966 Recruit School

Standing l to r: Constables Doug Trenham, David Pollock, Sergeant First Class Charles Porter; Constables Brian Craig, Bob O'Keefe, Chris Crellin, Brian Aitcheson, Dave Dunstan, Jim Carstairs, Ray Weir; Doug Vallance, Ray Wein, Bob Haydon; seated: Sergeant Second Class Frank Cronshaw; Inspector Jim Mannion, Policewomen Constables Marie Christophersen, Diana Tracey; Commissioner Clive Graham, Policewomen Constables Jean Lilley; Patricia Keaton and Angelina Butta

(Policewomen were attached to the CIB and did not wear uniforms)

three men and one woman to Alice Springs. We were a little surprised that only a week or so into the recruit school we were asked if any of us would like to apply for these positions. So we had a couple of days to think about it and a typing session to prepare an official report making the application. I put my name down for Tennant Creek and Alice Springs, I really didn't want to stay in Darwin, I felt that I would be a whole lot more comfortable 620 or 950 miles (1,000 or 1,530kms) away from the Darwin headquarters and I also felt that I'd like the life better in Alice Springs, and that there and Tennant Creek would provide a lot more opportunities for varied work plus they had a "winter" ... and there was Australian Rules football in Alice Springs during winter, not this rugby league rubbish.

To our greater surprise, the day after we made our applications Sergeant Cronshaw announced who was going where – Jim Carstairs was going to Tennant Creek; while Patricia Keaton, Doug Vallance, Ray Weir and I were off to Alice Springs. A reason for the early arrangements was to allow us to be measured for the making of winter uniforms. While in Darwin, the Northern Division of the force as a whole, wore the same khaki uniform, comprising open neck shirt (you wore a tie to Court or some official function only), light weight long trousers with a brown buckle belt, brown shoes, and a *"Kimberley Downs"* model Akubra by day and a peak cap by evening. Those stationed from Tennant Creek south had a winter uniform for the months of May to August which was a unique brown colour with both trouser and tunic and worn with the normal khaki shirt and tie. The closest I ever came to describing the brown colour of the uniform was to compare it to the brown of the Pioneer Tour drivers. The issue of one tunic and two pairs of trousers each year was tailor made at John Martin's, Adelaide. Another member of the force in barracks, Constable Bob Kucharzewski, born in Scotland of Polish parents, with as broad a Scotsman's accent as you could wish, was a qualified tailor and he was organised to measure us up.

The Northern Territory police emblem, about two-and-a-half inches high, commonly described as featuring a kangaroo scratching itself, standing on a scroll with the word "POLICE", surrounded by a laurel wreath and surmounted by a crown, was the hat badge. On both collar points was an identification number, and on the shirt shoulder epaulettes was a small silver coloured badge – "POLICE".

During recruit school we wore plain clothes the whole time, in fact we did not get an issue of uniform (for most of us just enough to keep us going) until the afternoon of the second last day of recruit school, just in time for us to iron, adjust and be able to wear it to the graduation parade. The initial uniform issue was six shirts, four pairs of trousers, two ties, two pairs of Julius Marlow shoes (we got an order for them and went and bought them at Heaven's shoe store) a cap and the *"Kimberley Downs"* Akubra hat which needed to be steamed to get it into the *'right'* shape, oh and a leather belt and a plastic raincoat.

There were several examinations during the recruit school. The first was on the Friday of the second week, then the Friday of the fourth week and early in the last week of the school. Thankfully, Good Friday was the sixth Friday of the recruit school so exams were abandoned that week. The first two exams were a single paper we did in the morning, getting the results the following Monday morning. The final exams started with a fingerprint exam, then a written law and a written practical exam, each of three hours, on successive mornings.

I felt pretty pleased with myself scoring 73 in the first exam, the top mark was 75 and the lowest 34. In the second exam I topped the school with 83 with the next mark 79. This time around lowest mark picked up to 50 which pleased Sergeant Cronshaw no end. In the fingerprint exam I managed equal third top mark with 77, the top being 81. In the written law exam I was also third with 79 while the top mark was 82 and the second highest 79. At this stage Jean Lilley had an aggregate 5 marks above my total and I was resigned to not making it Dux of the recruit school, not that it was something I had set out to do, in fact it was one of the last things on my mind. What did bother me was that if she was to be dux, she would be the first woman dux, and a real fuss was being made of this prospect.

To give Sergeant Cronshaw time to finish marking the last exam papers (remember, he had 17 papers each of a 3 hour duration to process) we were sent to the pistol range under the guidance of Sergeant Barry Tiernan, a rather portly officer known commonly (I am not sure if ever to his face) as "Tubby" Tiernan. Sergeant Tiernan was officer-in-charge of Special Branch, one of two officers whose responsibilities covered sensitive security matters, army deserters, illegal migrants; and security of dignitaries, visiting ambassadors or even members of the Royal Family. The story was told that once in a briefing he said to fellow officers to ignore him, not recognise him in the gathering where a dignitary was to visit. *"Just think I am a refrigerator in the corner of the room"* he told them.

I'd never had a revolver in my hand before, the closest thing being my brother's cowboy six shooter cap gun, in fact the first time I had any firearm in my hand was a few weeks earlier when another of the recruits, Jim Carstairs, had bought a .22 semi automatic rifle and we had gone down the track to some bush and had a shot or two.

I was pretty pleased that with my first six rounds of standing shot, I not only hit the target five times, but once a bullseye. I didn't fare so well in the rapid fire but more than half my shots at least hit the target.

With the graduation parade and the end of the recruit school getting closer the real effort now was to get everything together for the graduation night party to be held at the barracks. Liquor and food had to be secured, we all had to put in toward the night. As the better typist in the group, I'd been given the job earlier in the piece to type the official invitations to the Commissioner and others. The night before the party, the barracks hall was appropriately decorated. I'm convinced that as Friday morning dawned, many palm trees around Darwin felt a little naked.

The final morning of recruit school was taken up with a rehearsal of the passing out parade and getting back our final exam results – the practical law paper. I managed a mark of 76%. Minutes later when all marks were written up on the blackboard I found I had managed to scrape in as dux of the recruit school – an average of 77.7 compared to Jean Lilley's 76.8. Inside myself I was feeling pretty proud when at lunch-time I sent a telegram home to my parents, remembering the knock-backs I'd had along the way and the struggle it had been to make the recruit school at all.

The afternoon saw us all together in uniform for the first time. Individually, we each stepped out to receive from the Commissioner our official ID card, then after a short speech from the Administrator, Roger Dean, he presented me with the dux prize – the book *"Patrol Indefinite"* with the inscription *"Presented to D. L. Pollock Dux of the Northern Territory Police Recruits. 22nd April, 1966"*.

Then there were more official photos, group photos and an informal chat with the Administrator plus photos for the local newspaper. As I was formerly a journalist this gave them a special story line with reports on both ABC and the local commercial radio news plus a write-up complete with photos in the Monday's *"Northern Territory News"* and the Alice Springs *"Centralian Advocate"* the following week. One thing the media were particularly interested in was the issue of a new design cap ... like other police forces around the world, the Territory was moving to have a blue and white band. It was something that was going to make the recruits stand out as the "new boys on the beat". Fortunately, a few weeks later, as the annual uniform issue was made, all other members had the new design caps to wear on evening and night shifts.

For me, the disappointment of the passing out parade was the non-attendance of Chief Inspector Bowie. He was said to be ill but I noticed he manage to get to the graduation party at the barracks that evening.

Being one of the recruits with a car, one of my jobs for the party was to go to the RAAF base and pick up a car load of girls from the single quarters – not one car load but two trips! Then I was rostered to help with the bar.

More than 200 turned up for the graduation party. There was heaps of food, including a pig on a spit, which had met its fate at the barracks the previous evening. There was 110 gallons (500 litres) of draught beer not to mention the special brew punch which knocked many stupid after only a couple of small glasses. The hypnotist Frank Johnson was in Darwin at the time and had that evening put on a performance to aid the Police Boys Club. After the show he came to the barracks and joined in the party. I called it a night at 2.30am. I still had not had a drink.

I was the only one from barracks to go to breakfast next morning. In fact, when I left there were still two or three in the barracks hall who had not even gone home. There was a hell of a mess to clean up but I was surprised how people came to life and the job was done in no time. It was a great party, with not even a complaint from Douglas Lockwood.

It was time to pack, to move on, to take up my appointment in Alice Springs. The Monday morning was ANZAC Day and as the morning passed Jim Carstairs and I headed for Katherine and next day to Tennant Creek where I left him before continuing to The Alice.

CHAPTER 4

Constable Pollock reports for duty

I arrived in Alice Springs and reported to the officer-in-charge, Sergeant First Class Allan Metcalfe, then made my first Journal entry. *"Constable Pollock reports arriving at Alice Springs at 2.30pm".*

I was shown to the barracks, which were just through the back yard of the station, but with a separate vehicle access off Gregory Tce. I was issued with my linen – two pairs of new sheets, pillow cases and towels ... but the urgency was not so much to show me to the barracks, rather to pass on a message that the editor of the *"Centralian Advocate"*, the Alice Springs weekly newspaper, wanted me to contact him urgently as they had a printing press problem and Jack Bennett had suggested they *"get David Pollock to have a look at it, he will be in Alice Springs today"* and see if I could solve the problem!

So within an hour of arriving in Alice Springs I was at *"The Advocate"* office to see if I could solve 'their problem'. The ink rollers on the printing press were not distributing the ink evenly across the print and thus on to the paper as it was fed through. Unfortunately I couldn't spot the problem. After all, I was a hand compositor not a trained machinist although I had plenty of experience on hand fed Platens and an automatic Heidelberg. But they did overcome the problem which was caused by inexperience and fixed by adjusting the rollers.

The barracks was no Hilton. In fact it was little short of a dump. It was built in the 1940's with a timber frame, fibro, flywire and a galvanised iron roof. An aged evaporative air-conditioner was mounted on top. There were about nine bedrooms which surrounded an open space, the common area with an excuse for a kitchen in one corner. There were a couple of good-sized refrigerators in the area with the centre feature being a slow-combustion wood heater. There was the typical '60's laminex table and chairs, a couple of vinyl lounge seats, and a bare concrete floor.

Most of the bedrooms were of good size, for one person, although most were designated as shared bedrooms. At the time there were enough bedrooms for each of us in barracks to have his own room, so there wasn't a need to share. The rooms had an open built-in hanging space, a wardrobe with more hanging space and a dressing table. The beds were steel framed with a wire mattress base, a good mattress at least, but the floors were again bare concrete except for a floor mat.

41

*In winter uniform outside the Alice Springs Police
Station, May, 1966*

The Todd River "Coming down" towards The Gap

At least the rooms were airy, with good outside light, big sliding, glass, flywired windows. There was a portable fan, and most importantly, a radiator. We would soon be needing it as the late autumn days approached. The walls were Canite in need of maintenance, the holes conveniently covered with posters. The whole building was in desperate need of maintenance, but at the time there seemed little prospect of any real improvement.

There were two bathrooms, one had a bath and a wash basin while the other had a couple of wash basins and two shower cubicles. There was only the one toilet. While there were about eight of us in the barracks, the facilities coped but it was wise to get in early for a shower to make sure you had hot water. The hot water system was a wood fired boiler which relied on the police trackers or members of barracks to keep it alight, and thus maintain the hot water supply. It was important that someone from night shift remembered to light the heater early in the morning so that those in barracks working day shift could have a hot morning shower. It wasn't that important during summer, but in winter a cold morning shower was out of the question, so it was wise to shower before going to bed. If someone from barracks was on night shift, there generally wasn't a problem, but when two married guys were working the night shift, problems arose.

Despite its inadequacies, the barracks was going to be home for the foreseeable future so there was no point in getting demoralised over the place.

Most members in barracks had been in the force a couple of years, some longer. Jim Berry had been in the force many years. Married and divorced, he had worked at many outposts but had plans to leave the force shortly. He was heavily involved with the up-coming population census and had a huge area to the west of Alice Springs to patrol over about three weeks. With that out of the way, and the extra travelling allowance to be earned for the job, he resigned, to take over a roadhouse at Threeways, 15 mile (24km) north of Tennant Creek, at the Barkly Highway junction.

Bob Henfry was originally from Perth and had an uncle who had played Australian Rules for Carlton in the VFL. At least he could in-part speak the same sporting language as me. Over the years, we became great mates. Bruce Wyatt was an ex-Sydney-ite but at least he didn't ram Rugby League down our throats. He was a good organiser and one of the driving forces in eventually getting improvements to the barracks. Graham "Dasher" Daly was a bit of a mystery man, hailing from Broken Hill, he seemed to have means of getting his hands on anything that anybody

The Todd River in flood at the Causeway

Aboriginal humpies, their homes, at Yuendumu, 1966

New homes under construction at Yuendumu, 1966

wanted, quite legitimately, although at times some of us thought it better not to ask questions.

Malcolm "Bluey" King had a bent on gliding and seemed to spend every spare minute at the Gliding Club airstrip, 16 mile (26km) north of Alice Springs, at the Alice Springs Emergency Airstrip. We didn't see much of John Oldfield; he was on relieving duties at Kulgera, 175 miles (280kms) south of Alice Springs. When he finished there, had some leave, he returned to resign although he did stay on to live and work in Alice Springs.

Of course there was Ray Weir and Doug Vallance, the other two recruits who had transferred to Alice Springs with me.

The policewomen had their own barracks, a part of an old house, the other part used as the CIB offices, situated diagonally across the road from the police station. Their facilities were also a little on the basic side, but with just the two policewomen, and being allowed to cook in their barracks, they sort of 'lived on the job'.

The Standing Order instructing that no meals were to be cooked in barracks (but remember you were allowed to prepare snacks) was applied in Alice Springs. It was always one of the many quirks of barracks life. The guys in barracks had an arrangement at the Mt Gillen Motel, at the time equally the best motel in Alice Springs, and part of the Ansett chain. Either lunch or dinner, three courses, cost us just $1. There was a table set in the corner of the main dining room for us to sit and be served. It was a pretty good arrangement. The only hassle was getting the meal served in the 40-minute break when you were on duty, not to mention being able to schedule the meal break with the meal time at the motel. When off-duty, everybody made an effort to dress smartly, after all, in a dining room of tourists, you were a little on-show. Heads would turn when, on duty, we would arrive in uniform.

One thing, you could get away with at barracks was cooking breakfast - crumpets, cereal or a winter favourite, porridge. Again, some pretty big lunch snacks were knocked up in barracks but nobody seemed to mind.

I hardly had time to get the car unpacked, sort out my room and get a uniform ready for duty the next morning. It was the start of a new fortnight's roster, so being on day shift, I was the first of the recruits to actually report for duty. Ray and Doug were on evening shift. In my first roster I had three day shifts – the Thursday, Friday and the Monday, a public holiday, May Day, then a couple of days off before being the first to front for night shift – seven nights straight. Duty was ten 8-hour shifts in each 14-day period with one of the off-duty days being a Sunday. All other duty was on paid overtime. There were no penalty rates for weekend work, evening or night shift but a minimum call-out of two hours at time-and-a-half if you were called to Court or called on duty for some reason.

At the time, the day shift was 8.30am–4.30pm; evening shift was 4pm–12 midnight, and night shift 12midnight to 8am except one fellow, known as the day reserve worked 8am–4pm. There was a virtual permanent day reserve Monday to Friday, a Senior Constable Dennis Connigan, known to all as "Dinny" Connigan. He was the front counter man, did the radio scheds to Darwin and the outpost stations in Southern Division.

So, Thursday, 28 April, 1966, a nervous *"Constable Pollock reports on duty at 8.30am"*. There was no time book as such; there was the Day Journal and the Complaints and Enquiry Journal or commonly known as the *C&E Journal*. The Day Journal recorded the moment by moment activities, like signing on/signing off duty, what you did for the shift, your patrols, arrests, and so on. The Complaints and Enquiry Journal recorded complaints and enquires made at the station on the left page and the action taken in response on the right hand page, with a cross reference to the Day Journal recording your duty.

My first shift sergeant was Sergeant Third Class George Simpson. He'd been in the force some years, had worked at several remote stations including Anthony Lagoon, on the Barkly Tablelands. As I recall, there were two or three other constables on duty in the general duties section.

First task of the day was school crossing duty ... off to either the corner of Todd Street and Wills Terrace where high school children crossed to the Anzac Oval complex, or outside the Ross Park primary school. It was more a ritual, a be-seen exercise, repeated at lunch time when school broke for lunch-hour, more than anything else. I guess that's why the task was dropped later in the year as pressure on time increased. As it was, on many a day, an incident of greater urgency left the school crossing unmanned.

Then it was back to the police station to ready the prisoners in custody for 10am court. The magistrate's court – the Alice Springs Court of Summary Jurisdiction – sat every morning Monday to Friday at 10am in the court house in Parsons Street some 100 yards (90m) diagonally across the road from the police station. The resident magistrate in Alice Springs was a Mr Godfrey Foy Hall SM known to all and sundry as "Scrubby" Hall, a reflection on his bush justice approach to his job.

A former solicitor from New South Wales, and a rugby league devotee, he had held the position a number of years. He had a circuit of Tennant Creek, monthly at the time, and later included Katherine, and if the need arose, he would also sit in Darwin. On these occasions local Justices of the Peace – two sitting together – would constitute the court.

I went to court for half-an-hour, then the shift sergeant paired me up with Constable Graham "Dasher" Daly, armed us with the warrant book and sent us on a patrol to Amoonguna aboriginal reserve, some 8 miles (11kms) south east of the town. We had a summons to serve and the patrol also gave us the opportunity to check if there were any aboriginals at the settlement who had outstanding warrants for either unpaid fines or non-cash bail forfeitures. "Dasher" had been in The Alice 18 months or so and had got to know the regulars. A few enquiries to those in charge of the settlement or amongst those living at the settlement would soon show if anybody with an outstanding warrant was about.

So off we headed, in a cage – a Holden panel van – down Gap Road to Heavitree Gap, then east crossing the Todd River and heading through the farm area to the end of the bitumen, then three or four miles of sandy dirt road to Amoonguna. However, I was soon to learn a little more about "Dasher". First stop was the Gap Store, half way to The Gap where his good mate Bill Hill ran a service station and store. A cuppa and catch up on gossip was the order of the morning. Then it was on to Amoonguna.

Heavitree Gap, about a mile (1.6km) south of the main town centre, was an imposing feature. It was a break in the Macdonnell Ranges which allowed access for not only the Stuart Highway from the south but also the rail line and most impressively, the dry 50 yards (45m) wide bed of the Todd River.

The ochre coloured broken rock of The Gap sides rose several hundred feet either side as the Ranges ran east-west for miles. Immediately through The Gap, the Ross River Road headed west over a single-lane concrete causeway, across the bed of the river. The Pitchi Ritchie Sanctuary featuring works of sculptor Bill Ricketts, famous for his sculpture sanctuary in the Dandenong Ranges out of Melbourne, and the Heavitree Gap Caravan and Tourist Park were the properties across the river. Next to Pitchi Ritchie was a date farm, then the only commercial date palm plantation in Australia.

Then there was the Heenan family's vegetable gardens growing fresh lettuce, cabbage and other goods for the local market with surplus supplies being sent to Tennant Creek or Darwin in the north. There were also groves of oranges and mandarins coming into season. The citrus in the area was equal to the best I ever tasted. There were a few other vegetable farms, an olive grove if I recall correctly, but all still showing the stress of a long drought only recently broken.

Amoonguna aboriginal settlement was an eye-opener. Smart grey cement brick government style houses occupied by European staff contrasted with the galvanised "William's Huts" that they used as offices. The kitchen and dining hall comprised a large silver painted galvanised iron shed. At the bottom of the scale was the aboriginal housing – rows of untidy sheds with extensive verandahs, wire clothes lines and mobs of barking, skin-and-bone dogs of true "Heinz" breed.

As I recall, we spent a fruitless hour checking the warrant book and returned to town in time for school crossing duties. Much of the afternoon was spent on a firewood collection patrol. In an old Land Rover utility I took trackers Larry Jabarula or Snowy Harris to the north of town to collect firewood, mainly drought-dead mulga, for the police station open fire which was in increased use in the evenings and night as May approached. Of course we needed wood for the barracks hot water system too.

Firewood collection was something the chaps from barracks frequently did in their off-duty hours. It provided a chance to get out into the solitude of the bush, provided some exercise, and if nothing more, something to do! I made many a patrol during the winter months, usually with Bob Henfry. We always took at least one of the trackers. Although they usually knew in good time that we would be going to collect wood, they never had the axes sharp and ready.

Few Australians realise how bitterly cold it can be in Alice Springs in winter. Clear-air overnight temperatures were around freezing early into the evening with solid white frosts in the morning, down to 27 or 28F (-4 or -5C) quite common, even three or four mornings in a row. Generally, overnight temperatures are lower in Alice Springs than Hobart. July's average minimum in The Alice is 40.2F (4.1C) while in Hobart it is 40.7F (4.5C).

It was a 15–18 miles (24–30kms) trip out north to the firewood collection area and I can always remember Tracker Larry waiting until our arrival to sit down to sharpen the axe, 10 minutes of wasted time. I remember we would be approaching the collection spot and Bob would say *"If Larry* (who would be riding in the back of the Land Rover) *sits down to sharpen the axe when we arrive, I'll wrap the bloody thing around his neck!"* Sure enough, Larry would sit down to sharpen the axe, with Bob mumbling on!

Mulga is a tough wood, (I guess it has to be tough to withstand the rigours of the Central Australia climate) slow growing, and it is relatively shallow rooted, with L-shaped roots from its trunk just below the surface spreading in several directions. This tree trunk-root shape provided a strong grain for the making of the traditional Central Australia hook or killer boomerang, the idea being for the boomerang in its L-shape to be thrown and end up wrapped around the neck of an emu or even a kangaroo, breaking the neck to kill it.

The dead mulga was mainly still standing, trees 10–15 feet (3–4m) high which a couple of us could usually push over; then chop the branches, and load it up, rope it down and back to the station where over the next few days, the trackers would further chop the wood for use at the station, in the hot water system or for themselves in their own quarters.

At most police stations the trackers lived on site but in Alice Springs the trackers lived at Amoonguna settlement and travelled in and out of town by bus unless we needed their services out of hours when we would have to go and collect them at dawn, or take them back at dark.

There was time for a patrol of the hotels too – but I didn't make an arrest on my first day of duty.

⋙·◦·⋘

The first day on the job behind me, I quickly settled into the routine. Next morning I was on day shift again, there was the school crossing routine and time at the station to learn a little more of just what went on. There was great interest in the "radio sched", where "Dinny" Connigan, the day reserve officer, first talked, at least tried to talk, to Darwin and then to the various Southern Division out-stations using short wave radio. There were vehicle checks to be done, fuelling vehicles, having the vehicles washed, helping get any prisoners in custody to Court and so on.

I attended my first motor vehicle accident ... a municipal worker, Ningah Tuit, driving a tip truck backed into the Mini Minor used by Sister Eileen in Parsons Street, opposite the entrance to the barracks yard, less than 100 yards (90m) from the police station. I walked to the scene and completed my first accident report. The damage was minimal but with two Commonwealth "Z" plated vehicles involved, the full accident report had to be completed. In addition, the brief, complaint and summons for Tuit on a charge of "driving without due care, attention or consideration" had to be prepared.

Ironically, when the accident incident went to court, a few weeks later, Welfare Branch arranged for Ian Barker, the town's leading solicitor, to represent Tuit ... and in a manner so typical of Magistrate "Scrubby" Hall, he dismissed the matter ... he accepted Tuit had in fact used due care, he had looked, but it was just unfortunate that he didn't see Sister Eileen's car!

When I took the accident report, it was the first time I met Sister Eileen. She was a welfare officer with the Welfare Branch of the Northern Territory Administration (NTA). She had first come to work at Alice Springs with the Anglican church which operated the St Mary's Mission, on the southern outskirts of town, caring for many disadvantaged children, particularly aboriginal and part aboriginal children of Central Australia. Over the years we had many a contact as we dealt with either children or distressed, needy people.

The Welfare Branch offices were in a building first used as the home of the officer-in-charge of police at Alice Springs. In fact, the senior welfare officer at Alice Springs, Creed Lovegrove, who now lived with his family in a house opposite the barracks, had lived in the building as a child, his father being a former officer-in-charge at Alice Springs. Another welfare officer was Helanie "Lannie" Lane. She had grown up around Belgrave and had come to the Territory some years earlier as one of the first policewomen recruits of the force.

The old stone Stuart Gaol building, used as a store room these days, stood behind the welfare office, between it and the police station, but Creed Lovegrove would tell of days as a lad when he had seen prisoners in the gaol building.

The Northern Territory Administration comprised many branches. These covered all the State-like activities of primary industry, lands, water resources, motor registration, the police, fire brigade and prisons and in the town areas carried out all the municipal type duties of a town council like parks maintenance, garbage collection, street maintenance and cleaning. There was a central stores provider and a central government garage, but the Commonwealth Works department had its own garage for its heavy equipment maintenance. The Commonwealth was more directly responsible for construction issues, education, health and the courts.

The next day I was on duty was the Monday, May Day, a Territory public holiday. In Alice Springs the Rotary Club organised the "Bangtail Muster", a street parade of mad-cap floats and other entertainment all leading that year to Anzac Oval where the Apex Club and the Youth Centre conducted the May Day sports, the feature race of the afternoon being the May Day Mile.

I was put on point duty for the parade, not just some quiet corner, but probably the most significant traffic corner of the parade, in Todd Street, at the corner of Gregory Terrace. I'd never done point-duty before, we didn't have our uniform in time to do any practice during recruit school, just given some theory on the topic. But I survived! It was also a surprise when Mrs Edna Watt and her daughter Shirley, who had been on *The Ghan* on my trip north, came up and spoke to me. They had seen the write-up in the *"Centralian Advocate"* the previous week so knew I was in town and were keeping a look-out for me. They even took a photo of me . . . one of the first in uniform, on the job. As it turned out, over the years, scores of tourists asked to take photos, the khaki uniform and wide brim hat being so different to "down South". I had never expected to become a tourist attraction, it just became part of the job.

I then had a couple of days off-duty to be ready for my first stint of night shift, a 12 midnight start through to 8am for seven nights, or more correctly, mornings, in a row. It was the first time of my life I'd been awake most of these hours, let alone worked such hours. Two usually worked the night shift. My first shift was with Ewan Macintosh, a Constable First Class, a rank gained after eight years service. Obviously he'd had several years experience in both town and bush stations and was a conscientious guy. That week he taught me a lot.

First job of the night shift was for one of the two of us on shift to drive the evening shift members home! This would then extend into a patrol of the town and environs taking about an hour, usually incident free. The member back at the station would write up all the vehicle logs, record the mileages, tidy up the place, perhaps prepare the bail documents, and at this time of year, keep the open-fire burning!

The night shift had the task of fingerprinting the prisoners in custody, and granting bail to those considered eligible. I was working the second week of the fortnight roster, which was always the off-pay-week which usually meant a much lower number of arrests and people in the cells. Still, there were the regulars who would be in custody night after night.

Bail day was usually Tuesdays, so those in custody and with a record of honouring their bail were bailed out late morning while those with a record of failing to meet their bail would be kept in custody and face the magistrate later in the morning. Later this changed with people being bailed to later the same morning. It wasn't unusual for someone coming to town and hitting the grog to greet the night shift four or five nights in a row, each night having to be fingerprinted and bailed. But after a few days, the magistrate's patience would also be wearing thin and seven days in the "Big House" – the Alice Springs Prison – would sober them up.

No week of night shift could pass without a call or two, even three or four, from Miss Olive Muriel Pink, an eccentric woman in her 70's who lived alone on what was deemed to be a flora reserve for plants and trees which lived in the under 10 inch (25mm) rainfall regions of the country. She lived in a corrugated iron house surrounded by sapling gums; the 400 yards (365m) drive was an avenue of Bean trees, each named after someone who had at some time been in her favour, but unwatered and allowed to die when that favour was lost.

Between the expansion/contraction sounds of corrugated iron and the falling of twigs from the gums onto the roof of the her house, Miss Pink had developed a paranoia that people were spotlight shooting, and landing pellets on her roof which demanded the presence of police to apprehend these dastardly offenders! The trouble was, she had contacts in high places so ignoring her complaints caused more trouble that her initial complaint. At least, it broke the monotony of many a night.

Apart from her phone calls, Miss Pink was also a regular visitor to the station, calling to further complain about the *"goings on"* around the *"one million gallon water tank"* nearing completion on a hill to the east of her home or to leave a note for one of the members involved in following through one of her complaints. She was a diminutive figure, slightly stooped but still alert. When visiting the town area she invariably wore a full length grey skirt and featuring a white jabot on the bodice of her white blouse. In winter she more often wore an overcoat, and always a hat.

In the early days of decimal currency she refused to refer to any money transactions in the new currency, causing the lads at the Commonwealth Bank no end of trouble. Her current complaints seemed to centre on the "million gallon tank", anonymous phone calls and pellets from the guns of spotlight shooters landing on her roof. Previous complaints had been made against aircraft pilots flying east from the town airstrip *"perving on me"* while showering in her out-door, roofless shower facility.

Some years earlier, when the fire station had been located close to her home, she made constant complaints that the firemen were running an SP betting shop. She refused to believe the continual fire alarm test bell-ringing was not a punter ringing the station to place bets.

A couple of mornings into the shift all was quiet until about sunrise when the phone rang. It was the gaoler, he was short a prisoner; a European male inmate who had been bedded and locked in the kitchen overnight to make an early start in preparing breakfast for the prisoners. Somehow he had cut his way out and unnoticed, climbed over the brick wall to freedom.

First thing was to make an immediate trip to Amoonguna to pick up trackers Larry Jabarula and Snowy Harris and bring them to the station where detectives were waiting to take them to the gaol and commence to track the escapee. It was an intriguing display of the skills of the aboriginal trackers.

They went to the gaol wall where the escapee jumped to the ground and walked only a couple of steps to bitumen. They then fanned out checking street corner after street corner until some hours later, about a mile (1.6km) from the gaol, they found the same footprints in the dirt verge of the highway and along the unmade footpath towards the railway cattle yards. The escapee then skirted the town to the west, headed south and toward the MacDonnell range which he commenced to climb. By then it was dusk and the search was abandoned for the day.

Next morning the trackers did not continue from where they had left off the previous evening; instead they made the assumption that the escapee would climb the range and come down its southern side. So they commenced their morning search on the southern side of the range and soon detected the escapee's tracks which led them through the sewerage depot and back to the north-south rail line. The escapee headed back in toward the town, along the rail track and then diverted to break into a house and steal new shoes and some clothing. They found the discarded shoes and clothes under a bush and followed him along the rail line, ironically right past the prison and back to where he had been the previous day.

As he walked along the rail tracks he stumbled and fell; at least the trackers told the accompanying police that this is what happened. Later in the day the tracks led to a rocky out crop on the northern edge of the town. There the tracks were lost. But the trail had not gone completely cold. After circling the outcrop a couple of times Larry said *"He's in there boss"*. Bruce Wyatt walked to the outcrop, armed with a rifle and called on the escapee to surrender. He came out without a fuss.

As a test of the tracker's remark about the stumble and fall, Bruce asked *"did you hurt yourself when you fell on the rail tracks back there?"* ... *"How did you know I fell?"*, was the response.

The end of the night shift brought a new roster and a round of day and evening shifts. But before I could start the roster I was told I would be accompanying a detective out to the Yuendumu aboriginal settlement, 175 miles (280kms) north-west of Alice Springs. I had to go prepared to stay out a night, although we expected to get fed while at the settlement.

Detectives from the CIB usually investigated what was called "serious" crime. This could consist of a car theft, a serious assault or larceny, routine break, enter and steal matters and of course frauds and deaths. As it turned out a young aboriginal woman who had been assaulted at Yuendumu, had then come to town, and had died at the Amoonguna settlement.

So Friday afternoon Detective Sergeant "Monty" O'Mahoney and I headed for Yuendumu. It was a four-hour drive on a pretty good beef road which branched north-west from Alice Springs 15 miles (24km) north of the township. "Monty" O'Mahoney knew the superintendent of the settlement quite well, although the settlement was now a government settlement, once operated by the Baptist church. We were invited to stay overnight at the superintendent's residence. Having arrived late in the afternoon, we left our work to the morning.

While having breakfast, a settlement aboriginal came to the superintendent's house to collect some keys. The superintendent asked if Jimmy Cullen, the man we were interested in speaking with, was about. *"Yes, him down camp waiting"* . . . *"What's he waiting for?"* ... *"Those policemen fellows, him waiting for them"*.

It was my first visit to a remote aboriginal community. There were about 800 aboriginals at the time at Yuendumu. Most lived in appalling humpy conditions with no amenities of running water or electricity. About 70 "homes" were under construction at the time but while these would have had basic ablutions and running water, they were of solid cement brick, cement floor with a galvanised iron roof providing little more than basic protection from the elements. Still, they were a significant advance on the conditions most were living in. There was a community kitchen and eating hall where highly subsidised meals were provided to all who turned up to eat.

As soon as we had finished breakfast, we drove to the main aboriginal camp area. Jimmy Cullen walked straight over to us. We could not believe we had located the man we wanted to talk to so easily. It might have been quite different if he had known his assault victim had died. "Monty" O'Mahoney did all the questioning and formally made the arrest. I was there in uniform to be seen, observe and get the experience. We took Cullen back to Alice Springs where he was formally charged with manslaughter.

Duty in Alice Springs was always varied. Into May, the tourists were returning for another season, the annual show came around with not only police involvement in a display but also plenty of additional work through the influx to town of many bushies, many non-urban aboriginals who found difficulty handling their exposure to liquor. With the right to drink, many seemed to have the belief that the right to drink was an obligation on them to drink. Thus a few beers at the beer garden, a can or three at the show or sitting in the bed of the dry Todd River taking a few swigs from a bottle or the more popular flagon of "Reserve Port" soon had many of them drunk.

Over the years, show-time and the later developed Alice Springs rodeo provided big arrest weekends for the police. Those least able to handle the effects of liquor appeared to be the women who apart from their uncontrolled physical state would also react with loud and abusive language and by ripping their clothes from their bodies. One of my most embarrassing moments was to attend Todd Street, in the middle of the afternoon and take into custody a drunken female aborigine. She was not only a physical mess, but stark naked, screaming foul language and resisting attempts to place her into the back of a police van.

I recall another afternoon when one of the policewomen brought to the station a female aborigine, arrested drunk in a public place, screaming *"you got no Catholic in you woman ... !"*

———◦—◦—◦———

I was on probation for the first year in the force and always conscious that it was desirable to make a variety of apprehensions, not just the common drunk. When working in pairs with an experienced member if you made a traffic apprehension or arrested someone for theft or assault for example, the senior fellow would pass the matter to you so it looked good on your monthly service report submitted by the station sergeant through the Divisional Inspector to headquarters.

On returning from Court one morning, the station sergeant told me the Inspector wanted to see me. My immediate thought was *"what have I done wrong?"*. Instead, he wanted to ask me if I'd accept the Inspector's Clerk job for the rest of the year. The chap doing the job was keen to apply for a vacancy at a one-man bush station coming up, but the Inspector was not keen to release him before another chap designated for the position returned from special leave. There was also the carrot that at the end of the planned assignment, if I was keen to keep the job, I might stay in the job, or there might be a move to the prosecutor's office or the CIB. Oh, and there was $2 a week special duty allowance as well!

Being on probation, there was only one answer. *"Yes, sir"*. I only had to wait 24 hours to know I didn't have the job ... the present clerk's wife said "no way" was she going to the bush so his application for the position didn't get lodged!

My ability to type, to write a report, put a few words together and be precise, coming from my days working as a journalist, helped a lot and was noticed. My experience as a reporter in Court added to my training and helped me ask the right questions, to put things together.

This had been noted, it was a reason no doubt why I was considered for the Inspector's Clerks' job, just as I was later asked to work in the CIB offices for a few days to fix up some files, catch up on the paper work and accompany the plain-clothed policewomen to follow up some matters and make some visits to schools that had been requested by teaching staff.

One of these visits was to the Catholic primary school run by an ageing order of Nuns, all well-intentioned but unusually appearing to lack a little authority or standing amongst a core of students ... a visit by the police and some appropriate words on "wagging school" might help with behaviour. I didn't do any real CIB work and on reflection wonder really why I was seconded to the section for the week or so.

CHAPTER 5

The Alice ... Six months on

The days came and went and before I knew it, it was six months since I'd left home, six months since I'd arrived in Darwin, six months since I'd been sworn in, six months since I'd arrived in "The Alice".

I was adjusting to the life-style as well as the work. I quickly got to know that with a drop of rain, there could be wash-aways on the Ghan train link, so it was straight down to the store and stock up on some fresh milk before supplies ran out; the overland mails would also be late. If there was an airline strike (common at the time) the normal airmails would be disrupted and the newspapers from "down South" would be delayed as they were the first thing to be off-loaded if there was trouble.

Nearly everybody bought daily newspapers from "the South". With a predominance of people living in Alice Springs being of Adelaide/South Australia or Melbourne/Victoria, origins, the Adelaide *"Advertiser"* or the Melbourne *"Sun"* were the popular papers except on Sunday when the Sydney Sunday papers, along with the Adelaide *"Sunday Mail"* which carried the Saturday sports results, were popular. At the time there were no Victorian Sunday papers. Of course, all papers were "plus air freight" which made them more expensive.

There was only one newsagency in Alice Springs – "Marron's" – run by Ted Marron. There was no morning delivery of papers because if the papers arrived at all, it wasn't until after lunch on flights from Adelaide, on the days that there were in fact flights. However, Ted Marron did a paper delivery usually about four or five o'clock in the afternoon. He had a small blue coloured delivery van which had a hatch in the roof. Ted would drive the van while usually Dave Trend, a prominent local sportsman, stood on a stand, his body out of the hatch so that he could throw the papers into the yard or driveway. I'm not sure which was the most hazardous part of the operation – Dave throwing the papers or the other motorists trying to avoid the weaving van as it drove the streets "delivering" the papers. Then one day, Ted was driving the van to visit his good friends Bill and Dawn Prior at Hamilton Downs Station, to the north-west of Alice Springs, when he ran off the road, rolled the van and was lucky to escape without serious injury. That ended newspaper deliveries in the town.

I also got to know it was quicker to write home and ask my brother to buy an LP record and mail it up rather than order it through the local electrical store, not that I had a stereogram to start with, but you could always play your records on someone's 'gram. You needed to because there was no television, not even a commercial radio station. There was just 8AL, an ABC regional station, part of the Darwin based Northern Territory service. But still many of the programmes originated from Adelaide or even Sydney.

Because Territory time was half an hour behind Eastern Standard Time, even the ABC News was half an hour "early" compared to Melbourne – the 7.45am EST news was at 7.15am in the Territory. There was little popular music played. What there was, was usually played during "Housewives Choice", and that would be dropped if there was Test cricket or the Davis Cup. At least the Saturday afternoon sports programme provided a great coverage of not just the races for the fanatical race followers of the town, but also the Australian Rules football ... first from Melbourne, then the last quarter of SANFL football, from Adelaide to be followed by football from the WAFL, Perth, this coming via short wave to Darwin and re-transmitted. There was of course the Country Hour and "Blue Hills", the school programmes, good doses of classical music and on Sundays, "Divine Worship from ... "

At night it was possible to pick-up many of the southern radio stations. At the barracks we were assisted by the fact we were right under the police radio masts and an aerial out the barracks room window and up to the mast helped. I was pleased to be able to pick up 3DB Melbourne, particularly the football shows on Thursday evening when the teams were announced. I had not been away from Melbourne long enough to want to lose contact with what the football notables like Lou Richards were talking about. Sometimes the Mt Isa station came in good and strong, or maybe the Adelaide stations with some good music.

I also got used to the local power failures. When there was a problem with the British made generators at the power station it generally meant a part was needed from England, so for a week or two restrictions and interruptions would occur, not to mention blackouts caused once by a snake going across high voltage conductors. It was wise to always have a candle or two ready but I also bought a gas lamp attachment for the small gas bottle I had for a gas stove, which also came in handy to boil some water when the electricity was off.

This was all part of living in Alice Springs – "The Centre" during the 1960's.

The Alice Springs Police Barracks ... after a good paint job, 1966

"The Grandstand" at the Harts Range Races

It seemed each time I worked night shift it rained enough for the Todd River to flow or to "come down" as the locals said. During the first three night shifts I worked the Todd "came down" soon after dawn. The Todd River had a relatively small catchment area to the north of the town, but a very rocky area which promoted high run-off, so with an inch or so (25mm) of rain, the river could be expected to flow. It was a spectacular sight to see a "wall" of red-brown water, white frothing, and bubbling and about a foot or so high to start with, moving down the dry river bed, usually at about walking pace across the width of the river and quickly turning to a raging torrent.

Rain in the Centre seemed to either come as a thunderstorm, when the river could be expected to "come down" quickly, or start off lightly, then turn to more steady, soaking rain, which would then run-off and bring the river "down" slowly. Still, in most cases, however slowly the river "came down", it would soon turn to a raging torrent.

The "coming down" of the river had a fascination for me and most other people.. The town would turn out, particularly people new to The Alice, seeing the sight for the first time. A crowd would gather at the town causeway to watch the water arriving and give a big cheer as it crossed the bitumen. Then the water moved on to divide the town and reach The Gap.

Usually when the river flowed, it would cause the closure of the main causeway which linked the town area with East Side, sometimes for an hour or two, other times for days, but every time without fail, people would continue to drive across, despite warnings, until the first car was washed off the causeway, usually resulting in the need to rescue the driver and passengers. The police wouldn't make an effort to rescue the vehicle; it served as a warning to other fool-hardy drivers not to attempt to cross until it was considered safe.

People living on the East Side of town would prepare for the Todd flowing by parking a car on the town side of the river. With the river in flood, and the causeway closed, they could walk to the river, cross on the footbridge and then drive on to work. The fire brigade and police would take a vehicle and park it on the east side of the Todd ready for an emergency.

The flush of the river also freshened the whole place up. The dry river bed was used, particularly by day, as a campsite for drinking aboriginals who left behind their wine flagons, bottles, tinned meat cans and other rubbish. The flow of the river would wash it all away, envelop it all in the sandy bed and dry up in a day or so fresh and ready for new 'occupancy'.

Of course, the rains being experienced with such frequency also had a special meaning for those who had lived in The Alice for some time. Much of the previous six to eight years had been drought, severe drought in fact with little rain, infrequent river flows and dramatic dust storms which lasted for days on end. Much of the mulga scrub which dominated the landscape was dying. The rains brought new hope, green grass, wildflowers and restored the underground water table. The water supply for the town was drawn from a basin beneath the Todd River but when this was severely drawn down during the drought years an alternative supply was developed from an underground resource to the south of the town, partly discovered through oil exploration some years earlier.

I also got to check out the social life of the town, although as a non-drinker, life for me was a lot less boisterous than for many. Night life seemed to centre around two of the town's three hotels – on Wednesday nights at the Hotel Alice Springs, in the "Jet Bar" there was a band, dancing and drinking, interspersed with the occasional fight, and on Friday and Saturday nights much the same at the Stuart Arms Hotel, except that on Saturday night, like Wednesday night at the Hotel Alice Springs, the hotels had a late licence. They could go through to 11.30pm with people off the premises by midnight. On Friday night it was standard 10 o'clock closing. There were a couple of local bands which knocked out a pretty good rhythm and kept up with most of the current pop music.

The main draw-back about going to the hotels was that lack of anonymity. All the locals knew you were "a copper". As soon as there was a scuffle, half the eyes turned to the scuffle, the other half turned to you to see what you were going to do about it. You might be officially off duty but you were never off duty in the community's eyes.

The town had two picture theatres – the Pioneer "walk-in" and the Pioneer "drive-in". The "walk-in" was like the one in Darwin; an open air theatre with rows of deck-chair style seating. It only showed on two nights during the winter – Friday and Saturday – but in the summer, showed mid-week as well. In winter, it was freezing, even dressed in a jumper, sports coat, overcoat and blankets to cover yourself it still felt freezing. For this reason, they always showed the main film first with the 'support' shown second, so if you wanted to stay on and watch, you could. If it rained, the pictures were invariably cancelled.

At the drive-in, it could be just as cold but at least you had the car to preserve some warmth.

There were also always visitors to The Centre that I knew. One afternoon, not long after starting work in Alice Springs, I'd gone for a walk down Todd Street when I met three young fellows who I knew from the Young Farmers Association around Wonthaggi. Another day I met a school party being led by my Upwey high school form teacher, Mr Lithgo. There were always other friends or friends of the family passing through town who I would catch up with, take for a drive and a bit of sight-seeing during some of my off duty time.

One special visitor to The Centre was the Governor General, Lord Casey, and his wife, Lady Casey. As R. G. Casey, he was our "local member" at home, the Federal Member for Latrobe, and Minister for External Affairs in the Menzies' Governments. Through my family's involvement in local politics, I had helped in several of his election campaigns, folding and enveloping manifestos to be mailed to the electorate or handing out how to vote cards on polling days. He knew Dad well through involvement as a Shire Councillor and Shire President of the Shire of Fern Tree Gully, later the Shire of Sherbrooke.

During their visit the Caseys stayed at The Residency which was the equivalent of Admiralty House of the Territory. The Residency was the home of the Alice Springs District Officer, Dan Conway, and his wife Jilna. Originally built as one of the first government homes in Alice Springs in the late 1920's, it had been upgraded and was even the home of the Queen during her visit to Alice Springs in the early 1960's.

The Residency was virtually opposite the police barracks, a stark contrast in living facilities I can assure you.

One morning during their visit, I had the task of minding the gate as part of the security arrangements. I got talking to Lady Casey's aide and told him how, as a youth, I had helped in his election campaigns and that my parents were well known to them. When they came to leave The Residency to undertake one of their official engagements, I was called over and formally introduced and had a short chat. His Excellency remembering my parents and in particular asking if Dad was still on the council. It raised an eyebrow or two – *"how come you got introduced to the G-G?"* but I was really pleased, and proud, to be able to write home and tell Mum and Dad of the meeting.

Apart from making the easy arrests for "drunk in a public place", I was also getting my share of other apprehensions; liquor on a Reserve, offensive behaviour (urinating on a shop window), assaults, shop-lifting, larcenies, assaults and traffic offences arising from accidents and even a drive under the influence. There were no such things as breathalysers or .05 rules; a driver was either driving under the influence or drunk, the latter more difficult to prove. There would be all the usuals – *"I have been following you along Gap Road and noticed that your vehicle was wandering across the roadway, do you have any reason for driving this way?" "I can smell liquor on your breath, have you been drinking tonight?" " Where were you drinking?" "what were you drinking?" "Stubbies or schooners?" "nips or halves" "oh, doubles!" "who were you drinking with?" "how many drinks did you have?" "who was buying drinks in your 'shout'"? "How many rounds did 'x' buy?" how many rounds did 'y' buy?, "how many rounds did you buy?" "To me that adds up to . . . double what you said before, are you sure you only had three or four 'Bundies'?".*

There was the routine work of recovering a stolen vehicle abandoned along the highway, or another afternoon driving 20 odd miles (35kms) north to a culvert where it was reported some 'boxes' were stored under the road. They turned out to be cartons of new toasters and electric jugs, obviously part of a consignment in a container headed north but 'dropped-off' for recovery later by some thieving truckie.

There were the Government payroll escorts, wide load escorts through the town and "the Hills" north of the town, or security at the airport for visiting RAAF aircraft involved in an exercise.

One day, out of the blue, I was told that next morning I would be accompanying the police prosecutor, Sergeant Second Class Peter Haag, and the magistrate, out to the Finke River mission at Hermannsburg, some 80 miles (130kms) west of Alice Springs to act as court orderly. As part of the Mission's attempts to familiarise the aboriginal community with the workings of "the law", the idea was for several aggrieved residents at the mission to make "complaint" and have the offenders brought before the magistrate for sentence.

Instead of the police prosecutor being the complainant, six aboriginal residents at the mission "laid" the charges – one for assault, one drunk in a public place, two for fighting, one for offensive behaviour in or about a dwelling and one for indecent language in a public place. I had the task of reading the charges, asking the question *"How do you plead – guilty or not guilty?"* In each case the magistrate took a not guilty plea so that the complainant had to give evidence of what happened, when and where and the general facts about the incident along with comments from the accused. Each offender was duly convicted and either cautioned and discharged or fined. With the exercise over, we drove back to town in time to knock-off. I was pleased as each of the matters was added to my monthly probation report as an arrest for the month.

I also got to know some of the "bush station" chaps, in particular Constable Norm Wright at Ti Tree, 120 miles (195kms) north of Alice Springs. So when the opportunity came along to drive up and spend a couple of off duty days with Norm, and his wife and family, I did. He enjoyed having some vocational company, and I looked at it as a great opportunity to see how the bush stations worked. After all, I had a wish to do bush station relief in the years ahead. While there we would go for an afternoon's highway patrol up to Barrow Creek or out to one of the local cattle stations.

When John White, a member of my shift in Alice Springs, was transferred to Kulgera, the one-man bush station, on the Stuart Highway, or better known as the South Road, 175 miles (275kms) south of Alice Springs, and only about 15 mile north of the Northern Territory-South Australia border, I also spent a few days out of town with him. Kulgera was more of a "bush station" than Ti-Tree, at least I thought so, just getting there was by 170 miles (268kms) of unsealed road – it was the real 'outback'!

The first Monday in August was a public holiday – Picnic Day, and having the day off, I decided to drive out to Hart's Range, 145 miles (240kms) north east of Alice Springs where there was an annual bush race meeting over the weekend. There were about 100 station property horses there, each would run in at least one race on the Saturday and Monday, and with nine races 'on the card' each day, some raced more than once to help fill the fields.

There were no bookmakers on course, the only betting by means of a 50c manual tote, operated by the race club, but requiring the attendance of a police officer to oversee its operation. There were no pocket calculators around then, it was a manual job of taking the bets, recording them and after the race, manually calculating the dividends according to the formula set out in the Lottery and Gaming Ordinance and Regulations. It was a job, I am happy to say, I never had to do.

One frequent, and unpleasant job, was to deliver death messages, or other sad personal news to either people on tour to Alice Springs or people living there, about loved ones at "home". My first experience in this field was one evening when I received a call at the station asking us to locate an elderly visitor to Alice Springs. I had to advise him that his 9-year-old grandson had been murdered near Tatura earlier in the day. My patrol off-sider Doug

Vallance remarked *"wasn't that the name of a fellow 'paged' at the Gillen tonight while we were having dinner?"* So we drove to the Mt Gillen Motel, the office had closed but we got the manager from his residence who was able to confirm the gentleman was indeed a guest at the motel. We awoke him and passed on the sad news and helped him arrange through the motel office to contact home.

On the lighter side, I recall one Sunday evening I took a call at the station asking if we could locate a chap and his daughter, travelling in such-and-such a vehicle, expected to be in Alice Springs at whatever time and staying at a caravan park and tell them "Bessy" had died. After I took as much detail on the people we were being asked to contact, I asked *"what relationship is your husband to Bessy?"* *"Oh, Bessy is the cat!"* In the most polite manner, I told the caller our time was a little more valuable than to spend it on such an errand, but I don't think she quite understood.

Another Sunday morning I recall receiving a call from Navy Headquarters, Darwin, advising that a rating had gone AWL and that a warrant had been issued for his detention. After a detailed description of both the rating and his vehicle, the officer remarked *"You won't miss him, he looks like a stunned mullet!"* The truth was that the rating had not gone AWL. With a mate from the navy base he had driven out of Darwin and his vehicle had broken down on a back road. They were found near– perishing several days later.

One of the 'plagues' of being new in town, and in the public service or the police force were the life insurance agents. At the time there was no AMP or other life insurance agent in Alice Springs; they would make periodical visits from Darwin, spend a week or so in town and always visit the police barracks. First it was the AMP representative who thought that I should dispense with the policy I already held with AMP and take his recommended policy. Very nice for him, a nice new commission! Then a couple of weeks later it was the MLC representative who thought the original AMP policy I had was *"ideal"*, I should just boost it up with a policy he recommended which would be just $2 a week from my pay.

A year or so later, came a move that shocked most in the force, the local Detective Sergeant resigned to become the Central Australia representative of AMP, and did so extremely successfully. Mind you, most of us were pleased he left the force as few of us had any genuine rapport with the man.

One thing that I noticed was the short spring season. The weather seemed to quickly move from the distinctive winter weather to a milder, warmer to hot days and mild nights. First came the days when the station open fire was not left burning from night shift, that it wasn't lit in the evening and then not lit at all. There was also the move from winter uniform to summer uniform, first the day and evening shifts before night shift also moved to summer uniform but with a winter tunic jacket handy for that odd cold night.

Typically for spring, bees would swarm, and when a swarm passed through the back yard of the barracks it caused quite a commotion. I grabbed a tin and started to bang it, the noise was said to 'drown' the noise of the queen bee and cause the swarm to settle or land. It did. But the noise of the banging on a tin attracted more than the bees with heads from the adjoining fire station and welfare office all peering out to see what was happening. However, before a bee keeper could come and collect the swarm it moved off again.

The tourist season seemed to end fairly abruptly in September, the last of the features of the season being the Henley-on-Todd regatta held in the bed of the dry Todd River. With lots of ingenuity, the local Rotary club had organised all sorts of traditional regatta events in formats that meant a lot of hard work for those participating, and lots of laughs for those who watched. There were yacht races with teams of four holding around them the flimsy frame of a yacht complete with sails, there were rowing 'fours' in cut-in-half 44-gallon drums, joined and on track and wheels, shovels being used to 'row' the 'boat' along. There was the greasy pole and a 'sea battle' to conclude the day with plenty of flour and smoke bombs to cause mayhem.

The introduction of the first Boeing 727 jets to Australian airlines during the early part of the year extended to the Northern Territory in September, 1966. With no curfew at the Alice Springs or Darwin airports, the jets could be utilised for the Territory during the night hours, leaving Adelaide before the evening curfew, flying to Alice Springs and on to Darwin, then waiting until time to fly from Darwin back to Alice Springs and on to Adelaide to arrive just after the morning curfew was lifted.

Each airline at first operated the 727 jets one night a week. Of course, the extra passenger and freight capacity reduced the normal daytime air services with a resultant 25% or more drop in mail and newspaper deliveries. The move wasn't popular, not the least amongst the business community which found it difficult to get orders through by mail, and air-freight from Adelaide as quickly as before. Added to this, it was something like 4am departures from Alice Springs to travel South.

A change at the airport which effected us at the station more was the increased use of the facility by international originating flights which meant quarantine and customs clearance status for the airport. On occasions international flights from places like Singapore, heading for Sydney, which has a morning curfew, would be forced to land in Alice Springs when Sydney airport would be fog bound and the availability of Brisbane airport as an alternative was in doubt. At the time, Melbourne's new, Tullamarine airport, almost fog-free, was still under construction, so when a Qantas or BOAC Boeing 707 jet had insufficient fuel to continue to Sydney and circle for maybe hours, they would put down at Alice Springs and wait for a clearance.

This resulted in a call to the police to provide security at the airport while the quarantine matters in particular were attended to. Each passenger had to disembark and produce a valid International Health Certificate for at least smallpox and cholera. An invalid or suspect certificate resulted in on-the-spot vaccination. It was then realised that the police, guarding the facility were not themselves vaccinated so as a result we were all lined up on a couple of afternoons and given both cholera and smallpox vaccinations, and certificates, to safely continue the work. For those who had not previously had a small pox vaccination it was a wait for 10 days for the fever attack surrounding the build-up of the immunity, and the large festering sore on the upper arm where the vaccination was given.

Life at the barracks was also changing. An extensive renovation project was at last completed. With vinyl tiles on the floor, strip heaters, a new evaporative air conditioner and a complete new paint job the place was really livable. Then one afternoon there was a sudden realisation that the wood-fired hot water system was a fire hazard, and within 24 hours it was converted to an electric system! Bliss.

The numbers in barracks also reduced with two more being sent on bush relief – Malcolm "Bluey" King to Avon Downs, on the Northern Territory-Queensland border for four-and-a-half months and Bob Henfry to Lake Nash, south of Avon Downs, also near the Queensland border for three months. He was at Lake Nash only a few weeks before being selected to represent the Northern Territory Police in the Australian Police Contingent at the Montreal, Canada, "Expo 67". He was transferred to the Darwin CIB for additional training and experience before going to Canada.

These staff losses, along with other leave and some sickness really ran the staff numbers down at the station to the degree that some shifts were being worked with only two members on duty. Inevitably, on these shifts all hell broke loose. One evening shift had hardly started when we got a report of a three-year-old child missing near Simpson's Gap, having wandered away from a tourist group. Fortunately before I arrived with trackers, other local aboriginals had helped track the lad and found him safe and well. That under control, there was a report of a light plane with a pilot and two passengers missing. As plans started to come together for a search we learned that it had landed safely just as dusk fell at a property a little out of town and the local cattle station people were looking after the occupants.

The police station wasn't the only place that seemed short-staffed. At the Northern Territory Administration District Office, where they handled the motor registration and driving licence matters, there was an unusual call for help ... they needed someone for half an hour or so to help, so the story went. So I was sent to 'the rescue'. When I walked into the District Office foyer I saw a Mrs Diano, a middle aged Italian lady, a bundle of nerves and well known to be very highly strung. She was there for her driving test.

The truth of why I had been sent to help quickly became clear . . . nobody at the District Office wanted to take her for the test. I don't know if she had been before, but I was quickly given the job and ushered out to Hartley Street to her car, a tiny European make. I could hardly fit into the back seat, and felt most uncomfortable. She was extremely nervous, I was more in fear than anything else, but we proceeded on the test. I am not sure if I took sympathy on her, or I couldn't put anyone else through the trauma of testing her, or I feared her outburst in Italian and broken English if I failed her, or I wanted to get my own back on District Office by getting me over on the pretext of being busy. Anyway I passed her. I just hoped and prayed that when granted her licence she would improve. I was relieved to see in the years ahead, her driving did improve, but I'm equally sure that I heard a few ghosts say *'who the hell gave her a licence?'*

It was also becoming time for me to be thinking about applying for my first leave as I wanted to return to Melbourne for my sister's wedding in mid-February, 1967, a fortnight before my probationary period would actually be completed. I spoke with the Inspector, my plans were approved at the local level and sent on to the Commissioner for a change to the general leave roster to accommodate my need.

This was no sooner done than the Inspector called me aside to say he had me in mind to go relieving in January, at Anthony Lagoon, on the Barkly Tablelands. This would mean I'd have to change my leave plans although it could still be possible for me to fly from Mt Isa to Melbourne for the wedding. However, a week or two later I was told the Superintendent did not consider I was experienced enough at this stage to relieve at such a remote location, a decision deep down I was happy with as I was really starting to look forward to 'going home' for my sister's wedding.

One thing I really wanted to do before I went home on leave was to go on a mission patrol. The patrols hadn't been as frequent as usual because of staff numbers and then when one came along, it was only a three-day patrol compared to the normal four or five day patrol. Still, I wasn't going to knock back the offer, even if the patrol ran into some of my rostered days off before I started another dreaded night shift.

The patrols were done in one of the station's 4-wheel-drive vehicles, with a police tracker coming along as a guide, an interpreter and for the company. On this patrol I had the use of a Toyota Landcruiser, tray-top, equipped with short-wave radio, long-range fuel tank and fresh water tank. You never relied on the tank, always carrying additional fresh water in some container, along with your swag, camping gear and food in case you had to 'sleep-out' or didn't have hospitality extended at one of the overnight stops, usually visiting staff quarters at one of the aboriginal settlements along the patrol.

After the patrol, I submitted my report –

```
Southern Division
Alice Springs Station                          October 22, 1966

Officer-in-Charge
Police Station
Alice Springs

Report of: Constable D. L. Pollock, Reg. No 262

Subject:    Patrol of Government Welfare Settlements and Missions
            Alice Springs Police District, October 13, 14, 15, 1966

I have to report that on Thursday, Friday and Saturday, October 13, 14
and 15, 1996, in Toyota vehicle ZBD 229 I carried out a patrol of out-
lying Government Welfare Settlements and Missions in the Alice Springs
Police District.

2.  Police Tracker Sonny Woods was in my company

3.  A journal of the patrol is as follows:

4.  Thursday, October 13: After conveying Tracker Sonny from Amoonguna
    we departed Alice Springs at 9.20am and proceeded to Milton Park
    Station where I first spoke to Mrs Milton Willick who's husband had
```

written to Mr S. Calder in regard to literature of a Communistic nature being distributed to aboriginals. Mr Willick was mustering about 15 miles from the homestead. The Native who had passed on the information to Mr Willick, Peter Lou, was also in the Mustering party. As some time had elapsed between when the original letter had been written and my visit to Milton Park I though it best the matter be attended to now so proceeded and located Mr Willick and Native Peter Lou. I have made the matter a subject of a separate report, attached.

5. Then proceeded to Yuendumu Settlement where on arrival I spoke to Mr W. Frazier, Superintendent, who stated apart from firearm and dog registrations there were no matters requiring police attention.

6. Enroute to Yuendumu endeavoured to make radio contact with VL5HE with negative results.

7. Road conditions: The road from Alice Springs to Yuendumu is generally good. However, the standard within 20 miles of the settlement is not as high as nearer Alice Springs. Total mileage for day: 268 miles.

8. Friday, October 14: On duty 8am. Registered two .22 rifles and 27 dogs.

9. I then made a patrol of the camp area and spoke to several natives. There were no complaints. Some 72 new brick homes for natives are nearing completion at the Settlement which will give many more families a higher standard of accommodation to the present numerous bag and bark humpies.

A new kitchen and bakehouse is also near ready for occupancy

10. Radio contact was made with VL5HE through HF(Kulgera) at 9am. No traffic.

11. At 10.20am departed Yuendumu for Papunya Settlement. On arrival at Papunya I spoke to the Superintendent, Mr P. Petersen who stated there were no matters requiring Police attention. However, he requested I speak to an assembly of school children in regard to vandalism and truancy.

12. This request was complied with. It appears many children are on a rampage of stone throwing and window smashing, the school building being the central target. The headmaster, Mr. Gallagher stated there was only about 80% daily attendance at school, compared to 98% at Yuendumu. The Papunya settlement with its larger numbers of primitive Pintubi tribe natives is faced with a difficult task of encouraging full attendance. Only a fortnight ago a truck load of natives, not previously known to have come into contact with whiteman, were brought to the settlement. On the day I visited the settlement one of these new arrivals was attending school for the first time.

13. Shortly before 2pm I departed Papunya for Haasts Bluff. Enroute endeavoured to make radio contact with VL5HE with negative results. On arrival at Haasts Bluff spoke to the Manager who stated apart from the registration of two rifles there was no matter requiring police attention. Two rifles — one .22 and one .310 were duly registered.

14. Served Ordinary Summons 528/66 and State of Queensland Warrants of Apprehension 394/65 and 1950/65 "A" and "B" on M. S. Maidens, mechanic at the Settlement. The Warrants of Apprehension for the sum of $70.11c were settled by the payment in full.

15. Then proceeded to Areyonga Settlement and on arrival at 7.10pm spoke to the Superintendent, Mr R. Houldsworth who stated apart from firearm registrations there were no matters requiring Police attention.

16. Road conditions: The road from Yuendumu to Papunya is in fair to good condition. Care has to be taken in some sandy patches between Central Mt Wedge Station and Papunya. From Papunya to Haasts Bluff and on to Areyonga the roads are good, having just been graded. However, between Papunya-Hermannsburg Rd., turn-off and Areyonga there are several very sandy sections which come with little warning. Much care is needed on this section of road. Total mileage for days: 237 miles.

17. Saturday, October 15: On duty 8am. Registered one .22 rifle. Made a patrol of the camp area. Spoke to several natives. There were no complaints. Several natives were spoken to about a large number of dogs in the camp.

18. Endeavoured to make radio contact with VL5HE with negative results. Contact made with GU (Harts Range)

19. Departed Areyonga for Hermannsburg where on arrival at 12 noon spoke to the Superintendent of the Lutheran Mission, Mr G. Stoll. Mr Stoll stated there were no matters requiring Police attention. Executed U.J.S. Warrant of Commitment 284/66 on Lindburg Inkermala. Payment was made in full.

20. Then proceeded to Palm Valley Chalet. With the tourist season finished this chalet is closed. a care-taker is in residence. On departure at 2pm vehicle ZBD 229 gave mechanical trouble. This was traced to the carburettor. Some 2 hours later this trouble was cleared. I attribute the trouble to the standard of petrol obtained at Areyonga on this day.

21. Endeavoured to make radio contact with VL5HE at 3pm and 3.55pm with negative results.

22. Then proceeded to Jay Creek Settlement where I spoke to the Superintendent Mr A. Probin. He stated there were no matters requiring Police attention. Made a patrol of camp area and spoke to several natives. They had no complaints.

23. Returned to Alice Springs at 6.55pm. Tracker Sonny was then conveyed to Amoonguna.

24. Road conditions: Road traversed were generally good except the section referred to previously on the Areyonga Road. The road to Palm Valley is still only suitable for 4-wheel-drive vehicles. Total mileage for the day: 183 miles

25. General: The country is at present looking quite prosperous. There is much vegetation and feed for stock. Stock is in prime condition.

26. Behaviour on reserves at present appears good, the only trouble seems to be arising from the occasional conveyance of liquor onto Areyonga and Jay Creek settlements and to Hermannsburg Mission. Taxi drivers are in the main blamed for this. It is reputed that the driver of Alice Springs Taxi's car 4 will convey liquor to pre-arranged places on payment in advance. Super-intendants and staff are on the look-out for this and feel the offenders will be caught "red-handed" before much time has passed.

27. An increasing dog population on reserves seems to be Superintendent's main groan. This appears worst at Areyonga where the dog population is estimated to be twice the aboriginal population of about 280. From my observations this would be correct. As this patrol was made in an off pay week for the settlements visited natives generally were without funds for dog registration fees, if time had have permitted any effort of a mass registration.

28. Three days is insufficient time for this patrol. It does not allow sufficient time to patrol native camps etc. If any one settlement had had a matter requiring investigation it would not have been possible to complete the patrol in the three days allotted. For the Constable making the patrol it is one of near continual driving on roads that whilst good, need considerable more care in negotiation than bitumen.

29. Vehicle ZBD 229, apart from the matter previously mentioned performed well. Tracker Sonny also carried out his duties as required.

Submitted for your information

David L. Pollock
Constable, Reg. No. 262

The patrol was a great experience, I couldn't wait to conduct another, just when I would have to wait and see. The "literature of a communistic nature" turned out to be a mailing of publicity brochures for the "TIME" magazine publication "Russia". TIME frequently mailed nearly everybody on the electoral role promotional material on one of their publications, trying to encourage receivers to buy the various books and publications they put out. The superintendent at Hermannsburg mission told me later that they frequently just trashed all similar letters because of the confusion it caused amongst the receivers who had no understanding at all of the mail-outs.

I got to see a lot of new country which was looking great after winter and spring rains. At the gates of Haasts Bluff, I got tracker Sonny to take a couple of photos of me standing beside the vehicle, radio aerial in place. I sent the photo to Jack Bennett at the *Free Press* who included it in his "Uphill and Downdale" weekly segment along with some of my letter " ... *You couldn't wish the country to be looking better. Many areas were covered with three feet high vegetation and others were a mass of wild flowers. At one place on Mt Wedge Station the ground was so white with flowers you would have thought it has snowed. The skeletons of the dead mulga (which died during the drought) and the green and gold Christmas bush made the scene even more impressive".* I used the photo on my Christmas cards I prepared a month or so later.

At least the night shift after the patrol gave me a chance to attend to all the paper work, write my report and have everything tidied up. Still, there were interruptions, like a wailing young aboriginal woman coming to the station screaming "rape". CIB and the policewomen were called out in the middle of the night but at day-break we had the police trackers on the job. Checking the site, they translated quite a different story and when confronted with it, she admitted it was all a fabrication.

———

You could never be sure what lay ahead. It was Sunday, I was off duty and really just filling in the day. I'd ironed some uniforms for the next few days, and was thinking of wandering off to watch the guys from the station playing cricket. Then a call-to-duty. There was a message from the Royal Flying

Two forms of boating on the Todd River – at the "Henley-on-Todd" Regatta in the dry sand bed of the Todd River and the fool-hardy in their aluminium row-boat when the river was in flood

74

Doctor Base that an aboriginal man had drowned in a dam at Yuendumu. So I, in uniform, was sent with Plain Clothes Constable Terry O'Brien, to investigate and recover the body. It was nearly 6pm before we left on the 186 miles (300kms) drive to the settlement.

On arrival we were relieved to get the news that the body had been recovered; it was all neatly laid out in a plastic zip-up body bag. Next morning we took a multitude of statements from witnesses and I took some photos for a report to be prepared for the Coroner. It was my first experience with an aboriginal death, many of their customs surrounding death were hard to understand but had to be respected.

When it was realised the man had drowned in the dam, there was a wake or "sorry" through the whole community of nearly 800. Aboriginal men assisted in the search in the dam for the body of the drowned man but when they located it, they left the water and indicated to the European staff at the settlement where the body was. They would not further assist in the recovery until the body was partly lifted and appeared out of the water; then they jumped back into the water and helped lift it out.

Custom demanded that the women of the tribe must sweep away the foot tracks of the deceased. Because he had been to the communal lunch at the kitchen/dining room at the settlement, and the women had not had time to sweep, only a handful of the normal hundreds who could have been expected to eat dinner at the dining hall that night came for a meal.

Nobody was allowed to mention the name of the drowned man. While taking statements from aboriginal witnesses we had to refer to him as *"that man", "that bloke"* or more commonly, *"that fella".* When we went to the aboriginal camp to collect any belongings we found everything had been burnt, all the camps/shanties for a hundred yards or so had already moved. For months, no aboriginal will go to the shed where the body had been kept for the night. There was a long hot summer ahead but until it rained and flooded and flushed the dam of the man's Spirit, nobody swam in the dam, normally a popular swimming spot.

My first birthday away from home passed. Some goodies, like a large fruit cake and other sweets arrived. My dilemma was whether to get stuck into them now or hold off until Christmas. They didn't last to Christmas. There were further rains interrupting the road and rail links to the south. This was not only a frustration for Christmas supplies, but kept me wondering what conditions would be when I was due to go home on leave in mid-February.

On another three day break I tossed up whether to go north to Ti Tree or south to Kulgera and spend a couple of days at one of the bush stations. This time I decided to go to Ti Tree. It rained there but only about half-an-inch over the two days I was there. At Kulgera there was a storm and six inches of water ran through the police station.

The warmer weather was more encouraging to go to the open-air movies, that is when it didn't rain, and as the Christmas period approached the school broadcasts also lightened off, so we had a little more daytime music on the only radio station we had in town. Work also started on a new cell block in the back yard of the station, a double storey block to cost $67,000, able to hold 100 or more short-term prisoners, complete with male and female "drunk tank" individual cells and a reception/charge room so that prisoners did not need to be taken through the station offices.

Several were going on recreation leave, including the station sergeant which resulted in the Detective Sergeant First Class Phil McLaughlin moving into uniform and taking over the station for the three months Sergeant First Class Metcalfe was to be on leave. This reduced the CIB staff 25%, left them with only three men and it was made even worse when another was put off sick with suspected hepatitis. So early December, I was moved back to CIB, but this time, in plain clothes. The CIB had unmarked, plain number plated cars as distinct from the normal police vehicles which were Commonwealth "Z" plated.

The work was mainly day shift as the CIB worked only a couple of evenings a week. Most tasks were fairly straight forward, some minor thefts, even investigating the theft of a Bible which someone had hidden as a practical joke (but it was a 'clear-up!) and the odd vagrant. Then I received a call from the Northern Territory Administration advising that their electrical meter reader had gone to a home to make a routine reading and found a knitting needle stuck through the top of the meter, thus preventing the meter from revolving and registering electrical use. The meter reader had called his boss first who attended and took a photo of the needle in the meter but by the time CIB was notified and I arrived on the scene, the needle was gone. Of course, the householder denied all knowledge of the matter, so innocently asking "why on earth would anyone put a knitting needle like that in a meter?"! To top it off, when they checked the water meter, they found it was fitted backwards!

As the prosecution was handled by the Crown Law office, the case took months to come to court. Then when it did, the case was dismissed! The defence solicitor, Brian Martin, virtually admitted the Crown had a good case but said the Crown had presented documentation that the defendant was responsible for only one of the two meters at the site and not necessarily the meter which was subject to the alleged offence. *"It looks like red tape has fallen flat on its face again"* the Magistrate, Mr Hall remarked as he dismissed the matter.

I never ceased to be amazed at the sheer stupidity of some supposed criminals ... like one afternoon, just as I had finished for the day I was walking though the station when the phone rang. It was a local bank manager who wanted to urgently talk to a member of the CIB. The phone was passed to me ... a client had two cheque forms stolen from her cheque book, they had each been presented and cashed in town for $20. The client was well known and respected, there was no need to suspect anything wrong with the cheques when cashed. The person who had cashed them had then written an address on the back of each of the cheque ... so half an hour later, in company with the Detective Sergeant, we called at the address. We couldn't believe that the offender, the gardener at the home from where the cheques had been stolen, answered the door! We later charged him with larceny of two cheque forms and two counts of false pretences for which he was sentenced to a month's imprisonment.

Christmas was rapidly approaching. I had a mate, Bob Fraser, who I'd gone through trade school with print me up some nice cards and on to them I pasted a photo I'd had the tracker take while on the mission patrol. I was also thrilled to get so many cards too, and strung them up in my barracks room. There were the Christmas parties. The police party was a pretty dull affair but at least everybody kept themselves 'nice'. Then on Christmas Eve I was invited to the prison officers' Christmas drinks to which I went with my Detective Sergeant boss. I was still a non-drinker but made the effort to join in; those who knew me always had a Coke or lemon squash handy, others shook their head when I declined a beer. As I left the prison officers' party, the Gaoler, Mr. Vince Seymour quietly spoke to me *"call in and have a 'soft-ie' with the wife and I in the morning"*. I felt privileged.

It was where my Christmas Day began; a "softie" with Mr Seymour and his wife, then off to Harry Belton's place where he and his wife, and daughter Gillian, not only had a traditional Christmas spread in preparation, but also had Bill Frazier and his wife, the superintendent from the Yuendumu Settlement, staying with them for the weekend. It was 100F (37.8C) plus but with the air-conditioning, I didn't mind. My father had sent up some fresh strawberries on the plane and although they had been delayed along the way, they were still great to have as a special 'add-on' after the main roast and plum pudding. The married members at the station made sure all the single members went somewhere for a Christmas meal.

Later in the day I went and had another "softie" at the home of my CIB boss but for evening meal, I went with a couple from barracks to our traditional eating place, the Mt Gillen Motel. There was a sort of tradition that the single members would work Christmas Day to allow the married men to be with their families. Then on New Year's Eve, the single members would be off duty and be able to get out and enjoy the night. This year it was a more unusual New Year's Eve as a late afternoon storm saw the Todd River flow once again, just before midnight. I stayed quietly in the barracks and listened to the cricket from South Africa, then at midnight the fire siren sounded, car horns went off everywhere, there was a hell of a noise. Another year had begun.

My new year started with a trip to Papunya, 150 miles (240kms) west of Alice Springs, after a complaint that an aboriginal woman had thrown an empty jam tin at one of the nursing sisters at the settlement. Because of the cut on her head she had been evacuated by Flying Doctor plane to Alice Springs. It was the first time the police had been to the settlement for some time, so it was no surprise to find on arrival I had a few a few jobs to handle. Another aboriginal had given his wife a beating the week before. On word of my arrival, he went bush taking his wife with him, which made it pretty difficult to follow the matter through. Two others, also aboriginal, who had been banned from the settlement for 30 days for "disrupting the good order" of the place had returned and ended up in my custody. I had the mission patrol box with me and registered a few firearms, .22 rifles were popular amongst the aboriginal people, they were allowed to have them, and were much more effective for capturing bush tucker such as kangaroo or emu than a spear. I did a few driver licence tests, to make staff at the settlement 'legal'. Then I had one old man bring me his wireless to register.

The jam tin thrower was an older woman from the Pintubi tribe. She claimed not to speak or understand English so I had to use an interpreter to question her. She freely admitted the offence and realised she had done wrong. It had all been explained to her that she would need to be punished and I would need to take her to Alice Springs to court. She was sentenced to a month's imprisonment.

My sister was getting married on 18 February and as the middle of January passed and the weather was continuing erratic with storms and road and rail closures, I was beginning to wonder just how I was going to get away on leave on 14 February. One week I was thinking I would drive the South Road, rather than take the car on the train, or fly home. I was only going to fly home as a last resort as I wanted a car on leave; I couldn't think of anything worse than being home for nearly six weeks without a car.

I had another hurdle to jump as well. I was still a probationary constable, my appointment would need to be confirmed 12 months after commencement, the probationary period extended six months or be considered unsuitable and virtually sacked. My monthly reports had, as far as I knew, all been good, to me my main concern was still my height. I had another medical to face before 'confirmation'. My heart jumped a little when the sister doing the preliminaries marked my height as 5 feet 8 inches. The doctor completed the examination and remarked *"no problems, I couldn't be fitter myself" "Doc"* I said. *"I have to be 5 feet 9 inches tall"* (175cm) *"Oh, do you lad – fixed"* as he noted the document. The other pleasing thing for me was that I now weighed more than 12 stone (76kgs), I had put on more than a stone (6.4kgs) in a year. What amused me more though was that the two others who had been sent for medicals were told they were overweight and given diet charts.

What I didn't know at the time was that the acting officer-in-charge, Sergeant First Class J. P. (Phil) McLaughlin, was recommending against my permanent appointment. He didn't believe I would make a good *"street policeman"* . . . Constable Pollock is not . . *"aggressive enough to handle the coloured population of Alice Springs"* he wrote in his recommendation against me. His decision was over-ridden by Superintendent Bowie with comment *" . . . how can the man be given a good report all year, recommended for relieving duties at a bush station, be placed into CIB for relieving duties and then not be recommended for appointment?"* It wasn't until years later I found McLaughlin's comments on my file. Few in the force had a good word for the man, but, mistakenly, I had been prepared to give him the benefit of the doubt. Thankfully, I have never set eyes on him since I discovered the truth.

On patrol, near Haasts Bluff

At Areyonga, Donkey Donk Number Two demonstrates the use of a woomera he was about to sell me

Staffing at the station was becoming a real problem, not just with those who had gone on leave but coupled with a couple of resignations and a couple off sick, the night shift went back to one-man for a couple of weeks. I was brought back to general duties – uniform section to get another night shift out of me before I was also going on leave. It had been a quiet shift, I'd even had time to sit down and write home. Then I thought with the night jet services operating, if I drove out to the airport about 4am there might be someone travelling I knew who could post the letter in Adelaide or even Melbourne, and get it home a little quicker.

So I 'organised' a mobile patrol just after 4am. As I drove south along Todd Street, heading for the airport, I noticed a wisp of what I first thought was steam coming from the side ventilator high on the wall of a block of three shops. Then I thought, was that steam or was it smoke? I stopped and quickly discovered that the middle of the three shops, "Centre Jewellers" was in fact on fire! The shop was full of smoke, the window black and near breaking point. Obviously, the fire had been burning inside the building for some time, but starved of fresh air, it had burnt quietly building up quite a heatbank. I immediately radioed the station; then the fire alarm sounded and in minutes the brigade was on site. The Fire Chief, Lloyd Allen, said later that the whole building would have exploded within another three or four minutes. Remarkably little structural damage was done to the shop or smoke damage to the adjoining shops; the smoke had gone through the ceiling and out the end vent of "Don Thomas' Stockman's Outfitters". Inside the jewellers it was a blackened molten mess, crystal and glassware in particular ruined. Metal trophy cups and the like had fallen apart as the solder had melted in the heat. Water damage added to the mess.

I was proud as Punch to read the next issue of the *"Centralian Advocate"* ... *"An alarm sounded by an observant policeman . . ."* Even Miss Pink rang the station to congratulate me.

The fire also strengthened a friendship which I cherished with Don Thomas who operated the Stockman's Outfitters next to the jewellers. Don was a real pioneer businessman of The Centre, a gentleman with a friendly disposition always with a few spare minutes to have a yarn. A few years later when he died, I was taken aback when his son, Glen, approached me and said *"Dad thought a lot of you, you were good mates, you were always happy to have a yarn with him; I'd like you to be a pall-bearer at his funeral"* I willingly accepted, feeling very humble amongst the company I was with as I helped carry his coffin from the John Flynn Memorial Uniting Church, virtually opposite his store.

Now with less than a week before I was due to go on leave it became apparent I had no hope of driving south; the river crossings wouldn't allow it, but the Ghan was still running. Another chap at the station was going on leave the same day, Tony Stenhouse, also headed for Melbourne. He had sent his wife and child south already and wanted to take himself and his Morris Mini on the train. We got our heads together and at the railway booking office did a deal. His car would be a 'trailer' to mine, thus with two adults travelling in my car, we would get a concession.

Still there was time for the best of plans to be destroyed, and I soon thought they would be. A couple of CIB fellows had been flown to Areyonga settlement to investigate a breaking into the settlement canteen. They had been charter flown to Areyonga as the road was impassable following more rains. Next day a telegram arrived at the station *"Have nine prisoners, please send pick-up vehicle"*. A look at the roster, I was working the Saturday and Sunday, so I was given the job of taking one of the Toyota four-wheel-drives out to make the pick-up.

Then a second telegram arrived *"Send two cartons of fruit with escort"*. Two cartons of fruit? What do they mean? are they going troppo? It was an hour or two before the penny dropped. Only European staff at aboriginal settlements had permits to keep and consume intoxicating liquor on the aboriginal reserve. With no transports to the settlement for a week or more, someone was obviously getting thirsty. They could not send a telegram *'send two cartons VB'* ... so here I was ... a 'grog runner', tee-totaller and all.

The trip to Hermannsburg (80 miles (130kms)) was OK, although there were a couple of creeks or rivers like the Hugh still running. The Finke River at Hermannsburg had been feet deep but was now passable. *"There's been one vehicle through to Areyonga"* the manager at Hermannsburg remarked *"The secret is to drive through the water, don't try and drive around it, you will bog, drive through it, there's a hard base and you'll get through"* This was sound advice. The 60 miles (100kms) on the Areyonga were a nightmare.

Areyonga is a God-forsaken place, built in a narrow valley. On one side there was a rocky cliff face 100-200 feet (30-60m) high; on the other, a creek. It could be hellishingly hot or in winter freezing cold. Why anyone had established a community there, I would never know. On arrival I was ushered into the staff quarters *"want a cuppa, want something to eat?"* – *"Yes please"*.

Then without warning there was consternation ... *"Boss, boss, them boys run away"!* Seven of the nine youths who had been held in custody in a shed overnight had bolted. They had run to the cliff face, scaled it and were gone!

The rest of the afternoon was spent up down and over the rock-face, chasing the escapees in a near fruitless exercise. They knew every nook and cranny of the rock face; it was only with some luck and great assistance of some of the aboriginal community elders that we caught four of them, and went back to Alice Springs next day with a little dented pride.

I was never so relieved to hear the Ghan whistle blow and the wheels move under the carriage as I left on leave, 12 months to the day since I'd left home for the Territory. Through The Gap, past Ewaninga, Deep Well, Rumbalara and across the Finke River before a short stop at Finke and the chance for both Tony and I to say a quick *"hi"* to the local officer Charlie Tailor, then on across the border and on to Oodnadatta. We woke next morning with the news the train was virtually on time as it rolled into Marree.

We had both booked only as far as Marree where our cars were waiting at the unloading ramp. We couldn't sign the consignment note quick enough to get on the road. I planned to make Adelaide and try to get to John Martins before closing time so I could get a personal fitting of my winter uniform. John Martins tailors made the winter uniforms and I needed mine to be just that little bit better fit, after all, I'd put on a good stone since last year's issue. The gravel road from Marree to Leigh Creek, 60 miles (100kms), wasn't too bad, then past Leigh Creek and the open cut brown coal mines which fuelled the power station at Port Augusta providing South Australia with most of its electricity. The road was still gravel, but much better.

The Flinders Ranges flanked me on my left most of the way, the creek beds, gums and countryside so much like parts of Central Australia but yet still so different. At last near Port Augusta I struck the bitumen and it was on to Adelaide. I made it in good time to "Johnnies". They were a little surprised to have me walk in and ask for a fitting, it wasn't everyday they had a Northern Territory policeman call for a fitting, in fact, very few took the trouble. Jim and Pearl had the gate open ready for my arrival; they were more excited than I was, with so much to tell me about what they had been doing and wanting to ask me about my year in the Territory.

Jim had again been out fishing and Pearl served some up some great South Australian garfish for dinner. We sat and talked, and even watched the TV News – yes television, it was 12 months since I'd seen television. Next morning a hearty breakfast and on the road again, through the Adelaide Hills, Murray Bridge, the border could not come soon enough. The Victorian Wimmera was hot and dry, the wheat stubble golden yellow. The Melbourne peak-hour traffic was horrendous, but I managed to negotiate it safely, my NT number plate excusing me when I was in the wrong lane. I pulled into the kerb at home, it really didn't look a lot different to when I'd left, but yet so much had changed. While some might have thought I was "home", I was only "home" on leave, there was never a thought in my mind of not returning to The Alice.

CHAPTER 6

The second year

My sister's wedding in February, 1967, went well, a sunny summer day, she looked the lovely bride. I got to speak to many relations and friends. I knew the time would flash by so I wasted none to get around and see as many friends as I could. I went to athletics on a couple of Saturdays, spending most of the time talking with friends, I went and had a night down at Wonthaggi with the Featherstons and caught up with Tom Gannon and the crew at *The Express* and had a wander through the shopping strip speaking with some of the people I used to call on to pick up advertising, or the occasional news story, even called at the police station. My first boss Norm Gill arranged for me to be a guest at the Rotary Club of Belgrave and to speak on the year I'd had in the Territory. But the news from The Centre was about record rains and flooding, particularly of the Finke River which had again destroyed the railway bridge at Finke, and flooding that caused miles of rail track washaways. As it turned-out, I had left Alice Springs on the second last Ghan passenger train to leave before the flooding. I would return six weeks later on only the second train to return to town.

A couple of weeks into my leave I got written advice that my appointment had been confirmed.

When I went to book to return, I was told the first class sleepers were fully booked. Although there was room for my car, I would have to travel back economy class although there was a chance I could get an up-grade when I got to Port Augusta. In fact, I had no trouble at all, of the 150 bookings for the train, only 50 fronted up to board, so I was able to change to a first class roomette without any trouble. Despite the rains of the past six weeks, the trip through to Oodnadatta ran pretty well. Then we started to slow, at one stage it took 1 hour, 55 minutes to travel 22 miles (35kms). At another time we travelled 115 miles (185kms) in six hours. The delays added up and instead of arriving in Alice Springs about 11pm Tuesday night, it was well into the early hours of the morning before arrival. We were allowed to sleep on the train until 4.30am, then I walked back to the barracks to get a little more sleep before morning.

There were changes at the barracks, new recruits – Ross Kerr, Les Perry, Kevin Morris and Jim Andrews – and a couple of transfers, Dudley Mardling from Darwin to bolster the CIB and another from Tennant Creek – Jim

At the Mt Gillen summit cairn
l to r: Ray Wein, Jim Carstairs, Winston "Lofty" Moffat and myself

Carstairs who a year earlier I'd dropped off at Tennant Creek as I'd moved to The Alice. Dudley Mardling despised Alice Springs, not the least for its weather, but even more so the people who had transferred him from Darwin very much against his will. Still, he was a very competent detective. He was one of the few English born members of the force, bringing another sense of wit to barracks life. Jim Andrews had come from the a sawmill office at Wauchope, on the central coast of New South Wales. He was even quieter, more reserved than I had been. Unfortunately, he found the job and living conditions more than he could cope with and left us a couple of months later.

When I got to barracks soon after sunrise, some of the chaps were organised to climb Mt Gillen, part of the Western MacDonnell's, 1,500 feet (460m) above the surrounding plain overlooking Alice Springs. As I'd never climbed the peak, I decided to join them. We drove about six miles (10km) out of town to the base of the range and began to climb. It took about an hour to reach the summit, the last few hundred yards (metres) along the top of the range from the actual point of assent to the summit marker/trig station. The views were spectacular, both back to the east and across Alice Springs, and to the west, where the razor like range ran as far as the eye could see. The colours – the red and orange ochres of the ranges close by to the blues of the distant ranges were no less spectacular. The plain below was its own unique orange sand colour scattered with mulga and the dull greens of scrub.

The summit itself was a rugged outcrop of ochre colours with a battered black trig marker firmly staked in place.

I never climbed to the summit again but on many night shift mornings, in all seasons, I took the opportunity to drive to one of the vantage points around town, like Anzac Hill or the hill behind the power house, to see the ribbons of morning light run across the range, changing its red and ochre colours like you have never seen.

The climb took the tension away from an incident which was alleged to have happened the weekend before I arrived back. A part aboriginal had made a complaint that he had been assaulted while being arrested. He had gone to the media and a solicitor; there was all-hell-to-pay, culminating in a special identification parade of all police on duty at the time to allow the victim to mark his alleged assailant. The members at the centre of the inquiry were from barracks. As I wasn't even in town at the time, I didn't get involved. By coincidence, the member involved was about to go on leave. He left, saying nothing, just leaving his typed resignation in the station sergeant's file overnight. We never saw or heard from the young member again and what had been a promising career was cut short.

Another day to settle in, then back to work. While I had been on leave, apart from changes at the barracks, there had also been a few changes to the uniform. The wide leather trouser belt had gone, replaced with a military type webbing belt with a police badge mounted on a silver buckle. The collar numbers had gone with a single ID number on the left hand breast pocket flap. My pocket number was 332. As the numbers started at 201, I had a seniority of 132 below the commissioned officer rank of Inspector. Another change was the roster with the new recruits meaning there were now a few members below me in seniority. I became the senior man on some shifts, particularly on a Sunday.

We also had a new Commissioner, Mr W. J. (Bill) McLaren, recruited from the Victoria Police where he and his brother, both police inspectors, were said to have vied for the job. He was never a popular commissioner. To this day, there are some who say the Department of Territories mixed up the applications and recruited the wrong brother!

It wouldn't be long now to the winter tourist season getting into full swing so if I was going to get some good aboriginal water colour art, from the "Hermannsburg School", the Albert Namatjira type water colour paintings, I would have to move pretty quickly. Once the tourist season started and demand for the art work increased, the quality quickly fell away. I got out and bought a couple of paintings from Maurice Namatjira, a nephew or cousin of Albert, I'm not sure which. I also got a beautiful wide landscape by Claude Panaka and another by Benjamin Landara who at the time were considered two painters producing the best in the style. From time to time I'd bought a few paintings in the style and sent them home to my father or to my brother who got to sell them on at his shop or amongst workmates. When times were hard for the painters they would turn up at the police station or barracks and try to sell. I made it a policy to buy at a fair price and often refused to buy when the asking price was 'over the top' for the quality of the work, the price being dictated by the unmentioned need for money to buy liquor and hire a taxi to take it out bush which would have only led to trouble.

Night shift quickly came around but at this time of year it was quiet, in five nights the phone rang once, and that was the indomitable Miss Pink again complaining about someone shooting near her reserve. *"It must be policemen shooting at rabbits"* was her latest claim. At least it was a change from past stories.

It was soon May Day again; this year I was on evening shift so the station sergeant asked me if I would help him and others on the Youth Club stalls at the sports day after the Bangtail Muster parade. I ended up with the Territory member of the House of Representatives, Sam Calder, cutting rolls for the hamburgers before moving on to the "knock-em-down" stall. I was never so pleased to go off to work, the only trouble with work was that by evening many had over-indulged, the hotel bars were spilling out drunks and it was all a bit hectic. In fact the whole weekend was hectic ... a woman went to sleep on the middle of the road and was run over, and killed; an 81 year old tourist walked on to the street and was hit by the bull bar fitted to an army Landrover (he died a few days later) and a stolen car caused a three-car head-to-tail accident right in front of a couple of us as we did an evening street foot patrol.

It was good politics to respond to the request for help by the station sergeant for one of his pet projects in town, the Youth Club, not that I minded at all. In the year or so in The Alice I really had not got into any community affairs apart from helping to start up a local amateur athletic club. It paid off when he wandered into the barracks next week and half asked, half instructed *"You'll be right to go on a mission patrol next week, won't you?"* Of course I was. On the other hand, I was a bit concerned it might also lead to a transfer to Tennant Creek where a vacancy had occurred with a member in barracks at Tennant Creek being selected as the Northern Territory representative in the Australian Police contingent to Cyprus.

This time the mission patrol was to be 5-days, starting on a Sunday. I took the same tracker, Sonny Woods, with me but I reversed the trip from my first patrol, heading out first-up through Hermannsburg. We had lunch beside the Finke River. The river was still flowing nearly a foot (.30m) deep. That was well below its peak of more than 18 feet (5.5m), and hundreds of yards wide in late February and early March. I spent the first night at Areyonga, then went on to Haasts Bluff and on to Papunya where I stayed two nights before going on to Yuendumu. Again, as there had not been a police visit to the settlements for some time, there were lots of routine matters like dogs galore and firearms to be registered and driving licence tests to be done. At Yuendumu they had five chaps lined up for truck driver's licence tests, all aboriginals. In each case I told them to drive me from the settlement office, where I had set up "shop" to the hospital ... I thought *"well if anything is going to happen, at least I am part of the way to hospital!"* They actually were pretty good drivers, they had been driving for ages but there was a need to make it all legal just in case there was an accident, after all, they were driving Commonwealth vehicles!

At Areyonga one old fellow, Donkey Donk Number 2, with his mud curls in his beard, came down to me with a spear and woomera under one arm and his .22 rifle needing registration under the other! I bought the spear and woomera off him for $1, then took 25 cents back to register his rifle.

The weather in May is usually great, in particular the first half of the month. It was no exception on the patrol with lovely sunny days and mild nights making the trip great travelling. Such weather at this time of year could only mean one thing – it would have to build up and break, and it did with an evening thunderstorm like I hadn't seen for ages.

The Alice Springs Show came around again, this year I was on evening shift, which gave me the opportunity to have a look at the Show during the day, then work the evening shift and have to 'clean-up' the drunks around town to the stage where there was only standing room in the cells. I arrested 11 drunks myself including a late afternoon arrest at Traeger Park, where they held the Show. Ada Baxter was quite an articulate aboriginal woman but frequently arrested for drunkenness and other street offences. She also frequently pleaded "not guilty" as she did on this occasion. So I was hastened to court to give evidence. In a rambling way she told the Magistrate *"he hit me and he kicked me and he ... "* with the Magistrate interjecting *"and he hit you over the head with a baton"* an obvious reference to the accusations against police earlier in the month. *"Guilty ... fined . . ."* he concluded.

On my first trip up to Ti Tree after returning from leave I could see the change in the country side after the true drought breaking rains. The country was looking great and the wildlife was returning. This time I saw many kangaroos, and even emus, compared to the odd sighting the previous year. It made night driving very hazardous and to be avoided if possible.

One of the fellows from barracks had been sent to Finke to relieve for three months. While the rail went directly south to Finke, road access was the 175 miles (275kms) south to Kulgera and then 90 odd miles (145kms) east to Finke. The Finke vehicle was in for repair at The Alice and he had a loan vehicle so it was arranged that I and another chap from barracks would drive the Finke vehicle down one Friday afternoon and return on the Sunday. We got to Finke about 8.30pm and almost immediately left to drive the 20 odd miles (35kms) out to New Crown Station and on to a mustering camp set up at a bore-windmill-stock watering site and camped around a fire for the night.

Next morning seven of us, in a couple of vehicles set out to find some feral camels which were known to be in the area. They had been breaking down fences and causing general havoc for the cattle station property owners. The trouble with camels was they did not run in a straight line, they weaved, so when they hit a fence line they would not run through the fence once and break it but run miles weaving back and forth through the fence breaking it repeatedly. The cattle station owner wanted to get out and shoot a few and hopefully not only send the rest of the mob deeper into the nearby Simpson Desert region but reduce the fence damage.

We drove from 8.30am to about 3 o'clock and didn't see one camel. In fact, we didn't even see the sign of a camel. I just felt I'd been riding one all day, bouncing about in the four-wheel-drive. We went cross country, up sandhills, across dry river beds and along all sorts of bush tracks. At one stage we followed the Northern Territory-South Australia border for about 20 miles (32kms). We must have visited South Australia about 490 times as the track also weaved from side to side along the border marked by white marker posts every half mile with a 10 feet (3m) wide cleared strip marking the "line". The road along the border crossed in and out of South Australia three or four times every hundred yards or so (100m). At times I didn't have any idea where I was, and I'm sure most of the others didn't either.

I was really pleased to get back to Finke about 5 o'clock, the thought of a good hot shower uppermost in my mind except at the police residence there was no shower, just a chip heater over a galvanised bath. Well that was even better.

That night there was a community farewell at the local hotel for Mrs Colson, who with her late husband (but more recently with her son, Tim, newly married) had run the local general store for many years. She was retiring and moving to town. Everyone for about 100 miles (160kms) around turned out for the function. The music was all country and western, played on a scratchy radiogram. Although I had heard of him, I didn't really get an introduction to the music of Frank Ifield until that night – *"I Remember You"*, *"Lovesick Blues" "She Taught me How to Yodel"*, *"I'm Confessin'"* and the like. First thing I did when I returned to The Alice was go and buy the record. Next morning we went for a drive around Finke which was dominated by a row of railway employee houses and the strip with the police station, post office and telegraph repeater station, and the most modern building in town, the school. At last I saw a camel, three of them in fact, but they were domesticated, in the charge of an aboriginal Nicodemus, a genuine old fellow who obviously had a great affinity to his camel herd. I was tempted to ride but decided to leave that to another day. We went and had a look at the twisted wreck of the Finke River railway bridge. It was amazing to see how the forces of nature had up-rooted the concrete supports of the bridge, twisted the rail track and thrust it aside. Ray and I got ready to leave when word came on the radio that the Inspector said it would be OK for us to stay on and come back on Monday morning, in departmental time. We had to take the vehicle we were taking back to Kulgera and swap it for that station's vehicle and nurse it back to town for repair.

So we went fishing in some of the river lagoons that still existed from the summer floods. We netted 50-odd small fish the size of sardines, ready to be transported to a nearby cattle station dam. The fish had come from up-stream permanent water holes and washed down the river in the flood. As the water holes along the river dried up they would have died.

Night shift went quickly when there were a few incidents. The first night I found a man in a public toilet drinking methylated spirits, the ring of white around his lips, let alone his breath and the metho bottle in his hand immediately giving him away. He was in a bad way, seeing things, like a pack of dogs in the corner of the station office ready to pounce on him. He would have got at least a month's gaol to sober him up. Then on the Saturday morning we had to go to the airport for three hours when a Qantas 707 with 106 passengers en-route from Singapore to Sydney was forced to land in Alice Springs because of fog in Sydney. All passengers had to have their Australian entry health checks made as it was their first point of entry. They would then only have to clear Customs in Sydney.

With that done, we were invited on board and shown over the aircraft, given a soft drink, a pair of bed socks and some small Qantas pins. It was something different for the night shift. What wasn't different was Miss Pink phoning to again complain about shooting on her reserve. Earlier in the evening she had rung to comment that *"Constable Pollock is the most useless policeman in Alice Springs"*. I'd copped the blame for failing to apprehend the 'shooters' the previous evening. When next she rang and I spoke with her, I told her, in a quite serious tone, that I was considering instituting legal proceeds for defamation of my character. This kept her quiet for a while.

Another night one of the more respected aboriginal workers around town, Smiler Major, walked into the station to say he had just killed his wife. *"You proper kill her, or just a little bit"* the Constable asked. *"Proper"* he relied.

"Where?" the Constable asked *"At my camp"* he replied. *"Where is that?"* ... *"You know the hill where the sun come up, well just this side of that!"*. Smiler was subsequently convicted of manslaughter and sentenced to a short term of imprisonment. At the gaol he continued his work as a gardener and was often seen working outside the gaol as a 'trustee', a prisoner who was trusted not to escape, working in the orange grove or grounds of the Gaoler's yard.

Rowdy behaviour caused by liquor or intoxicated persons entering the Amoonguna aboriginal reserve was causing some problems to the degree that on pay week Friday and Saturday evenings two of us were sent there for a few hours to try to maintain some degree of decorum. The first Friday night I went out we arrested two for being drunk on the reserve and two for unlawfully taking liquor on to the reserve. Next evening as we arrived we were confronted with a screaming aboriginal woman, her clothes torn off, being chased by a man, who turned out to be her husband, armed with a nulla nulla (a piece of solid mulga wood, two to three feet long, up to a couple of inches thick) with a couple of blows clearly landing on her head. Fortunately, he only caused a small cut to the head and no serious injury. I arrested him and charged him with aggravated assault (an assault on a female). At Monday morning's court he was sentenced to 14 days gaol. After hearing the police summary, after a guilty plea, the magistrate, again Mr G. F. Hall SM, commented *"It might have been an expression of undying love ... or is this the way you win friends and influence people at Amoonguna?"*

The magistrate was resident in Alice Springs and on call at any time. I remember one morning, about 2am, having court in his kitchen, he in his dressing gown, as he signed a warrant to allow me to enter a property and investigate a report of a suspect mental defective. Sadly a man had become mentally disturbed, but he was not "wandering at large", he was in a caravan in the yard of his son's property. The Northern Territory laws on mental illness at the time were draconian. The process was that a person suspected of being a "mental defective" had to be arrested by police, be taken to a court where if the magistrate or justices were satisfied there was a prima-face case, an order was made remanding the person to the gaol where he would be examined by two medical practitioners. They were required to report their opinion to the court within 14 days. If they considered the person mentally ill, the court made a further order declaring the person a mental defective and in turn the Administrator of the Territory issued an order to remove the person, usually to Adelaide, for further treatment. All this could take weeks, and often did.

In this particular case, it was an unpleasant duty but one that had to be done – taking a man from his home to the police cells, then next morning to court. The magistrate made the appropriate order and the doctors quickly examined him and reported him being mentally ill and in need of transfer to Adelaide. They began treatment themselves and by the time all the orders came through, the man seemed quite well. However, a couple of weeks later Constable Les Perry, who had assisted me in the initial arrest, and I escorted the man to Adelaide where he was again taken into custody by South Australia police and in turn handed over to the mental health authorities in that State. At least we got a jet flight to Adelaide, two nights accommodation at Adelaide police headquarters and the chance to do some shopping in Adelaide before flying back in a prop-jet aircraft to The Alice.

Government housing was always in short supply, and not the least for newly married members of the force. I could not always fathom some housing policies, in particular one which allowed a department to maintain occupancy of a house vacated by say a member who had resigned by filling it with a member transferred into the town from another centre waiting for a government house. If nobody was transferred to the empty house, only then did that house fall back into the pool with the next government employee, from any department, on the waiting list being allocated the house.

So when a married member living in a police house in Alice Springs resigned, the department would transfer another married member, usually from Darwin, who was living in rented accommodation, to Alice Springs, to take the house and keep the house within the Police Branch of the Northern Territory Administration. It also usually meant that a single member in Alice Springs would have to be transferred to Darwin to maintain the balance in the numbers.

It was no surprise therefore, when Acting Inspector Metcalfe turned up at the barracks one morning and asked *"which one of you wants to transfer to Darwin?"* Nobody wanted to transfer to Darwin but it boiled down to the fact it would be one of three of us, the three who had transferred to Alice Springs at the end of our recruit school last year. I had a look at the leave roster for the year ahead and could see there were quite a few bush stations in the Northern Division where the officer in charge was rostered for leave and would need to be relieved by a single member so when the pressure for a volunteer to transfer was put on a few days later, I said I would be prepared to transfer to Darwin on the understanding that within a reasonable time I would be given the opportunity to go on bush relief. *"I'll tell them, but I'm not sure they will be prepared to make a commitment like that"* the acting inspector said.

Ten days or so later as I walked into the station from court the Acting Inspector called me into his office. I always remember he was standing in the station sergeant's office, which was across a passage from his office. He saw me, and with just eye contact and the come here movement of his index finger, moved to his office and sat down as I walked in. *"Yes Sir"* I quietly said, *"Well lad, you are going on a temporary transfer to Darwin, but before you get there, you have to go to Maranboy and relieve Constable Eckert, then you will go to Larrimah and relieve Constable Burgdorf, and if you don't stuff them up, you might go on to Elliott and relieve Horrie Prew. The paper work will be down in a few days but you can start to get organised".*

All three stations were in the Northern Division, thus the temporary transfer to Darwin. Maranboy was 30 miles (50kms) south of Katherine, and 12 miles (20kms) east off the Stuart Highway into the bush. It was regarded as the pick of bush relief stations as apart from being off the highway, the relieving officer also took over the duties of postmaster and mail contractor, normally carried out by the policeman's wife. Harry Belton, now stationed in the Alice as a Senior Constable, had been officer-in-charge at Maranboy for the four years before a transfer with Colin Eckert and his wife and two children eight months or so ago (Harry and Colin effectively swapped houses under the transfer/retention of housing policy) so I was able to get a good briefing about the place, what I would need to take and so on.

A day or two later the official advice arrived;

"You are advised that you have been selected for temporary transfer to Darwin.

2. *Prior to taking up duty in Darwin, you will be required to perform relieving duties at Maranboy and Larrimah Police Stations. In this regard you are to depart Alice Springs in sufficient time to enable you to travel to and reach Maranboy Police Station on 10th August, 1967.*

3. *You will remain at Maranboy Police Station during the period Constable*

Eckert is on recreation leave (14th August, 1967 to 6 November, 1967 inclusive) and will then proceed to Larrimah Police Station where you will relieve Constable Burgdorf whose leave commences on 11 November, 1967.

4. *Consideration is being given to granting you a further period of relieving duties at Elliott Police Station and you will be further advised in this regard.*

S. J. Bowie
Superintendent of Police."

So I'd leave Alice Springs in four weeks, four weeks that I'd have to watch that I didn't get involved in anything that would jeopardise the transfer, but still time to whip me in for another night shift before heading north. I packed some aboriginal spears I'd collected, in particular a couple of fine shovel nose spears, frequently used in fatal pay-back spearings, and sent them home to my parents. I started to get a few provisions together, they would be much cheaper in Alice Springs than in Katherine, where I would inevitably have to buy supplies later. I wrote home that I'd been able to buy a couple of dozen tins of Monbulk jam for 28c a tin, which included four tins of strawberry jam normally selling locally for 52c a tin. *"I'll use the strawberry jam, I'll use the other for rations"* I wrote home.

One of the responsibilities at bush stations was to provide the rations for the tracker and his family. At Maranboy there was just the tracker and his wife so I would get a weekly allowance of $11 odd to provide rations which would include tea, sugar, flour, jam, rolled oats, baking powder, salt and a few other things, now and then replacing the jam with golden syrup and the rolled oats or Weet-bix, depending on the tastes of the tracker. Then there was also beef, potatoes and onions to be provided so there was nothing really left of the $11. You had to shop wisely to provide the most. Then of course there was yourself to feed, there was no Mt Gillen Motel down the street or cafe across the road.

I was also determined to see Ayers Rock before I left Alice Springs. Although I was on a *"temporary transfer"* to Darwin, there was no certainty I'd be back to Alice Springs for years. The Rock was a rough 275 miles drive (440kms) south west of Alice Springs. I wasn't keen to drive there, in fact, I hardly had the time. Then I struck on the idea of speaking with my mate Ossie Watts at the Aero Club as I heard that some members were prepared to take a trip to Ayers Rock to help get up their flying hours for their pilots licence. I found someone to share the cost of the plane hire, then arranged with Paul Egar, one of two brothers, Paul and John Egar who ran a couple of businesses in town, including a supermarket and pharmacy, "The Egar Beavers" to fly us out. We left about 8am one morning for a two hour flight to The Rock in the Cessna 180. First we flew west along the MacDonnell Ranges, over Palm Valley and then south-west to The Rock which (along with The Olgas, 20 miles (32kms) west of Ayers Rock) we could see for miles as we began to descend.

The landing strip was right beside The Rock with one of its features, "The Brain" dominating the monolith. I was determined to climb the Rock, so straight after landing I headed off on foot to "The Climb", and climbed. It was over an hour to the summit, assisted in some sections by chains set into the side of the rock to help pull yourself up; then as you reached the top of the rock, a dotted white line, like a road marking line, across the top of The Rock to the summit and the visitor's book. The views were spectacular, across the plains, towards the Olgas, to the west, Mt Connor in the east, they are virtually beyond description.

It was a little quicker coming down, but you always had to be careful. Brass plaques at the foot of the Rock, at the start of the climb – *"In loving Memory of . . .who died while climbing . . ."* – were a grim reminder of the need not just for care but not to over exert yourself on the climb or descent.

I made it back to the airstrip and to one of the motels nearby where our pilot was waiting. A drink and a bite to eat and we were back to the plane for the return trip. It was a little more direct, across pastoral country, making a re-fuelling stop at Curtin Springs (the fuel was cheaper at Curtin Springs than Ayers Rock) and on to The Alice before dusk. Paul went on to fly regularly, in particular when he based himself back in Adelaide. He would fly himself up and down to Alice Springs on business trips. Sadly, in the early 1980's he was flying back to Adelaide when the plane struck bad weather over the Flinders Ranges and crashed, killing all on board.

The last weekend I was in The Alice was the first weekend of August, so it was the Picnic Day public holiday on the Monday with the Harts Range picnic races on the Saturday and Monday, the big Harts Range races ball on the Saturday night with most of Sunday to recover. Even the acting station sergeant, Sergeant First Class Len Cossons, who was down from Darwin on relieving duty, had gone out to Harts Range for the weekend. As a young constable, he had been stationed there and thus knew many of the locals. It was a great opportunity for him to see old friends. I worked both the Saturday and

*Looking from the summit of Mt Gillen on the northern side of the range,
east toward Alice Springs*

Sunday, then had the Monday to pack, load the car and be ready to leave for Maranboy first thing on the Tuesday morning.

Sunday shifts had a reputation of being either dead quiet or being run-off-your-feet. This particular Sunday promised to be the latter. Some of the chaps from barracks, after working the day shift on Saturday, had left to go to Harts Range and join in the festivities. They arrived just after a shooting murder in the aboriginal camp, in which an ex-police tracker had been shot dead and as I recall, an aboriginal woman badly injured from gun fire. It was a matter of all hands on duty with a couple of them needing to travel back to town with the body and the wounded woman before going straight back to Harts Range.

I was at the station attending to routine matters, cleaning up the last of my files, when the phone rang. *Flying Doctor Base here ... we have a message for you ... two of your members have been shot at Hart's Range and are being evacuated by air to Alice Springs. They are not believed to be in a serious condition ... no, there are no names available at this stage, they do not want to give them over the radio"*

A few minutes later the RFDS rang again ... *"We can tell you the registered numbers of the members shot are 36 and 163"* A quick reference to the seniority list in the Police Gazette told us those shot were Sergeant Cossons and Constable Blake Jobberns, who was at Harts Range for the races.

Both had been shot by Billy Benn, the murder suspect, armed with at least one .22 rifle, possibly two. After the early morning shooting he had been tracked to a hillside and as the search party approached he opened fire. The bullet that hit Blake Jobberns hit him in the chest, to one side, with the bullet running around his rib cage and out his back. He wasn't even admitted to hospital, little more than a band-aid at the point of entry and exit of the bullet along with a couple of injections. Sergeant Cossons was more serious. He had been shot, as he took cover, in the lower back, the bullet shattering inside with some remnants resting inside his rump area for the rest of his life. He was admitted to hospital and underwent surgery to remove some fragments but again he was lucky not to have been more seriously injured.

With no idea of the extent of injuries, we advised the hospital early in the piece that if they required blood, to advise us from their records the names of members with the same blood type so we could quickly arrange their attendance to donate. The hospital kept virtually no blood supplies, only calling on donors when blood was needed. It might take hours to get enough donors of the right type, even in an emergency.

I remember later that afternoon Sergeant Third Class Allan Lake and a constable, whose name I can't recall, were called to donate blood. They returned to the station, with their arm bandaged as it always was in those days after a blood donation, Sergeant Lake, extending his blood donor arm and patting the bandage with his other hand, in his grating voice, proudly saying, boasting, *"I've been down to the hospital lad, to donate blood for Sergeant Cossons"* I didn't have the heart to tell him, in his case the blood was for a young aboriginal man severely injured in a motor vehicle accident the previous evening! Sergeant Cossons had a less common blood group, O Rh Positive. It was common for Mrs. Pat Newman, Harry Birtwhistle and the District Officer Dan Conway to meet, often in the middle of the night, at the hospital, all called when their blood type was needed as it was for the Sergeant

So with the murder and two police shot, a search for the culprit began. It was a gruelling 10 days before his capture, a story in itself but one in which I took no further part as I left Alice Springs on my temporary transfer.

CHAPTER 7

My first command ... Maranboy

It was an easy day's drive – 315 miles (500kms) – north to Tennant Creek where I spent the night. The next evening I was spending with the Burgdorfs at Larrimah, where I would go to relieve in three months. They had asked for some *"Tennant Creek bread please"*, the baker at Tennant Creek having a reputation, in particular for his sliced loaf, wrapped in a solid greaseproof wrapper. It not only had a good texture and tasted great but it seemed to keep fresher longer. A few last minute purchases and then on the 300 miles (480kms) to Larrimah. Along the way I took the opportunity to stop at Elliott and have a look at the station there, and have a word with Horrie Prew as I felt confident I'd be relieving him in six months time.

Next morning it was another 60 odd miles (100kms) north to the Maranboy turn-off. The 12 miles (19kms) from the Stuart Highway, along the Mainoru beef development road, wasn't too bad, although it was very dusty with a couple of significant patches of "bulldust", fine powdery yellowish-red dust that seemed to soak in everywhere. Finally, the police station turn-of, and the station building dominating a hillside rise came into view, a blue gravel strip with a ring road around the station complex.

The main building was a former Australian Inland Mission hospital, built 50 to 60 years earlier and used as a hospital in the hey-day of the district. It was double story with a 360 degree view of the area. At the back of the station there was a garage complex, the cell clock (a single cell) and the tracker's quarters. On the western side of the building was an elevated tank stand which doubled as a tower for the radio aerials. At the rear of the building was the power house which housed the 240 volt lighting plant. There was no 12 volt power back up. There was the laundry entry and then into the kitchen which like most stations had both a conventional slow-combustion stove, which doubled as a hot water service and the gas stove. There were two large capacity kerosene refrigerators, both of which had freezer compartments.

The ground level was open plan with stairs to the first floor. A storeroom/pantry, and the police station office and post office, were on the western side of the building, the post office having a shutter window for customers. You had to walk through the post office to get to the police office. Upstairs was open plan too. The building was generally timber, iron, plenty of fly wire, louvre

The front entrance of the Maranboy Police Station and residence dominated by the water tower. The Post Office was in the front left hand corner of the building

windows and some canvas blinds. Being set on the top of a rise, it caught all the breezes.

There was lawn around the front and side of the building. There was a sort of fence surrounding the place, but really in need of some repair as I was to find out in a few days. There was no vegetable garden although there was an area half-worked up that was to be used as a vegetable garden. Of course, going on leave, Colin had not pursued much gardening in recent times. Perhaps his nick name "Speedy" reflected that. To the front of the building there was a small valley. Directly across the valley was the ruins of the tin mining battery, a relic from the days when the district produced much tin and had a flourishing community. Today there was only one tin prospector, and his wife, left in the district; an elderly couple I got to see each mail day. To the front left, you looked at the road rising on the Bamyili "jump-up", an aboriginal colloquialism for a sharp rising hill to another level.

As I drove up to the back of the station, I was greeted by a bounding golden labrador dog, which I later found I would have the task of minding while the Eckerts were away. The tracker, Frank, appeared from his quarters and Colin, quickly followed by his two children, from the back of the house, to greet me. You could tell the sense of excitement that I'd arrived. The time to when they would be on their way on leave was getting closer, it was past the talking stage, the reliever had arrived and they would be off as soon as time allowed.

A cup of tea and a quick chat, a quick familiarisation look around the station and then into the paperwork. The handover/takeover was a sort or ritual. First up, there was a check of the station inventory, a check that every chair, table, bed, office desk, cabinet, even the safe, listed in the inventory was physically there. Serial numbers of rifles and the pistol, along with the typewriter, had to be checked with a report submitted listing details of the last transaction in the inventory.

An inventory of text books on hand at the station had to be compiled, all accountable forms on hand, both used and unused, had to be checked, and a report listing them had to be countersigned by both the outgoing and incoming member. The same went for the stamp book (the stamp advance was usually about $8), dog registration tags and at stations where there was petty cash, probably about $4–$10, it had to be checked and verified. The vehicle had to be checked over, all accessories including in those days safety belts, the crank handle and the fire extinguisher, along with the "Police" sign, the tool kit had to be checked off and signed over. I had to sign for the copy of the "Police

Code". This was kept in the safe, a formula for a code used to compile confidential radio messages or to decipher coded messages received, particularly at locations where there was no other means of contact than by radio or private telephone. Any court exhibits or found property on hand also had to be listed and reported on.

The process was usually speeded up by the outgoing member preparing all the reports in the day or two before hand, checking everything off ready for the arrival of the incoming member. But it had to be thorough and accurate, the incoming officer had to have full confidence everything was in order, it would be on his head if the Divisional Inspector or government stocktaker or internal auditor walked in tomorrow and found a discrepancy. There would be a hell of a row.

We attended to most of the handover/takeover on the Thursday afternoon, completing it on the Friday morning. Then after lunch we attended to the fairly simple handover of the post office from Colin's wife to myself. There was little more than checking the postage stamps and cash on hand and showing me a few procedures. As the post office was a Commonwealth function, I had to take an Oath of Allegiance and sign other documents about secrecy and the like. From the time of my arrival, I was shown how the post office and telephone exchange worked.

Then we had a look at the lighting plant and the bore pump, a couple of hundred yards from the station, set up in a steel mesh cage with a tin roof to protect it from wandering livestock and to some extent the weather, and the watering system. We then drove over to Bamyili, the aboriginal settlement seven miles (11kms) further along the beef road, and met the manager and some of the staff, including the nursing sister, Sister June Eperjezy, who had a great reputation for supervising the training of young women at the settlement in home duties, washing, ironing, cleaning, even cooking. She was a no-nonsense woman but she had a real knack of being able to encourage people to help themselves to a better lifestyle. There were about 400 aboriginals at the settlement.

That evening we all went for a meal at Shepherds timber mill. Ron Shepherd and his son John and daughter June, came back home every Thursday afternoon or Friday morning with a load of cypress pine they had gathered around their bush camp; on Fridays they would do the final milling and have a load ready for transport out in the afternoon, the Darwin timber merchant eager to get the keenly sought after building and flooring timber. They were the only miller of this timber which they harvested over Crown land to the north of Maranboy. Then first thing Sunday morning they would be back to the bush.

They had a well trained group of young aboriginal men working with them who would travel in and out of the bush, and camp at the mill at weekends.

June was a great cook. Each weekend, usually on the Friday evening, she would prepare a roast. It became normal for me to be invited over, and a great time would be had by all.

Then on the Saturday morning, at piccaninny light, the Eckerts left, their Holden station sedan well packed, the four of them so looking forward to three months out of the Territory. At the morning radio schedule I sent this radio message to Headquarters *"Handover-Takeover Maranboy Constable Eckert to Constable Pollock completed 11.8.67 signed Pollock, Officer in Charge.* It was those words – "officer-in-charge" – that made me realise that I was really on my own. Here I was, a constable of less than 18 months experience in the force, 24 years old, the officer-in-charge of my own police station. I not only had a responsibility for those who lived in the 12,000 or so square miles of the district but I had the responsibilities of ensuring the efficient working of the station, that the lighting plant, the bore, the police vehicle, the buildings, were all cared for appropriately. They needed to be for my own well being as well.

I was not just the officer-in-charge of police. As at all the bush stations, I was the Deputy Registrar of Motor Vehicles, I was the Registrar of Dogs, Deputy Registrar of Firearms. At Maranboy I could also issue Miner's Rights to prospectors and so the list of tasks went on. There was also an underlying feeling that I was a Southern Division invader coming to take over perhaps the plum relieving station in the force.

Of course, apart from my police responsibilities, I was now also the postmaster, the local telephonist and mail contractor. The telephone exchange was only open four hours a day – 9am-11am and 3pm-5pm. – Monday to Friday, and 9am-11am on Saturday mornings. There were only three subscribers – the police station, the office of the aboriginal community at Bamyili, seven miles away, and Shepherd's timber mill.

Part of the post office arrangements was the mail contract, to take, and pick up, the mail four times a week from the mail contractor on the Stuart Highway. There were set times to meet the mail van but if the mail van was running late or ahead of time I usually got a phone call from Katherine when heading south, or Mataranka, an hour south of the Maranboy turn-off, when heading north. At the turn-off, actually beside the railway shelter as the rail line ran virtually parallel with the highway at this point, there was a large red painted, padlocked steel bin. If the mail van came through in the middle of the night I could leave mail in the bin or have mail placed there. Wridgways had the mail contract those days, the Ansett-Pioneer coaches having lost the contract earlier in the year. The post office, telephone exchange and mail contract was worth $32 a week, so it was quite a handy additional income for me.

The telephone switchboard was a pure plug system, no cords, just a pyramid of plug holes with calls being connected by inserting the plug in the hole combination for the call – from the exchange line to subscriber 1 or 4 or 5 with the capacity to also connect 4 and 5 internally. A pulse for an inward call would set off a buzzer, connected to a bell when away from the switchboard, allowing you to know when to plug in. If the call was from outside – Katherine – then I'd answer *"Maranboy"* with the telephonist at the other end saying *"5 please'* with my response *"calling"* as I inserted the right plug, gave a sharp twist of the handle to get a ring at the other end or if the call was from a subscriber, I'd answer *"number please"* and proceed to connect them through to Katherine in the next stage of getting the call through. If the call was for the police station, I liked to take it at the desk, so when I answered *"Maranboy"* and the telephonist would say *"4 please"* I'd respond *"connecting"* and proceed to plug the phone off the switchboard to the police station desk. I remember one morning as I responded *"connecting"* the telephonist in Katherine said *"But that's you isn't it?"* . . . *"Yes"* ... *"well ... "* a little perplexed but I sat down at the desk to take the call, able to take notes.

In addition there were the opening fee charges of 30c a time to open the exchange out of the set hours. I had to warn my parents that when they rang, which they were likely to do of an evening, always to preface their call booking with the words *"prepared to pay opening fee"* because, out of hours, the first words I would say when the exchange rang and I plugged in would be opening fee. I was ruthless on incoming calls; nobody got away without paying opening fee when they rang out of hours, that is except when I wasn't at the station/post office. At these times I would connect all subscribers, that is the settlement and Shepherds direct to Katherine, so they could ring to their hearts content. As it was, the Katherine exchange girls did all the call dockets, whether I was in attendance or not.

I had the weekend to settle in. With the Eckerts gone, I unpacked the car and set up home. It was customary for Frank the tracker, and his wife Nikapinni, to spend every second weekend at the aboriginal settlement with friends and relatives. On the other weekend, which was this weekend, they would spend it at the station and on the Saturday, perhaps even on the Sunday too, he would be given the station .22 rifle and a few rounds of ammunition to go hunting. It seemed no different if you gave him a packet of 50 rounds or just five rounds. There would not be a result from hunting until the last couple of shots, more likely the very last shot. With 50 rounds it was "bang, bang, bang, hell I missed". With just a few rounds left, every shot would count, and the very last, definitely count. He might be lucky to shoot a kangaroo, a bush turkey or a good sized goanna. *"How did you go today Frank?" ... "I got one kangaroo, but he didn't fall down".* In other words, he wounded a kangaroo and it ran away. His wife would be with him all the time. She was a quiet lass who had been well trained in domestic duties at the aboriginal settlement. She could wash and iron well, so for a few dollars a week, she would do my washing and ironing, do the kitchen washing up, sweep the house and the like. Every morning when I got up, the stove would be lit and the kettle boiling.

I wasn't going to have it easy at Maranboy. Because of a staff shortage in Katherine, both the members stationed at Maranboy and Mataranka, were each working one or two evenings a week in Katherine to allow two men to be on duty during the evenings. It meant I would leave Maranboy about 4pm, and take the hour to drive the 42 miles (67kms) to Katherine, work through to about 11pm and then drive home by midnight – an 8 hour shift. We didn't get paid anything extra for this, as overtime was an unheard of term for bush stations; members stationed at bush stations were virtually on call 24 hours a day, seven days a week. They could get a day added to their leave if they were required to work on Christmas Day or Good Friday.

At least the work in Katherine had its advantages and allowed me to keep up my supply of perishable items, fresh bread and milk and so on. Still, I would have rather just stayed at Maranboy. I had only ever stayed two nights in Katherine, one on my way to Darwin when I joined the force, and the other on the way back to Alice Springs after recruit school, both stop-overs doing nothing to let Katherine grow on me. The work in Katherine also allowed me to get a few repairs done to the vehicle, it needed a new speedo cable for one and a filter in the fuel bowl. So on the Monday, which was my first evening shift in Katherine I went in at lunchtime. Typically, the government garage couldn't fix the speedo cable, but then this had its advantages; there was no checking on my use of the police vehicle to drive to the highway to collect the mail. However, there was a good let out to coincide a mail trip with a 'patrol' of the Stuart Highway. There had been a recent special circular from the officer-in-charge of Northern Division noting a poor record by stations actually making a patrol of the highway. In the Maranboy police district there was a section of only about 15 miles (24kms) of the highway within the district. It was probably the best patrolled piece of Stuart Highway in the Territory ... every mail day.

Next day was monthly Magistrate's court day in Katherine, the Alice Springs based Stipendiary Magistrate, Mr G. F. Hall, flying up on the Monday afternoon Fokker Friendship service and returning to Tennant Creek on the Wednesday morning. The police would have to collect him from the airport and convey him to the Magistrate's quarters at the court house, adjacent to the police station.

It was near 11pm and I was starting to get ready to drive home to Maranboy when a phone call came to say there appeared to be a drunk lying on the high level railway bridge. I went with the other chap on duty to find that the drunk was in fact dead – shot with a .22 rifle, the gun lying beside him, an apparent suicide. We called the Magistrate, a coroner, to the scene for a first-hand look. This could save a of a lot of paper work, even an inquest, having the coroner visit the scene. The incident also meant I didn't get back home to Maranboy until 2am.

The Katherine high level railway bridge was planked for cars and pedestrian traffic, and used by many people living on the north bank of the Katherine River. During the wet season it served as the alternate river crossing. It is 60 feet (18.2m) from the river bed to the decking. In 1957, the highest recorded flood to that time, the river rose to lap the decking.

Back at Maranboy, I was getting into the routine, and found it a little more relaxing to run than I had feared. It really was a matter of having a basic routine and just keeping up with everything, writing up the day journal and getting the returns away on the appropriate dates. It was important to keep up with the 'paper work', not the least of which was filing the police gazettes from the various states that seemed to come practically every mail.

Dress around the station was generally casual, but respectable. You never knew when someone would call by. Full uniform was kept for when there was real work to be done. The normal daily routine would be to be awoken by the screeching of cockatoos and other birds as they watered early. There were flocks of budgerigars and finches as well as the larger birds. With the kettle boiling I'd have had a morning cuppa and some cereal before signing on at 8am and be ready for the 8.30am radio sched with Darwin. As a non-bitumen station, that is, a station not on the Stuart Highway, I only had a set radio sched at 8.30am and 3pm although I could also join the additional sched during the day for bitumen stations. In an emergency, I could virtually call in anytime during the day, but then again, I was fortunate, I had the telephone as well. With the HF (High Frequency) system, there was a base station at Darwin, for Northern Division Stations, and Alice Springs, for Southern Division stations. Each station had its individual call sign, for the station radio and another call sign for the mobile service fitted to the police vehicle. At Maranboy the station call sign was VL5HK and the mobile set 8SLK. The common usage call sign was just *"Hotel Kilo"* for the station set but using the full *"Eight Sierra Lima Kilo"* when using the mobile set. The police radio usually took pride of place in every police office, in particular at stations where there was no telephone. It also doubled to provide music and the news from the short wave networks of the ABC, either Australian or Papua-New Guinea based transmissions.

After the morning sched there might be water to be pumped, something to be done on the vehicle or around the buildings, like fixing the fence to stop cattle or the feral donkeys or brumbies coming on to the station lawns to eat during the night. I was at Maranboy only a night or two when I was awoken in the middle of the night by the noise of a number of feral donkeys fighting on the lawn of the station. The *"hee-hawing"* was thundering. I awoke with a hell of a fright wondering what on earth was going on before I realised what it was. I grabbed the station revolver and let off a couple of shots to send them thundering through the bush. In the still of the night I could hear them pounding away, saplings breaking as they stampeded into the distance. The worst thing I could do was actually shoot any of them on the lawn, I would then have had a greater problem in disposing of the carcass.

Being mid-August, the coldest spell of the "dry season" had passed even though at Maranboy, well inland and a little elevated, there was still a good nip in the night air. Still the mornings were above the 50F (10C) mark and the days were running up to the low 80's plus (27C). It was dry, there were constant south-easterlies which tended to keep things pleasant. There had not been rain for months and the countryside had well dried off. In the western distance there was a constant haze of smoke as uncontrolled fires burnt through the bush.

As soon as I had the chance, I ventured further from home and took a drive to Beswick cattle station, about 25 miles (40kms) on from Maranboy. The cattle station was operated by the Welfare Branch as a training station for aboriginal stockmen. George Bates and his wife were the manager and office manager. Some of the cattle raised on the station were slaughtered for beef at the Bamyili settlement to feed the community, including the staff. Just as in

Central Australia dogs were a problem and the management tried to keep the matter under control by insisting all dogs were registered. On every visit to Beswick, there were dogs to be registered.

My routine was made a little difficult by having to work in Katherine a couple of nights a week, even more when members went off sick or there was some special event like the races. Added to this was an ageing motor vehicle. I was at Maranboy only a week when it wouldn't start. I got the mechanic from Bamyili over. He took one look and diagnosed the timing gear had failed, a very common fault of that model Toyota Landcruiser in the mileage bracket of 40,000 – 42,000 miles (64,000 – 67,000kms). This vehicle had done 39,500 miles! (63,200kms) So the Works department sent a team from Katherine to recover the vehicle and take it to town for repairs, which seemed to take forever. With a shortage of government vehicles, I had to hitch a ride into Katherine to work, going in with people from the settlement attending the races and staying on for the movies. On another trip I had to stay in town a couple of nights and was loaned the street sweeper's utility to go home for a night to check things out before having to bring the vehicle back in town in time for him to do the street sweeping next morning.

The aboriginals at the settlement soon got to know what nights I was away, particularly on pay weekends. This inevitably resulted in liquor being taken on to the reserve, resulting in noisy fights. One day, with no vehicle, I had to use my own car to travel over to the settlement and question the offenders. It dropped a few chins when I returned a week later and served the offenders with a summons to appear in Katherine court. The next pay weekend Saturday night I knew I would be working in town so I went down to the main road an hour or so before leaving and set up a one-man road block to check vehicles headed for the settlement. Sure enough a taxi arrived, with five aboriginals on board with eight flagons plus a bottle or two of wine. They accepted my suggestion that they walk the last seven miles (11kms) to the settlement. I thought by journey's end there wouldn't be too much liquor left. I believe I was right.

It was common to get a taxi from Katherine to the reserve boundary, the taxi driver knowing it was too risky to travel further with liquor on board. He would drop the passengers within hearing distance, at night, of the police station, where they would sit and consume their liquor before inevitably getting noisy. Some would then get a lift on to the reserve with passing traffic, and cause a disturbance within the settlement. I recall one morning being woken at 1 o'clock, not by the donkeys feeding on the lawn, but by the settlement superintendent arriving with two drunken aboriginals; they had a swearing match outside his home and had woken him up so he decided to give me some business, bundling them into the back of his vehicle and delivering them to the front of the police station. I arrested them for being "found drunk in a public place". As it turned, out they were the tracker's mother and step-father – both very apologetic at breakfast time.

Another night, at 2.20am, I was awoken by the screaming of an aboriginal woman from the roadside near the old tin mine battery " ... *Constable, come and get me ... you useless bastard . .* " I didn't need a second invitation, I obliged. Again, at breakfast, she was not feeling so sure of herself.

An arrest of an unusual nature was a white sulphur crested cockatoo which one afternoon arrived at the station. It gave all the indications of having been a pet at some time, goodness knows where. The cockatoo, as bold as brass, just walked into the station house. Frank, the tracker, and I caught it, put it in a tea chest and I sent it over to the settlement to join some other captive parrots.

I came to loathe the local picnic race meetings. The first I attended was at Pine Creek, about 65 miles (105kms) north of Katherine. This was a one-day event, on a hot and dusty Saturday followed by a gymkhana on the Sunday. Most of the picnic race meetings were on a long weekend with the races Saturday and Monday and a rodeo or some other activity on the Sunday. At this race meeting there seemed more horses in attendance than spectators. Still, there was plenty of action with two nasty horse related accidents over the weekend. On the Saturday, a girl casually riding near the racecourse lost control of her horse which threw her off. There was a wait for the ambulance to arrive from Katherine. It took her straight on to Darwin, 160 miles (260kms). We heard next morning that she had been evacuated by plane to Adelaide with spinal injuries. On the Sunday a chap was thrown from his horse suffering a broken leg. Again the ambulance had to come from Katherine but this time they took him back there for treatment.

With little more than a month to go at Maranboy things were looking up ... I got a call to take my break-down prone vehicle to Darwin to be replaced with a brand new Toyota Landcruiser tray top. It only had 13 miles (21kms) on the clock when I took delivery at the Government garage. It then went off to the Department of Civil Aviation (DCA) radio workshop to be fitted with a new short-wave radio, the first of its type to be fitted to a police vehicle. The set had capacity for six frequency channels plus the broadcast band. In this set there were two police channels, two OPR (Overseas Telecommunications network or

Flying Doctor) frequencies along with the DCA nation-wide emergency channel. The radio operated on pre-tuned whip-type aerials which were screwed into a mount according to the frequency you wished to use.

Not only was I able to get a haircut in Darwin (there was no barber in Katherine) and some new supplies at significantly lower prices than in either of the two grocery stores at Katherine, but I also got a couple of bottles of gas organised for the station. As a single officer, I was entitled to an issue of gas free, while a married member had to supply his own gas. It was an odd arrangement but I didn't complain; neither did the married officer when he returned from leave to find a near full bottle of gas left for him. I also had the promise of a new refrigerator in a couple of weeks, one of the two at the station was quite old and not running all that efficiently.

Darwin had changed a lot in the 18 months since I'd last been there. Police headquarters itself had been relocated to the old Brown's Mart building, opposite the Motor Registry in Smith Street. But the barracks and Darwin station were still the same. At headquarters I renewed my acquaintance with now Inspector Metcalfe, my first station sergeant in Alice Springs and with Superintendent Bowie. His first question was *"Are you drinking yet lad?"* . . . *"No Sir"* ... He walked off shaking his head and muttering.

A new recruit school also graduated providing additional staff for Katherine. This, along with the transfer of Harry Belton, now promoted to Sergeant Third Class, to Katherine to fill the vacancy in the rank at the station eased off my need to travel into Katherine to assist.

It let me plan and proceed on a patrol of my own police district. I wanted to do this while still at Maranboy. I packed-up the whole station crew for the patrol – tracker Frank and his wife, Nikapinni, and the dog. Frank's wife had relatives at Mainoru Station she would like to see. We headed out along the track to Shepherd's mill where we camped the first night. In some ways I hoped the dog would get a bit of a razz from the other dogs at the mill, perhaps a bit of a hiding and quieten him down, but he was smart enough to behave and clear that hurdle. From the mill we went on across bush tracks to Mountain Valley station which had just been taken over by an American based farmer consortium. They had plans to undertake massive pasture improvement to allow greater stock carrying capacity along with improved genetics to improve the standards of livestock turn-off. They were in the midst of building two new homesteads for management staff.

As we approached Mainoru station I received a radio message from headquarters instructing me to proceed on to the Union Carbide exploration camp at Bulman, about 50 miles (80kms) north-east of Mainoru, to provide a report on a company vehicle which had been burnt out. Bulman was on the southern fringe of the Arnhem Land aboriginal reserve. So I left Nikapinni and the dog at Mainoru while Frank and I went on to Bulman.

Mainoru Station was a picturesque spot, the homestead on a rise overlooking a river flat, with a meandering spread of river lagoons with masses of pandanus palm along its bank. The cattle station aboriginal camp was on the edge of the river, an idyllic place for their pace and style of life. There was plenty of wildlife, duck, geese, fish and so forth right at the lagoon while they had station rations of beef as well.

Mainoru was still family owned and operated. A young woman, Heather McKay, ran the place with her widowed mother. They rarely left the property, and I could understand why. Why leave such a pretty place?

Armed with directions for Bulman, we soon came across herds of buffalo like I had never seen before. There must have been 400-500 buffalo in one herd we saw, many with horns four, five or six feet across. Some just stood on the road, to get them to move aside was a job in itself. The last thing I wanted to do, miles from anywhere, was to hit a buffalo and immobilise the vehicle. I remember as we came around one corner we met a buffalo tail-on, tracker Frank remarking *"Elephant I think boss, not buffalo . . . "* until it lifted its head to reveal its prominent six-seven feet (2m) spread of horns. We also saw kangaroos and quite a few bush turkeys (more correctly "bustards") but the number and size of the buffalos surprised me.

We had no trouble locating the burnt out remains of the exploration company's Land Rover, little more than the steel frame and engine block remaining, right in the middle of a bush track. With the tall tinder dry grasses of mid-dry season it was little wonder the vehicle hadn't set the countryside on fire. Obviously the vehicle crew had controlled that. In these conditions, with vehicles travelling across virgin land it wasn't uncommon for grass and light undergrowth to be caught and build up under the vehicle before coming in contact with the hot exhaust and catching on fire, burning the vehicle out. At least nobody had been hurt. We drove on to the camp site itself which was well set out with demountable buildings for the kitchen, dining room, offices and sleeping quarters for staff. There was a resident chef with supplies flown in regularly to a substantial airstrip adjacent to the base camp.

I got the paper work fixed up concerning the burnt out vehicle and was about to leave to return to Mainoru for the night when word came that a young man had gone missing. His name was Gerry Brett, 21, and he was on an exploration line exercise, about 75 miles (120kms) or so N-N-E of Bulman, in an area known as the Wilton River.

A line exploration was where a man would set off from a given point and follow compass reading for a pre-determined distance, along the line taking regular earth samples and placing them in sample bags. At a turning point, the man would walk a pre-determined distance to his left or right, at 90 degrees, and then return to the starting off line. Each of the soil samples would be subjected to analysis and a 'picture' of the mineral composition, the likelihood of finding certain minerals in commercial quantities, would be determined before more expensive drilling programmes. In this case, the field worker had not returned as he should have. A number of things could have happened, the most likely being that his compass had malfunctioned or he had misread the readings and got off track and become lost. Alternatively, he could have fallen and injured himself, could have been affected by the heat and/or sun and taken ill or even been bitten by a snake. The area was a habitat of the deadly king brown or even the taipan, which were both known as being fighters.

At this stage there was no point in me moving on to the area where the man was lost. It was about a four hour-plus drive as the road conditions were very poor. There was a helicopter based at the Bulman camp so it prepared and left for the area for a quick sweep before last light. I decided to stay at the base camp until there was further word. The site manager arranged a room for me in the quarters as well as for Frank.

Next morning we had a hearty breakfast, cereal, bacon and eggs, toast and all the trimmings. There was still no word of the man being found. A plane had come in from Darwin at dusk the previous evening so as soon as breakfast was over, it was decided we should take a flight over the search area and see if we could pick up any sign of the missing man. I prepared a police message to my Divisional Inspector in Darwin outlining the situation, to be sent via OPR (Outpost Radio) as soon as the Bulman camp could get through. It needed to go as a telegram in the finish, COLLECT, I never heard what the reaction was at HQ when the telegram was delivered.

It was only minutes by air to the search area where the twin-engine light aircraft made several low level sweeps of the area with sharp turns that soon had my breakfast in the only thing available – my hat! We saw no sign of the lost man and returned to the base camp. There was no good news there either – only word that the search helicopter was running low on its specialist engine oil.

So after lunch I set out by road to the search area, with a supply of the oil required by the helicopter. It was rough going along a bush track that seemed to be leading nowhere, except in the direction of the search area. It was all new country to tracker Frank, he had not been in the area before, and frankly wasn't too sure that he should venture into the area either. He expressed concerned that the "Giditcha" man would appear from behind a tree and "take him". When we were about 20 miles (32kms) from the base camp, to our surprise the helicopter came into view, it circled, and as we stopped, it landed in a cleared area close to the road. *"All's OK, we found him, he's OK, got his compass bearings messed up a bit"* was music to my ears. So it was then back to the base camp ... *"Any chance of you giving the tracker a ride?* I asked. *"Yeh, sure" "Would you like to go in the helicopter?"* I asked Frank. A surprised look on his face, I didn't need to hear his answer. He climbed on board, belted up into the middle seat, the engine revved and up it went. I still say to this day that Frank turned white as the helicopter lifted and flew away.

I drove back to the base camp where Frank was sitting up in the dining room, set up with tea and freshly cooked scones. A radio report to Darwin that all was well, a cuppa and we headed back to Mainoru and on to Maranboy, arriving back about 10.30pm. I was pleased to be back.

My time at Maranboy was quickly coming to an end. It was into November, the dry season weather had well passed, days in the mid-90'sF (35C) were common, the humidity was rising a little, the build-up for the wet season was getting nearer. So were the bushfires which had been on the horizon most of the time I'd been at Maranboy. They were getting closer and closer with the need to ensure none of the assets at the station were threatened. I was wanting some rain actually as Works department men arrived to replace the rain water tanks at the station with five brand spanking new 1,000 gallons (4,500 litres) galvanised iron tanks. In the process, I ended up with no rainwater at the house, having to walk 50 yards (45m) or so to the tracker's quarters to get drinking water, not a real problem for the amount I used or the time I had left at Maranboy.

It wasn't just my rain water tanks that were dry, the whole countryside was at its worst. The wirlies were blowing dust and leaves everywhere, the birds were all searching for water. There was a leak in the water main from the bore to the overhead tank at the station which provided a good watering place for birds. The only problem was that 50 black cockatoos watering made a hell of a noise, even 100 yards (90m) away.

My move to Larrimah was not going to be as simple as first planned. A couple of weeks earlier there had been a triple fatal accident on the Stuart Highway, virtually right outside the Larrimah police station. Three people in a car had driven head on into a road train. There was to be a formal inquest at the monthly Katherine Magistrate's Count a few days after I was originally intended to transfer to Larrimah. But that was overcome by me moving first to Katherine to works a few days before going to Larrimah after the court day, which I would have had to attend for other reasons anyway.

At Larrimah I wouldn't have the luxury of being able to go into Katherine regularly to get supplies, or be able to buy some items at the settlement store; there was no store at Larrimah. I would need to get more substantial provisions. So it was opportune that the manager of a large provisioner in Darwin – S. C. Eyles & Co Pty Ltd – came by on a goodwill trip as he described it, and I was able to give him an order which he arranged to be at Larrimah in time for my arrival.

As the last day of leave for the Eckerts drew close, I started to get the books all ready for the hand-over. At the post office it was also the traditional November count month where all inwards and outwards articles had to counted and recorded. As this was the basis of payment it was an important task. After all, while the Eckerts had been away, there was advice of a $2 odd rise in the weekly payment as a result of the previous count six months earlier.

Then as the Eckerts arrived home, so did the government stocktaker for his annual inspection of station property. This made practically a whole day's work, checking everything off. However, having three of us at the station – the stocktaker, Colin Eckerts and myself – he was able to have a formal Board of Survey where some items considered beyond economical repair could be condemned, a requisition made for a replacement and the old item destroyed. At least his visit simplified the handover-takeover of the station inventory.

I felt quite satisfied with my efforts at Maranboy and left for the drive into Katherine full of confidence. I could not wait to get to Larrimah next week.

CHAPTER 8

On to Larrimah

I wasn't really looking forward to the few days in Katherine before moving on to Larrimah, still it went well. I worked the Thursday and was sent on a prisoner escort north for about 110 miles (175kms), to Hayes Creek, where I handed the prisoner over to another escort who took him on to Darwin. I had the Sunday off. A group of us from the station decided we would make a morning trip up the Katherine Gorge. I'd never been up the Gorge. Nor had Ray Weir or his wife Annette. Ray joined the force and transferred to Alice Springs at the same time I had. He had just been transferred up to Katherine. He and Annette had spent a night with me at Maranboy only a few weeks earlier. Cec Parras, who had just transferred to Katherine at the end of recruit school, came along too.

The four of us joined a group of 14 for the two-and-a-half hour trip. The normal cost was $4 but the operator only charged us $2. March Motors, a car dealer/garage-cum-corner-store and cafe in Katherine, held the franchise to conduct the cruises on the Katherine Gorge. We did the trip in three stages; each stage in a different boat. The first stage was in near-open water using conventional aluminium boats seating about six each which took us to the first rocky ledge. Then there was a 500 yard (450m) walk to the next section where we used aluminium flat bottom punt-type boats for the short gorge, before another climb over another ledge and into similar flat-bottom boats to travel the main gorge. The boats were connected so we made a sort of road-train on the river, the leading boat being powered by outboard engines.

Some sections of the gorge are said to be more than 100 feet (30m) deep while the towering walls rose on each side of the river to provide a magnificent spectacle. The gorge was a focal point for the filming of the Australian epic "Jedda". One rock face was known as Jedda Rock, where she, or was it her lover, fell to their death. The red and ochre colours reflecting in the still clear waters were spectacular. It was hard to imagine how the gorge would look with a torrent of water flooding through in the wet season. As that time approached, the boats would be removed from the river and be made ready for the next season.

I guess one of the reasons we were given the concession rate for the gorge trip was the frequency the police were called to March Motors, where the cafe seemed to have that knack of attracting trouble. If it wasn't customers,

Larrimah Police Station (on right), court room and trackers quarters

The spectacular Jedda Rock, Katherine Gorge, one of the most photographed tourist attractions in the Territory

The billabong and pandanus palms at Mainoru – off the tourist track but a dry season oasis of luxuriant tropical growth

it was the staff! I remember one afternoon being called down by Eric March who reported a watch missing from the locked display case at the cafe-store. It turned out it had been stolen by one of the staff who at first hid the watch in the ice cream section of the store refrigerator. When the matter went to court I recall Magistrate Hall asking the police prosecutor, Sergeant Harry Belton *"Why on earth did he put it in the refrigerator?"* As quick as a flash, Harry replied *"Perhaps because it was a 'hot' watch Sir!"* as muffled laughter ran through the court room.

We got through court as quickly as possible on the Tuesday. As soon as the Inquest was over, both Gary Burgdorf and I headed for Larrimah. We arrived there in time for a meal and then got stuck into some of the handover-takeover paperwork, finishing it off on the Wednesday morning. There was time for him to show me the tricks of the lighting plant and the water softener and introduce me to the postmistress and her husband, the PMG repeater station technician, Pat and Peter Famillo, and the Larrimah Hotel publican, Mrs Pauline Rattley, and her husband, Reg The hotel was under some form of temporary management. Either the previous owner had died and a firm of solicitors were acting as executors, or the place was in receivership with accountants in Darwin appointing Reg and Pauline to manage the place until permanent managers or new owners took over. I don't exactly recall but it was one or the other. Before I left Larrimah new managers were to arrive and Reg and Pauline moved on to Elliott where friends operated another roadside inn, the Elliott Hotel.

While Gary and I had been attending to all the handover duties, his wife had been packing their Toyota short wheel base 4-wheel-drive. At the first opportunity after lunch, they were gone.

In contrast to Maranboy, the Larrimah station was one of the newer, modern stations. It was right on the Stuart Highway and coming from the north, the first buildings on the right. A gravel driveway separated the police station building from the court room, cells and tracker's quarters. Set behind a low wire mesh-galvanised iron pipe fence, the buildings were at ground level and of timber and fibro-cement sheet. The cells naturally enough were much more sturdy. The driveway led off to the right where 20 yards or so (20m) away was the residence, a typical Top End elevated house with plenty of fly-wired louvres. The house had four bedrooms, a smallish kitchen which opened to a nice big lounge living area. There was only a gas stove for cooking and no hot water system, the tap water being considered tepid enough to wash and shower with. The water supply came from the Commonwealth Railways system and needed to be processed through a water softener before use. There were tanks with rain water for drinking and cooking.

The house was fitted with overhead fans which you needed at night during the summer to help sleep. However, to have the fans working, you needed the lighting plant running and although it was 40 yards or so (35m) from the station, at times you wondered which was the worse of the two evils – the noise of the lighting plant or no cooling fan! However, as the wet season build-up continued, and there was no rain, the lighting plant noise won out, until about three in the morning when I would get up and turn it off. Gary had used his mechanical ingenuity to connect a cut-off cord from the back step of the residence to the lighting plant, a suitable tug on the cord, shut down the engine and thus the power. There was then no need to walk to the lighting plant to turn it off.

There was no dog to look after. Instead, there were two pigs, three goats and 18 fowls! At least I had plenty of eggs! They were all jobs for the tracker to help look after. The biggest task was keeping the food up to the pigs. Gary had relied on not just the scraps from his own household of himself, his wife and three children but also from the hotel/roadside inn. I had few scraps, especially so when I was away or invited to the hotel to eat and as the tourist season was well over, the scraps from the hotel lightened off at this time of year as well. The exodus from the Top-End before Christmas only brought straight-through traffic; a quick fill-up at the service station or hotel and on.

It was common for the tracker at a station to also take leave, or go walkabout at the same time as his normal boss would take leave. This was the case at Larrimah, but at least he arranged for a replacement – Powder – a young single chap, a relation. That wasn't so bad, except I was given an allowance of only $13 per fortnight to provision him! Well, at least the fowls would help. Actually, he told me he had a wife, she was at Nutwood Downs, a cattle station to the south-east, in the adjoining police district. The officer-in-charge was making a pre-wet season patrol to Nutwood Downs and I asked if he could pick up Powder's wife and bring her to town; I'd pick her up and they could stay together at Larrimah. It turned out his wife was only nine-years old! She was a 'promised' wife, still at school, where she stayed.

A plus at Larrimah was a good vehicle, only 17,000 miles (27,000kms) on the speedo, well fitted out with a "POLICE" sign and a siren. As Gary was a mechanic by trade, the vehicle was well maintained. Being right on the highway meant not just extra radio scheds but also that extra lookout of what was passing by. The radio scheds could be quite lengthy because for some reason, as the wet season built up interfering with radio frequencies, Larrimah seemed an ideal location for the wave length. Some days I would be the only station able to read Darwin clearly while I could also hear and speak to other stations clearly, thus I'd end up relaying messages all over the place. Being right on the highway, and having a 70 miles (110kms) stretch of the highway in the police district also made the station vulnerable for having to attend road accident call-outs at any time.

The nearest station south was Daly Waters, 60 miles (100kms) south, then three-four miles (5kms) off the highway to the town. It had an airport, still used weekly by Ansett-ANA, servicing the town with a once-a-week Fokker Friendship F27 service, both northbound on Sunday afternoons and south-bound mid-week. There was a hotel while the post office was attached to the police station. However, with a much larger telephone exchange, a married reliever was sent along whenever the normal officer-in-charge took leave as was the case at the time. Constable Bob Kucharzewski (who had been in the force about a year longer than me) and his wife were down from Darwin for three months, his wife running the post office and exchange. Bob was of Polish parents, raised in Scotland, with as broad a Scot accent as you could wish for. For a stranger, it was hard enough getting a tongue around his name, let alone understand him as he spelt it for you.

Only 27 miles (44kms) south of Larrimah was the Maryfield cattle station, one of only two or three real cattle stations within the police district. The manager kept in touch and was always generous with a supply of beef whenever they had a kill. Sometimes they would drop-off a supply which made me feel like a butcher shop. The first week I was there I ended up with two big topsides, a rump and a fillet of steak along with other meat for the tracker and the pigs! It was more than I, or the tracker, could ever eat. Fortunately, there was an electric deep-freeze at the house. It did mean running the lighting plant longer but with the summer weather and the need for fans, that was going to happen anyway. Still, none of the meat went to waste, there was always some poor soul that could do with a piece of meat.

I'd only been at Larrimah a week when the Divisional Inspector made his annual visit. Inspector Allan Metcalfe, who had been my station sergeant when I first arrived in Alice Springs, had been promoted and moved to Darwin following the accidental death of Inspector Lou Hook earlier in the year. Inspector Hook had been killed in a car accident on the highway between Katherine and Darwin after he had been south on station inspections. I was relieved to find everything was in order as far as headquarters was concerned. The Inspector stayed overnight. I remember we went to the hotel for the evening meal *"Let's go down to the pub and show the flag lad"* were his fatherly words.

The next week he stayed over again as he took another trip to the more southern stations at Daly Waters and Elliott. He no sooner left than the phone rang. It was the officer-in-charge at Mataranka, 47 miles (75kms) to the north, Constable Geoff Hoskins, to say he had a job on, the suspected illegal use of cattle by a cattle station within my district. So I headed off to meet up with him at Elsey Station. In the end we did 270 miles (430kms) through Elsey, Roper Valley, Hodgson Downs and Hodgson River stations to come to the conclusion there was no basis for the complaint. Illegal use of cattle was a common complaint amongst neighbouring property owners at mustering times. The action surrounds the use of some quieter cattle from an adjoining better managed station as coaches to get wilder cattle from a less well managed station into cattle traps – yards, where they can be handled to brand and ear mark and if required, castrate. The cattle are not being stolen, they are just being used. The common defence of a station owner using cattle in this way is that he has only mustered up cattle from an adjoining property which have strayed on to his station and he is keeping them yarded until there is an appropriate opportunity to return them back to their rightful owner. The questions that come up are how long the neighbouring cattle have been yarded and what efforts have been made to notify their rightful owner of their detention. When communications are poor, there is no telephone, no radio and no inclination, it becomes a matter of judgement with the benefit of the doubt always going the other way.

It was after 10pm when we got back to Larrimah, dusty, dirty and hungry with my vehicle still at Elsey station. I went and picked it up next morning, then took the opportunity to make a quick visit to Katherine for some fresh supplies.

The wet season build-up continued, the days got to 108F (42C), the storm clouds built up but there was no rain. Although there was no aboriginal camp or community close by, public drunkenness and unruly behaviour had to occur wherever there is licensed premises. In the climate, some people just don't know when enough is enough; thus the call came and down to the hotel I went to find two drunks staggering about the street, my first arrests in Larrimah. One worked for the railways. As I arrested him he offered me $10 to let him off. *"If you don't, I'll get Paddy Carroll onto you!"*. Paddy Carroll was a reputed communist, the North Australia Workers Union organiser in Darwin, and leader of the wharf strikes common at the time.

Next morning I gave them breakfast, then did the morning radio sched before I got around to fingerprint and bail them out. Then the phone rang; it was Plainclothes Senior Constable "Saus" Grant from Darwin CIB on the phone ... a Mini Moke on hire, not supposed to leave the Darwin area, had broken down at Daly Waters ... the hirer had telephoned the rental company to say that unless they arranged to have it fixed straight away, he would burn it! ... the officer-in-charge at Daly Waters was away from the station, in Darwin, could I go to Daly Waters immediately and attend to the matter.

So it was a quick trip to Daly Waters where I found the vehicle parked outside the hotel, and the young fellow who had hired it sleeping off a session on the grog. We agreed the best thing was for me to put the vehicle into safe keeping at the police station and for him to move on as quickly as he could arrange it! With the help of a local, I towed the Moke to the police yard, and returned to Larrimah and rang through to report the vehicle was safe.

Of course, the locals catch on pretty quickly when the local cop is out of town. The afternoon hadn't passed when I go another phone call, this time from the Daly Waters publican to say he was having trouble with three or four young fellows who had got on the booze and were now causing a disturbance around the hotel because he wouldn't serve them any more. Truth probably was he had served them too much in the first place. So it was back to Daly Waters again, another hour trip. Naturally enough, by the time I got there, the trouble-makers had well dispersed. All there was for me to do was have a lemon squash myself and drive back to Larrimah.

Before the day was out, I made it a trifecta to Daly Waters ... about 10 o'clock the OIC at Daly Waters, his wife and child arrived at Larrimah, in their own vehicle, experiencing engine troubles of some sort ... I ended up driving them home to Daly Waters, the third trip for the day. At least my trips to Daly Waters had let me find out about the Ansett-ANA flight on Sundays, which I could tell my parents about, and would enable them to send me some fresh strawberries up for Christmas, now only weeks away. The flight was reliable for perishables, after all, it called only once a week, so it needed to be. The freight rate from Melbourne was 38c a pound (84c a kg).

The publican's husband, Reg Rattley, was a Justice of the Peace. After my two arrests a week or two earlier, which I bailed to Katherine court, he was a little chuffed that court had not been held at Larrimah. *"But you need two Justices of the Peace to hold court Reg, there is only one here in Larrimah, you, and that is one more than normal anyway"* was my response. As soon as he heard of my next arrest, an aboriginal woman who had more than likely over-indulged at the hotel, he couldn't tell me quick enough *"Dave . . there will be two Justices available next Monday morning for court"*; he had organised one to come up from Daly Waters and sit with him! So it was to be, the first court sitting in Larrimah for years. I don't remember if I arrested her for drunkenness or disorderly behaviour; I suspect the latter as they fined her $10 with $1.50 court costs, in default six days hard labour.

Before the Justices could close the court she piped up *"Oh, Reg"* (one of the Justices) *"can I borrow the money to pay this?"* Next day she left town for a short time, remarking *"Too hard a copper in this place!"*

As Christmas drew closer, the excuse for all the locals to get together was ready made. First there was a race club meeting with people from Daly Waters and Mataranka coming first to the meeting followed by the children's Christmas Tree. Even though the community was small, there was still a strong community spirit to get together in a traditional way. After all, why should the kids at Larrimah or Daly Waters miss out on Father Christmas? It all took a bit of organising, gifts for the kids, a Christmas stocking each plus drink and food. The surprise for me came the day before when I was asked if I would be Father Christmas! There was one important qualification, *"Don't wear police uniform shoes, last year the kids picked Peter Hamon because he wore his police shoes"*.

It was 107F (41.6C) in the shade and here I was, with a pillow strapped around my gut to give some effect, whiskers and all, in traditional red pants and a long red coat, appropriately trimmed with white, perched on the front of a 5-tonne railway crane, arriving at the hotel, under police escort (Bob K from Daly Waters), not sure whether to *"ho-ho"* or pray. At least I fooled the kids as well as most of the parents (which was even more fun, until some big-mouth let the cat out the bag). Even Powder the tracker, didn't twig.

Next afternoon I drove my own car down to Daly Waters to meet the Ansett-ANA flight and pick up my fresh strawberries. The car hadn't moved in the month I'd been at Larrimah, I even had to charge the battery to get it going for the trip. Not unusual – the flight was a little late and it was dusk as it came in to land. The Daly Waters power supply was provided by the Department of Civil Aviation and the town knew when flights were coming in, or departing, as the town supply was cut off for 10 minutes or so at landings and take-off while the power supply was diverted to light the airstrip. The airstrip was quite large, one of a network of airstrips along the Stuart Highway, built for the RAAF during World War II. Daly Waters was one of the few still used. There was another airstrip just a few mile north of Larrimah. Unused for 20 years, it still had a good concrete north-south runway, with a maze of bitumen roads running off it, through the bush, to former workshop sites, ammunition and fuel dumps. The remains of the control tower were still standing.

The strawberries, and two other parcels of Christmas gifts from the family, arrived on the flight. Some of the strawberries were a little crushed, but I turned them into pulp and an ice-cream mix. It was a lovely pre-Christmas treat from home. The two accompanying parcels were also marked *"Perishable"* which gave me the perfect excuse to check them out, although having ascertained they did not in fact contain anything too perishable, other than a Christmas cake, I left them for full exploration on Christmas Day.

I got home to lie in bed and listen to the late news, news that the Prime Minister, Harold Holt, was missing, presumed drowned off Cheviot Beach, Portsea. It was Sunday, 17 December, 1967. Even though the event occurred thousands of miles away, it had a significant effect on everyone, even in Larrimah, with people eager for news on just how it had happened, as to whether or not his body had been found, who was running the country and who was going to succeed him as there seemed no logical successor. The following Friday most of us gathered at the hotel to listen to the memorial service broadcast from St Paul's Cathedral, Melbourne, on ABC short-wave radio. I had to fly the flag at the station half-mast for three days.

Christmas Day was hot and threatening but still no rain. I had Christmas dinner at the hotel. Despite the weather, it was a traditional Christmas dinner, a real family day. On Boxing Day I'd no sooner got lunch out of the way when a passing motorist delivered a man suffering injuries received in a motor vehicle accident, south of Dunmurra, 85 miles south, on Christmas Eve. With dried blood on his face and his arms and obviously in quite a bit of pain, the man had spent Christmas Day at Dunmarra. As the telephone was again disconnected at Dunmarra, the operators of the roadside inn, "Ma" and "Pa" Healey, had no way of notifying police of the accident, or sending for medical help. In all likelihood, nobody at the inn would have been sober enough to have acted responsibly. I was able to speak with Katherine hospital who arranged for an ambulance to come and collect the injured man. It was my intention to head north and meet the ambulance. Just as I had that arranged, I had further word ... the dining room at the Dunmarra Inn had burnt down earlier in the day, and as the officer-in-charge at Daly Waters was away (again) could I attend?

It was near a 90 minute drive to Dunmarra. The inn had quite a reputation for unreliable service, drunken parties and non-compliance with regulations, a reason why the telephone was disconnected. The inn was the only stopping place right on the highway between Larrimah and Elliott, about 80-85 miles (130-135kms) either way. The Healeys had operated the roadside inn for years, they were two characters of the Territory. There were stories of "Ma" Healey's food preparation which would make your hair curl. Whether they were true or not was never really debated, reputation was enough for acceptance that the incidents did happen. The best two I remember were someone ordering a cup of tea which was served at the bar. Remember, the place held a roadside inn licence, which obliged it to serve at least sandwiches and a hot beverage between 7am and 11pm and placed meal obligations on the premises at other times. The story goes that the customer asked for milk. "Ma" Healey, without a blink, raised the cat's saucer from the floor and poured it into the cup!

The second concerned someone who had asked for a sandwich. So "Ma" went off to the kitchen and returned to the bar with the ingredients to make the sandwich, placing the bread, sandwich filling and knife on the bar, then from her cleavage, the butter! Well, she only had two hands like the rest of us and wasn't going to make two trips! What always horrified me was that all so innocently I had stopped for lunch at Dunmarra on my first trip north, to join the force.

On arrival the place seemed deserted. It took me some minutes to locate Mrs. Healey who immediately went into a state of excitement *"Oh, the poor man, he was here all day yesterday, we had no way to get medical help for him, I hope he is OK ... "* I interrupted *"I'm not here about the accident, I'm here about the fire"* I started to explain. *"Oh, the fire, the fire . . . Noel said to everyone 'stand back, stand back'. . . "* as she started to head me in the direction of the dining room. As we walked through the shade-house covered is wisteria, an obvious drunk, sleeping it off, was lying on the concrete path. As she nudged him in the ribs with her foot she tried to whisper to him, but couldn't *"George, move, George, move, the police are here, you can't lay here like this!"*.

The dining room was an old Sidney Williams hut, detached from the main buildings and converted to be used as a dining room. It was fitted out with stainless steel tubular tables and chairs with laminated seats and tops. There had once been a linoleum cover on the concrete floor. As we approached the main entrance all "Ma" could say was *"Noel kept on saying, 'stand back', 'stand back' he thought the place would blow up! ... someone got some cutters and cut off the power but Noel was calling out 'stand back', 'stand back'"*.

The building was not that badly damaged after all. As it was built of corrugated iron, steel frame and fly-wire with a concrete floor, there wasn't much to burn. The cause of the fire soon became apparent ... the kerosene refrigerator, in the far left hand corner of the dining room, just near the entrance to the main kitchen area. I walked to the 'fridge and opened the door. A cold Christmas ham, still on its carving plate, half consumed, was sitting there on the middle shelf. Kerosene refrigerators were temperamental at any time, and the least disturbance gave the best results. It was always best to try to fill the fuel tank, a weekly job, without disturbing it; you only pulled out the tank when the flame needed a trim or replacement. In his exuberance to help after a great Christmas Day party that had obviously gone well (probably all day and into the night) one of the locals had decided to fill the kerosene refrigerator. With the wick burning, the tank full, it had been moved. The kerosene splashed out, ran across the linoleum floor which ignited and the whole lot burst into flames. As a result, between the kero and the lino it produced masses of black smoke. With the fuel burnt, and a splash of water the fire was soon put out.

I took a few photos; made a few notes and returned to Larrimah. "Kutch" could prepare the report for the Licensing Inspector and Coroner when he got back to his station.

The weather continued to be stifling hot with storm clouds building each day but passing. The weather had to break soon ... it was the end of the week ... Friday, 29 December, 1967 . . . perhaps it would be tonight ... and it was. As dusk came a typical tropical storm moved in from the south east, lightning, shuddering thunder and teeming rain. It was such a relief. I went to the hotel for tea and stayed talking until the rain had gone. Around the house, the chorus of green frogs was deafening, but it was pleasantly cool; no need for a fan tonight.

The storm had passed so it really didn't interfere with the radio reception as I lay in bed and listened to the 10.30pm ABC news, first the national news followed by the Territory news. The major item was a report of a light plane believed to be carrying six men, which had left Darwin about 3pm, that afternoon for the Macarthur River, east of Daly Waters but because of bad weather in the area decided to attempt to reach Daly Waters. It had failed to arrive. Both in the news and in a special announcement after the news, anyone who knew anything of the whereabouts of the plane, or had heard it during the evening, was asked to contact the Department of Civil Aviation.

After hours I had a direct telephone line to the Katherine exchange, so I got out of bed and rang through asking if anyone had been looking for me this evening. It was one of the beauties of a manual exchange; you could come back to the station and ring through to the exchange and ask if anyone had been wanting you. Alternatively, you could also leave a message with the operator as to where they could find you in an emergency. *"No, no-one has been calling you"* was a relief, but deep inside, if the plane was missing, I knew it would be only a matter of time.

Next morning I got up a little early, tidied up a few things, checked the vehicle over ... and sure enough, the phone rang. *"Metcalfe here young Polly"*. It was the Divisional Inspector, one of the few who called me Polly. *"A plane has gone missing ... "* he related the story *"I can't get on to Kucharzewshi, could you go down there and start a bit of a search along the roads, in particular drive out a bit along the Borroloola Road, see if you can see anything ... you better stick together, there's six in the plane, if you find anything, you'll need a bit of help for each other"*.

Half prepared I hastened to leave for Daly Waters ... another hour drive. As I pulled up in the yard of the police station, Bob appeared at the back door of the residence, a towel around his waist, half shaven, cream down one side of his face *"What the hell are you doing here?"* he asked. *"'Fangs'* (Inspector Metcalfe) *rang me, he couldn't get through to you; there's a plane missing ... "*. *"Yes, I heard something this morning on the radio, but nobody's said anything here"* *"Well, he wants us to go out the Borroloola Road and look for it ... "*

There was time for a cup of tea, and we set out in our vehicles, out to the Stuart Highway, south the few miles to the Borroloola Road turn-off and east. Remarkably, the road had dried well, there were some wet patches, a little water lying, at least no dust. We drove out 25-30 miles (40-50kms) but there was no sign of life. We met a vehicle travelling west; they had not seen anything either, so we headed back to Daly Waters.

By now there was increasing activity at the airport manager's office. There was still no sign of the plane. All that was known was the pilot had been unable to land at McArthur River. After a suggestion from the pilot that he head for Normanton, in Queensland, the Darwin Flight Service Centre suggested he should try to fly to Daly Waters. That was about 7.20pm. Ten minutes later the pilot reported he had set course for Daly Waters. At 7.55pm he reported his remaining fuel was *"probably enough for about 60 minutes"*. At 8.05pm a *Special Weather* for Daly Waters was passed to the aircraft, giving wind from 150 degrees at 13 knots, gusting to 21 knots, visibility 800 yards, with two-eighths of cloud at 1,500 feet and six-eighths of cumulo nimbus cloud at 5,000 feet. The pilot reported he was flying in cloud and was descending to 1,000 feet. Ten minutes later he said he was at 1,300 feet, in and out of cloud, and flying in rain. At 8.17pm he again reported he was descending to 1,000 feet, presumably in an attempt to remain clear of cloud.

At 8.25pm the pilot informed Darwin that the aircraft's port tank had run dry and that, as he had no fuel indication on the starboard tank gauge, he was uncertain of the amount of fuel remaining. Two minutes later, the pilot said that from moments of visibility during lightning flashes he could see the aircraft was getting close to the ground and he thought it inadvisable to descend any further. The aircraft's ADF (automatic directional finder), the pilot said, was still not giving any positive indication.

When asked at 8.30pm as to how much fuel he had left he replied *"about 10 minutes, but I think not much"*. Darwin then told the pilot that if he was forced to land, he should listen on 122.1 MHz. At 8.36pm the pilot advised he was still flying in cloud and rain, he was maintaining a heading of 260 degrees and that his ADF was now giving some indication that the aircraft was heading towards Daly Waters. Asked at 8.40pm if he could see the ground he replied *"negative"*. The pilot was then requested to try calling Tennant Creek on 122.1MHz and at 2041, he acknowledged the request.

Nothing more was heard from the aircraft. It didn't arrive in Daly Waters and thus the Department of Civil Aviation search processes were put into action. After closely examining the information transmitted by the missing plane, it was considered the area of probability was an area 55 miles (90kms) to the east of Daly Waters, 30 miles (50kms) to the south and 12 miles (20kms) to the north. It was after lunch before the first search aircraft were in the area – a Department of Health De Havilland Dove and a charter Beech Barron from Darwin and DCA's Aero Commander from Adelaide. Despite the distances, and a delay in leaving Darwin, again because of bad weather, most of the probability area had been flown over before the day was out, without any trace of the lost plane.

For us it was a waiting game. We just had to sit at Daly Waters and wait. In the evening I returned to Larrimah for the night, returning to Daly next morning a little more prepared to stay a day or two. On the second day, New Year's eve, four aircraft operated in the search area, re-checking and gradually expanding the area. DCA's Fokker Friendship, based in Melbourne, readied to fly to Daly Waters via Brisbane where it picked up officials to fly to the search area to assist in both operations and enquiries when the plane was found. Darkness brought no sign of the plane. There was even an after-dark flight over the area in the vain hope of seeing a campfire or similar indication of a crash site.

Everyone was invited to the local cattle station for a New Year's eve barbecue, the Daly Waters population being substantially increased by the search parties. But is was a quiet affair, everyone starting to think the worst, increasingly wondering just what had happened to the plane.

On the third day, the search force was reinforced by the DCA Fokker Friendship, an RAAF Dakota, two De Havilland Herons from Connellan Airways in Alice Springs and a Cessna 337 from Darwin. The search area was extended even further. The crew brought in by DCA had the flight centre at Daly Waters fully operational with much of the search being co-ordinated in Daly Waters rather than Darwin. Additional police arrived from Darwin on the RAAF aircraft, including Detective Sergeant Bob Jackson and I remember Jimmy Green who joined the crew of observers on the DCA Fokker Friendship.

Then the break-through ... at 12.20pm the wreckage of the missing aircraft was sighted, lying in timbered country north-north-east of Daly Waters and only eight miles (13kms) east of the Stuart Highway. I remember Jimmy Green, the first person to site the wreckage, as 'proud as Punch' ... *"I thought, 'what's those beer cans doing out there in the bush', then I realised, it was the wreckage scattered over the ground"* There was no visible sign of life at the site.

Both the Daly Waters and my police vehicle were commandeered to proceed to the search area. Sergeant Bob Jackson took over and left me behind; the seats being taken by himself as the senior investigating police officer, and other DCA accident investigation personnel who had already been flown-in in readiness. The first vehicle was guided to the site by one of the search air-craft while the second proceeded a little later. The ground party had great dif-ficulty reaching the site, penetrating the thickly timbered bushland, making a track as they went. Although they got to the site in the late afternoon, they were unable to establish radio contact with either Daly Waters or the second rescue vehicle. As it became obvious that the rescue vehicles would be out overnight, it was decided to attempt to drop the rescue party a "store-pedo" a three feet long tube about 12 inches (.3m) or so in diameter filled with emer-gency rations, blankets, water etc., from the Fokker Friendship. I went on the flight. It was getting toward dusk, we circled around the second ground party, and got ready to drop the "store-pedo". One of the crew was strapped into a seat beside the rear door of the Fokker, the "store-pedo" was set beside the rear door, a rope attached to pull the rip-cord and open the parachute as it was pushed out. The back door was opened and the "store-pedo" thrust out. As it rapidly fell from the door, friction on the rope designed to pull the rip-cord caused it to snap. The "store-pedo" crashed to the ground, away from the res-cue party, a total waste.

The Fokker pilot was a Scotsman with a beautiful Scots accent. I still hear his words *"what a bloody shame"* as we related the failure to him.

The DCA *"Aviation Safety Digest"* March 1968 issue reported:

The Cessna, had crashed in flat country lightly timbered with trees up to 40 feet and covered with dry grass up to four feet. Numerous fallen tree trunks lay hidden in the long grass. The aircraft's initial impact had been with branches of a tree 35 feet high. There was evidence the pilot may have unsuccessfully attempted to lift the port wing over the tree at the last minute.

The impact broke off the trunk and several heavy branches and tore off the port wing of the aircraft outbound from the lift strut. Seventy feet further on, the aircraft collided with a dead tree ten feet above the ground and, after a further 80 feet of travel, struck the ground heavily at a shallow angle of descent and at comparatively high speed. Sliding and tumbling, the wreckage then continued along the ground for a further 270 feet striking logs and othe trees, and disintegrated as it went.

Examination of the wreckage indicated that the flaps were almost fully extended at impact, and the propeller was rotating, but not under power. No trace of fuel could be found in the fuel system. Although the cockpit area was demolished, it was possible to determine that the master switch had been turned off.

The six occupants of the plane - Peter Limon, the pilot, and his passengers Barry Sullivan, Don Smith, Michael Breenie, Noel Healey and Peter Kay, were all dead. They were all in their 20's to early 30's, the passengers all from around the Bunyip area of Victoria; the pilot from Croydon, near Melbourne.

Ill equipped, the rescue party used the victims' sleeping bags from the wreckage to lay them out and load them into the back of my police vehicle. At least it had a covered tray. It was 27 hours from the time the wreckage was located until the rescue party returned to Daly Waters with the bodies of the crash victims. In the 100F (38C) heat, the state of the bodies, which had lain in the bush in similar conditions since the crash was beyond description. Fluid was dripping through the floor of the tray of the vehicle. The stench of death was over-powering. The bodies now needed to be taken to Darwin.

The bodies were in an unfit condition to be loaded into any aircraft. They were in my vehicle; it was now my turn to contribute to the search effort ... I would have to drive them to Darwin *"You are to stop only for fuel"* was my instruction.

The trip into the bush had taken its toll on the vehicle. The tie-rods were bent, the front wheels were out of balance, in general the vehicle had done a real bush-bash to get to, and then back from the crash site. A speed over 50 miles per hour (80kph) was going to be dangerous. The general condition of the vehicle was such there was a fear it would not even make the 400 miles (645kms) journey to Darwin. I was told that Constable Geoff Hoskins, from Mataranka, who had also been sent down to assist, would escort me through to Katherine.

I quickly packed my gear and set off for Darwin. It was 4pm. I thought a steady pace would get me there in 10 hours. I stopped briefly at Larrimah to get a fresh change of clothes to take with me to Darwin, I had no idea how long I would be away. As I headed on to Mataranka, there was no sign of Geoff. He had stayed on at Daly Waters to have a beer with those of the search team still at the airport. In a real tortoise and hare situation, I plodded ahead until he caught me not far out of Mataranka. The trouble was, in his haste to catch me, he nearly cooked the Toyota he was driving. In fact, I ended up towing him into town.

I refuelled at Mataranka, just a quick stop before I headed on the hour plus to Katherine where I reported to the police station and set about getting something to eat. Then station sergeant, Sergeant First Class Noel Owens arrived and said *"I can smell the bodies in my house* (50 yards (45m) away) *would you please keep on moving!; wait out of town and the boys will bring you out something to eat".* So on I travelled, crossing the high-level bridge and waiting on the north side of Katherine for a sandwich and a drink. The vehicle didn't get any better to drive. Then as I approached Pine Creek another hour plus north of Katherine, one of the officers at Pine Creek, Constable Bill Stevens, met me. *"Stop and have a drink"* he said, escorting me to the middle of the sports field, on the lee-ward side of the town to protect it from the stench of death. He then took me to the OIC's house, Senior Constable Kevin Smith for a hot cup of tea before I again headed north toward Darwin. While there, the Darwin police rang to ask if I had been sighted; how was I travelling *"He's here, he's pretty tired"* – *"OK, well, we will send someone down The Track to meet him".*

I was through Adelaide River, with 80 miles (130kms) to go to Darwin when relief arrived; someone else, I think it was Charlie Taylor, took over the driving. I stayed with him and we talked as we travelled those last miles and in the cover of morning darkness drove into Darwin, direct to the hospital mortuary, where further assistance was on hand to help unload the bodies.

There was a last minute bureaucratic hitch before the bodies could be placed in the mortuary. They had to be certified dead. A resident doctor was got out of bed, he walked to the Toyota, lifted the flap of the tarp, looked into the tray top, quickly walked to the nearby lawn and in a soft voice declared *"They're dead.".*

I didn't have to unload the bodies. To this day, I have the greatest admiration for the hospital orderlies and the two police, Sergeant Third Class Primo Bonatto and Constable Bryce Fardell, who undertook the most unpleasant task anyone could have imagined. Some people have the ability to undertake such tasks without showing any emotion. They did that. They deserved a medal. I know I was grateful that having driven the bodies the 11 hour trip from Daly Waters, I didn't have to unload them.

I then took the vehicle and parked it on the foreshore cliff-top opposite the barracks, found a spare room, showered and tried to sleep. It was only an hour or so to dawn and noise of the first of the chaps getting up for day shift had me up and about too. I dressed and went to Smith Street and had some breakfast, then went on to headquarters.

There was an unusual quietness, and on reflection, perhaps an unaccustomed feeling of compassion, not just for the tragedy and the death of six bright young men, but also for all those of us who had the experience of dealing with them in the way we had. The first task was to arrange to clean-up the vehicle, still contaminated with body fluids and even maggots. It was decided the best thing would be to have the fire brigade use a high pressure hose to flush out the back of the vehicle, around the spare fuel tanks and the water tank and to burn the canvas cover over the cage on the vehicle. This was all arranged until we hit a bureaucratic snag. A public servant staffer said that to burn the canvas cover would be unlawful destruction of government property. I thought Inspector Jim Mannion was going to explode! We needed a Board of Survey to give the appropriate authority. Inspector Mannion instantly declared the three of us – all public servants – a Board of Survey. Within 60 seconds we formally authorised the destruction of the canvas cover for health reasons.

So I took the vehicle to the open grassed area at the back of the fire station, we cut off the canvas cover and with a splash of oil, set it alight. The firemen used their high pressure hoses to clean-out the back of the vehicle which I then took to the government garage where nobody was keen to touch it. The transport manager said *"Come back in the morning, we will have a vehicle organised for you to take home until we have the repairs done"*.

Next morning I had a brand new Ford Falcon utility to take home. The only trouble was, it had to be run-in which meant for the first few hundred miles, I couldn't exceed 35 miles per hour (60kms) then move up to 50 miles per hour (80kms) until it had a 500 miles (800kms) service. So it was a slow trip home. At least the visit to Darwin had let me get another hair cut, and do some shopping at "Tom the Cheap's" grocery. I put it in mind that I'd make up a list for when I was next in Darwin, to pick up my vehicle, and I'd be able to get some supplies too for my next stop, Elliott, where the tracker was not only married but had seven children.

When I got home, there was a pile of mail, not to mention the washing and the routine matters to be attended to. Amongst the mail was a letter from my mother with a newspaper cutting from the front page of the Saturday evening *"Herald"*, a report from Douglas Lockwood in Darwin about the missing plane. In part it read *"Constable David Pollock and Constable Robert Kucharzewski. of the NT Police, are at Daly Waters waiting to begin rescue operations on the ground if the plane and passengers are found"*. Mum would have been so proud and no doubt was kept busy telling the neighbours, and family, of up-dates after I had phoned them from Darwin.

There was also news that while I'd been away, an aboriginal stockman at the Maryfield cattle station had accidentally shot and wounded himself with his .22 rifle. However, things didn't quite add-up and with a little inquiry I got to the truth. In a drunken domestic dispute, his wife shot him. As he wouldn't make a complaint or provide a statement, there was little I could do. The rifle was registered but it was unsafe, giving me grounds to seize it.

The next few weeks were relatively routine. There was a fellow who went troppo on the grog at the Works department road gang camp, some children of the town who were caught sneaking into the hotel and stealing a few loose change 20c pieces, their mothers administering justice after a lecture from me. The main frustration surrounded the return of my vehicle from Darwin. First I swapped the Ford Falcon utility for a new vehicle destined for Elliott, then the old Elliott vehicle before a false alarm trip to Darwin to find that my vehicle was not ready at all, so I was given another loan vehicle. Then when I got my own vehicle back, it got back to Katherine and broke down right outside the police station – another loan vehicle.

On one of the trips to Darwin I picked up a sprouting coconut palm, and planted it in front of the police station office, giving it a good salt water drink to encourage it along. After all, there was no salt air sea breeze at Larrimah. In fact the wet season finally started to arrive with good heavy falls right across the Territory, and south of Alice Springs, interrupting trains and food supplies. At one stage there were no potatoes between Alice Springs and Darwin, nearly 1,000 miles (1,600kms)! We were thankful for "Deb" – the powdered potato that substituted well for the real thing.

With the size of the force continuing to expand, a whole new group of vacancies was created, with a special radio message seeking application for 16 Constable-Relieving Duties positions formally created. Ten positions were in Darwin, four in Alice Springs and one each in Katherine and Tennant Creek. We were given four days to apply. I applied for one of the Alice Springs positions, not that I really thought there was any point applying. Headquarters had a reputation for going through the formalities of calling applications, then appointing whoever they liked anyway. In any event with the change of policy in the last year to accept married men as recruits it meant there were fewer single members in the pool for bush relieving duties anyway.

The opening of the new police station complex at Mataranka, 47 miles (75kms) north of Larrimah, gave me a new neighbour – Roy "Bluey" Harvey. He had been in the force 10 years or so, was a Constable First Class. He and his wife had been given the opportunity to move into a brand new house, with new station facilities, modern lighting plant and all. They invited me up for dinner one Sunday evening; "Bluey" knew a reliever like myself enjoyed a break from home, not that I had been stuck at Larrimah at all.

Still, it couldn't keep me away from work. I no sooner arrived at Mataranka than we saw a car pull up in town, driven by a suspect for the theft of a refrigerator from a Works department caravan eight months or so ago. He had been away in Queensland but we knew he would turn up again one day. We soon christened the new cell block.

No community, however small, seems to be able to escape some sadness. Opposite the Larrimah police station was a small petrol station with spare tyres, batteries, fan belts and the like, and a small open-air cafe to provide travellers with snacks, a drink or whatever. Peter ran the place, a quiet, pleasant chap, a European migrant along with his wife who was expecting their first child. She had gone to Katherine to await the birth; then word came that the child had died. Fortunately, it was the wet season with little traffic, and as he left to quickly join her, he gave me the keys of the place to serve any travellers in urgent need of fuel, a tyre or the like. I was able to keep one eye on the place and keep things at the station going without any trouble.

The road conditions didn't stop the folks I was relieving getting back. In fact they arrived two weeks early, with a 22 feet (7m) caravan in tow. They had bought it while on leave and used it as accommodation for much of the time, then brought it back to take to Darwin to set up and rent out at a caravan park. So I began to get ready to move on.

CHAPTER 9

I make it to Elliott

I was getting into the routine of handover-takeovers so the changeover at Larrimah was pretty quick. As soon as completed, I finished packing the car and left for Elliott, about a three hour drive to the south. I wasn't going to waste any time as I didn't trust the weather. As it was, at the Newcastle Waters causeway, there was three to nine inches (7cm to 23cm) of water across the road, for about three-quarters of a mile (1km)! A heavy rain in the catchment area, and it would have been impassable. In the floods the previous year the water had reached a depth of seven feet, and on the side-road to Newcastle Waters township, where there was presently six to seven feet of water across the road, it reached 15 feet (4.5m). Even now, the post office/PMG technician at the repeater station had to use a small boat to get to and from the township.

At Elliott, Horrie Prew had all the paper work ready. We completed the hand-over-takeover on the Thursday soon after lunch and he and his wife and children were gone, getting away a good day earlier than they might have expected.

The Elliott police station was on a side street to the highway, a street of government properties, with the school teacher's residence next door, along with the PMG linesman, a forester, a stock inspector and at the end of the street, the school. The residence was again an elevated house with the police office with visiting officer's quarters attached as well as a court room at ground level. Then there was the vehicle garage, storeroom and cell block. There was both town power and water, and the telephone exchange was open 9am-6pm weekdays and on Saturday morning. Out of hours I had a direct line to the Newcastle Waters exchange from where I could be connected to Tennant Creek, which gave me emergency communications.

It was one of the most distant stations from Darwin in the Northern Division which at times made radio communication difficult, often having to receive messages on relay. However, I had good radio contact with Tennant Creek and other Southern Division stations if the need arose.

The tracker, Pharlap, lived in the aboriginal camp, half a mile or so to the north of the town. It was a half-mile (800m) south to the hotel, a store-garage-post office and Peter Sherwin's livestock transport depot. The station was the most isolated I had worked at to date. It was 160 miles (260kms) south to Tennant Creek and 100 miles (160kms) north to Daly Waters. Within the police district were a number of cattle stations. Newcastle Waters covered an area of 4,005 square miles (10,400sq kms), and totally surrounded the Elliott township. To the north east there was Beetaloo, to the east Uckaronidge and Mungabroom and to the south, Helen Springs, one of the Vestey empire stations.

The hotel, which held a roadside inn licence, had recently been taken over by two sisters, Claudia and "Pos" Desailly, who had moved from Darwin. The Rattleys, who had been at the hotel at Larrimah, had also moved to Elliott in recent weeks, the four of them able to run the hotel. With both "Pos" and Pauline Rattley in the kitchen, they had the best meals of any roadside inn on the highway between Alice Springs and Darwin. They had a good bar area, including the "must" pool table and a juke box. The accommodation was half a dozen or so self-contained cabins in the rear yard area of the hotel. A little short of being half-way between Alice Springs and Darwin, Elliott was a popular stopping place for travellers, although during the time I was there, it was not the tourist season. In fact, the wet season rains made sure that at times there was little travel at all.

I was given a standing invitation to have dinner at the hotel for which I was most grateful. Not only did it mean I didn't have to cook, it was free. And I didn't have to provide myself with a range of cooking utensils. It was a standing order that when a single member like myself went to a bush station to relieve, the member being relieved had to give-up the house, except for the main bedroom where he could store their non-rented furniture and whatever personal effects they liked from the house. In most cases, as I had experienced at Maranboy and Larrimah, the members just left everything as it was, I just used a spare bedroom to sleep in, I had full use of all their household personal effects. There had been no mention that it would be different at Elliott, particularly as Horrie had wanted me, a non-drinker, to relieve him. He had even put his leave back a week so it would fit into the schedule. So I was a bit taken aback when I moved into the house to find the kitchen virtually bare; the crockery, cooking utensils, even the knives and forks all packed away! It was a lesson in human nature.

Although the meal at the hotel was free, I paid for it in kind. I used to try to arrive for dinner as close to 6pm as I could, then, having had my meal, I could relieve as barman while one of the others had their meal. I was helping out behind the bar one evening when a traveller walked in carrying a small mail bag ... *"I found this on the side of the road just out of town ... I went to the police station but there is nobody home there ... I was wondering if you*

A real "road train" with a Commonwealth Railways NT model locomotive being moved from Alice Springs to Larrimah by road transport. Note one set of the engine bogies (wheels) on the low-loader in front of the locomotive

"Fishing" at the Newcastle Waters Causeway. Tracker Pharlap and his extended family had another successful catch

could give it to the policeman when you see him ..." "Yes, sure, no trouble at all" I replied, taking the mail bag from him as he turned and left, so pleased with his public spirited action.

There was quite a bit of paper work at the Elliott station. In the first week I registered seven motor vehicles, did three driving licence tests and registered half a dozen dogs. I also had to make a trip down to Renner Springs, 60 miles (100km) south, and do the annual inspection for the race club's application for their racecourse licence for the annual Easter race meeting - races on the Saturday and Monday along with a rodeo on the Sunday. It was the social event of the district for the year, and would mean me spending Easter at Renner Springs.

I'd only been at Elliott a few days when I had to go back up to Katherine for court (the refrigerator case from Mataranka) but this gave me the opportunity to stock up on perishables, and a few household utensils. However, I didn't want to stay away long as I feared being stuck by floodwaters as the wet season rains set in. As it was, in Katherine there was 16 feet (4.9m) of water over the low level road crossing, 47 feet (15m) the previous week and by the time I returned to Elliott, rains had sent the level to 55 feet (17m) which meant if the river banks upstream broke, there would be water through the town. A tropical depression in the Gulf of Carpentaria coast had caused considerable rain in the catchments of both the Roper River, which ran into the Gulf of Carpentaria, and the Katherine-Daly River systems which had my colleagues at both Roper Bar and Daly River stations on full alert. In both cases the station buildings had been known to be flooded before. With high levels at Katherine there was time to warn people along the Daly to prepare, even evacuate. "Spud" Eggleton, who had been at Daly Waters some years always became a little excited you might say at rain and rising river levels, especially at Katherine. With no telephone, his police radio was a major source of information. I'm sure at times there were exaggerations of rainfall and river levels to get him a bit excited, still, he was always alert to the dangers and ravages of flood. The weather pattern also brought good rains to Elliott, 348 points (90mm) in one night.

This sort of rain soon had weight restrictions imposed on the highway in an effort to limit damage, hard lessons having being learnt from the previous year. At the time, the Commonwealth Railways were moving a number of locomotives from their Port Augusta based workshops to the North Australia Railway, to work on the Francis Creek iron ore trains. With no rail link between Alice Springs and Larrimah, about 650 miles (1,050kms), the loco-motives were moved on a specially designed low-loader, the train bogies (wheels) being on a second transport. They were usually accompanied on the journey by several Commonwealth Railway personnel, including the loco-motive engineer, "Snow" Andrewartha. On one trip the locomotive had reached Elliott when the highway load limit was imposed and all special per-mits cancelled, so the crew parked the locomotive on the special trailer in the Works department yard until it could travel again. It was some sight to see Commonwealth Railways loco NT 71 parked side-on to the highway hun-dreds of miles from any rail track.

The delay allowed the crew some spare time in Elliott, waiting to assess if the hold-up would be short or longer term, the latter meaning they would have to go back to Port Augusta and come back in a week or three to com-plete the job. The pool table received greater patronage with increasing chal-lenges between Mick Bailey, the stock inspector, Alan Wortley, the PMG linesman and the train crew, all under the eye of several from the aboriginal camp who kept the coins flowing into the juke box. It was never resolved whether "G3", Slim Dusty's "Road Train" or "A1", Johnny Farnham's first hit, "Sadie, the Cleaning Lady" was the most popular song at the time. I think the records just wore out before anyone moved onto another tune! One thing it also did was keep the supply of Southwark beer turning over - that's all the crew from Port Augusta would drink.

One thing the weather didn't stop was a medical team working the area on an anti-TB campaign. When they arrived at Elliott, the whole community lin-ing up for the well-known skin resistance test. Virtually nobody had a "resis-tance" reaction and near everyone went on to have the B.C.G. vaccination. We all knew this would develop to a watery lump on our left upper arm in a fortnight or so, then itch for weeks until it healed. The police station - the court room or visiting officers quarters - were used by the visiting doctor each three weeks for clinic. It didn't pay to get sick in between or it was a trip to Tennant Creek to see doctor.

A discussion at the hotel one evening, probably prompted by the wives, on how to pass some information around town on things such as the doctor's visit and the film night, got my old newspaper traits working, so with noth-ing better to do one afternoon, I sat down at the typewriter, and knocked up a one-pager *"Elliott News"*. It was a collection of nonsense and fact, report-ing on incidents around the village, like the school being connected to the telephone (Elliott 14), Claudia Desailly announcing she was going to plant "Billy Goat Stinkers" in the flower beds across the front of the hotel, and comments on the situation surrounding the town power supply which was having a few haemorrhages. The problem was that the automatic switching system was turning the whole town supply off for no apparent reason. After the local Works department officers, Don Robertson and Sid Weeks, had tried a few times to unsuccessfully reactivate the supply, technicians would have to travel, usually from Katherine, to try to rectify the fault. Fortunately, the hotel had a back-up generator, to keep its 'fridges and basic lights operating but the rest of town had to return to lamps and candles on-and-off for the best part of a couple of weeks.

The *"Elliott News"* was designated as priceless with copies run-off on the school spirit copier, one pasted on to a card and propped up on the hotel bar for all to read. One incident in town the *"News"* took delight in reporting, in a light-hearted way, was the visit of the Licensing Inspector, Sergeant Second Class "Monty" O'Mahoney. He arrived at the station and planned to stay overnight, so quite correctly he used the visiting officers' quarters. That was Monty's style - by the book. However, there were no showers in the visiting officers' quarters, so he asked to shower in the house. *"Sure, go ahead"* as I kept on at a few odd jobs around the office. A few minutes later I went to the house and realised Monty wasn't there; he wasn't at the station or the quarter's either. *"You there Monty?"* I yelled out. *"Yeh, up here, having a shower"* came back his voice! Only trouble was, he was next door, in the school teacher's house, having a shower. David Beaton, the teacher, who was half-asleep in the lounge, hadn't heard Monty walk up the back steps, walk down the passage and start to shower. The voice quickly brought him to realise someone else was in his house as a very embarrassed "Monty" met him at the bathroom door. The *"News"* reported a "quick arrest".

There were no court cases to report. I actually didn't have an arrest in Elliott itself the three months I was there. This disappointed Reg Rattley, the Justice of the Peace formerly at Larrimah, no end. However, he was quite familiar with the licensing provisions surrounding the absence of a licensee, so each time Claudia Desailly was going away for a few nights, he ensured the licence was transferred to someone else at the establishment. He would have to have court for that, and he would have to sign the respective authority. The only trouble was, between the weather, the rail crew and a few of the locals, Reg was in such a state of the shakes, sometimes I had to wait a couple of days after court for him to be fit enough to sign the court register or the authority.

Another visitor to town was the Roman Catholic bishop, on a highway pastoral trip from Alice Springs through to Darwin. A day or two before his arrival I had a phone call from him . . . he knew the Prews were away, a good Irish family, but didn't know if I was *"one of the flock"* and would like to attend a Mass as he passed through. I guess I disappointed him when I told him I wasn't one of his flock.

As the flood waters eased off, especially at the Newcastle Waters Creek causeway, there was a new interest ... fishing. There were thousands upon thousands of a silvery brown mullet-like fish, goodness knows what breed, that migrated north west from the waters of Lake Woods, east of Elliott, upstream to water holes or plain death. The creeks and rivers were destined to dry up in spring and early summer.. It is believed the fish spawn, which survives in the dry season mud, and then be flushed down to Lake Woods at the beginning of the next wet season with the cycle starting again. The fish swam up to the culverts, then attempted to pass under the highway and swim on upstream.

Using some wire netting, or just your hands, it was just so easy to catch them as many couldn't swim against the strength of the flow of water in the culvert, and were washed back to be caught. Still many succeeded and swam on. The fish were from about 6 inches to 10 inches (15cm-25cm) in length, many good pan size. So I took the tracker and his family, along with a couple of the older aboriginals from the village to the causeway several times. In an hour or two we would have caught an 'Esky' full along with two large stainless steel pails I had at the station. The kids fed several onto sticks (through their gills) while other bags and containers were also used to store the fish. It was then back to the aboriginal camp where the fish were all cooked and eaten on the one night. One afternoon we got back to find someone else in the village had caught a 4 feet (1.1m) goanna and had it on the fire cooking. Like the fish, they did not gut it, they cooked it whole, as it was, using any cooking dish they could find. Once I saw the remains of an old electric frying pan sitting on the hot coals. It looked out of place but it did the job.

Easter was in mid April and as the weather had improved significantly, there was a feeling that the 'wet' had passed. The Renner Springs race meeting and rodeo would be one of the last opportunities to relax before the mustering camps got into full swing during the dry. I made it a day trip on Good Friday as people gathered, many camping at the racecourse itself, a few kilometres to the south-east of the roadhouse, while others took over the accommodation cabins of the roadhouse or camped nearby to use the road-house facilities of showers, toilets and the like. On Saturday I, Constable First Class Basil "Bluey" Smith from Anthony Lagoon and Constable Dave Swift from Daly Waters met up at Renner to maintain law-and-order. The organisers provided us with one of the accommodation units, all self contained, which doubled as accommodation and police contact point if needed.

There were half a dozen or so local races for the day. With fields of up to half a dozen, some horses racing twice during the day. There were two on-course bookmakers, Eric Marks and Alf Chittock, both from Tennant Creek where they operated legal betting shops. Their main wagering interest was not on the local races but on the interstate races in Brisbane, Sydney, Melbourne and Adelaide, in particular the Sydney Easter feature races. "Bluey" Smith had a philosophy that he was prepared to bet and lose the equivalent of his travelling allowance, (T/A for short) an allowance we would be paid for meals and accommodation for the time we were away from home. This was about $6.50 a night at the time as I recall, so if he lost $20, he still considered himself even. I thought that wasn't a bad idea and decided to follow him, not that I had any idea at all about the horses racing. I picked something out in a Sydney race, at 10/1; Eric Marks gave me 12/1, he had a practice of giving the police a couple of points. My $1 each way was an instant winner and I ended the day $22 in front, nearly doubling my T/A. On the Monday my fortunes were not as good and I ended the meeting even, but had a lot of fun along the way.

The crowd, a couple of hundred on both race days, and about 1,000 at the rodeo on the Sunday, many making it a day trip up from Tennant Creek, were generally pretty orderly. We only ended up with one arrest. He was a guy who would not take the message to move on, and as he was known to be on a pro-hibition order we had no alternative but to arrest him. The cage on one of the vehicles served as the cells and when he was sober, we bailed him to the Tennant Creek Magistrate's Court - another trip to town.

We had our hearts in our mouths for a few moments on the Sunday, at least I did, when one of the sky diving team giving a demonstration jump as part of the rodeo programme, fell like a stone, his parachute not opening on command. As he fell toward earth all manner of thoughts raced through my mind, to be so relieved when his main 'chute fell away and his emergency 'chute mushroomed above him. We left it to his mates to rescue him from the bush. At the rodeo itself, a fall from a horse left one rider seriously injured, and needing to be flown out to Tennant Creek hospital.

I no sooner got home to Elliott late on the Tuesday morning when word came that an aged aboriginal woman had died at Beetaloo station, 15 miles (24kms) to the north on the highway, then 30 (48kms) miles north east to the station homestead. I needed to attend to be satisfied that her death was natural, really an observation that she had not been beaten to death, and to get together the particulars for the death file. I took along with me the Australian Inland Mission (AIM) Pastor from Newcastle Waters to conduct a service. It was the first natural death I had to deal with on my own, but everything fell into place, the formalities were completed and she was respectfully buried.

Notice formally came that I was being transferred back to Alice Springs as a "Constable - Relieving Duties" when I finished my duties at Elliott, so when I went to Tennant Creek the next week for court, I was pleased to meet the Inspector, Southern Division, on his visit to the area. He told me I could expect to go relieving soon after I returned to The Alice. It was surprising how quickly the tables had turned and how few single members there were to carry out the duties despite the fact the size of the Force was being further increased, to 201 in strength. The predominance of new members were married which was causing new problems in providing them with housing. I could see that there would be time for me to take a month's leave between when I would finish at Elliott and could expect to move to the first Southern Division relief at Finke, from 1 July. I thought that after more than nine months in the bush working by myself, I could do with a break. Although I wasn't eligible for a fare entitlement, I could afford the airfare. After all I had been on one form or another of travelling allowance all the time, plus I'd had the post office/mail contract income and it hadn't cost me a lot to live at places like Elliott. I'd paid off my car, even bought some shares and was feeling pretty pleased with myself.

Still, I didn't have the urge to buy a block of land in Elliott when the government released some home building blocks and auctioned them off, or more accurately, tried to auction them off. Only one buyer turned up. He only had to offer $1 above the reserve price and the block was his, the others being all passed in for later sale.

Although the dry season continued to approach, with the need to pull on a blanket in the late morning hours, there were still storms about. They always seemed to coincide with some form of emergency, this time the report of a young aboriginal woman, at Beetaloo, having difficulty giving birth. Of course, it was Saturday afternoon as well, and with the storms closing the highway to the south, the Tennant Creek ambulance was unable to travel north to assist. So between the welfare officer, Warren Smith, and I, we went to Beetaloo, across the black soil plain that separated the homestead site from the highway and conveyed her back to the highway, and north to meet a Katherine based ambulance. It was 3 am before I got home. The lass turned out to be only 14-15 years old, and to us, did not appear all that pregnant at all, but next day when I got Katherine police to enquire on her condition, they informed me that she had her baby an hour after arrival. *"Both are well"* was the report.

The Prews arrived back on their last day of leave, the handover was completed, I said my farewells and next morning left early and travelled right through to Alice Springs. Apart from some of the faces the barracks had not changed much. I nearly felt I hadn't left the place but I knew I would be there for only a night or two before flying out on four weeks leave on one of those horror 4am flights which were still operating.

I hadn't told my folks I was coming down on leave so I caught the airport bus into the city and the train out to Belgrave. The folks lived only a 100 yards or so (100m) from the railway station. When I got home there was nobody there. I guessed Dad would be at the milk bar at Upwey he was running at the time, so I went there. When I walked in he got quite a surprise, in fact he was so shocked, I decided I would never not tell them again.

CHAPTER 10

The Finke

My four week's leave flew by and before I knew it, I was back in Alice Springs. Although I'd been away nine months or so relieving, and now had four weeks leave, there were familiar surrounds and faces, it was good to be back. There were only four in barracks, which made it pretty quiet. Sergeant First Class Len Cossons was now in Alice Springs as permanent officer-in-charge. The town had grown with the increasing influence of the Joint Defence Space Research Facility (JDSRF) at Pine Gap, outside The Gap, off the main Stuart Highway South, to the south-west of the town. The tourism industry continued to build, there was increasing mineral exploration right across Central Australia and the pastoral industry was getting back on its feet with two good seasons that followed years of drought.

The general duties section roster for the next fortnight was out and although I was listed to go to Finke on relieving duties about the 29th of the month, the end of the roster period, nobody at the Alice Springs Station *"knew what was going on"* even though the office of the Divisional Inspector and that of the officer-in-charge of the station were only six feet apart. Relieving was a divisional matter and the Inspector was away for a few days at the Brunette Downs races. *"You will have to wait until he gets back to know for sure"* was the comment. It was a typical mind control exercise of uncertainty, that you could never be sure where you would be working, where you would be stationed, from one day to the next. It was like being a pawn in a game of chess.

Still, I was on the station roster to go to Finke on the 29th so that I could take over on the 30th with Constable Laurie Kennedy to officially commence leave on Monday, 1 July, 1968. It looked pretty good to me, especially when Laurie just happened to be in town for a night and had been told I was coming to relieve! *"I'll leave everything 'as-is' for you"* he told me, which meant I didn't have to worry about taking cooking utensils, bedding or anything like that.

On his return, Inspector Greg Ryall, confirmed I was off to Finke. We decided the best thing to do was leave my car in town and to travel down on the Sunday morning Ghan passenger train. While it was only 142 miles (230kms) by rail to Finke, the journey took about four-and-a-half hours. Still, it would get me there about lunch time and have enough time to get the

Three eras of The Ghan ... the camel before the 1927 arrival of the steam train and the water towers at every siding along the track and the diesel locomotive hauling the modern-day Ghan southward through Finke, August, 1968.

hand-over-takeover completed before Laurie's leave officially commenced. The rail fare was only $4 first class from Alice Springs to Finke.

The Finke township was on high ground, south of the mighty Finke River which by the time it reached the area near Finke, had been joined by its major tributaries and when in flood flowed on south east into the fringe of the Simpson Desert and disappeared. Thus the township itself was safe from flood, although it could be easily isolated by the Finke River itself to the immediate north, the Goyder and numerous streams to the south and any number of rivers and steams along the road west to where it joined the Stuart Highway, 98 miles (155kms) from Finke, a few hundred yards (metres) north of Kulgera.

The Overland Telegraph passed north-south through Finke where there was a repeater station, the first south from Alice Springs, the next at Oodnadatta, in South Australia. The telephone line ran on poles roughly beside the railway. The steel poles and single short cross bar, carried just four wires, but provided a vital link for both public and railway communications.

There was no railway platform as such at Finke. The station master's office was on the east side of the line with a row of half a dozen railway houses for the station master and other married staff like fettlers which ran north-south beside the line. They faced away from the station, each fenced, to a road, the "main street" so to speak. Facing them was the mission, the closed general store with the hotel on the south eastern corner of the street. At the end of the street was the police complex - a residence with office attached, the tracker's quarters, free standing single cell, power house and the galvanised corrugated iron ration store. To the east of the police complex was the repeater station, post office and residence and a hundred yards or so further on, the school complex. The school complex was the most modern government facility in the town with a fairly new brick teacher's residence, school building and facilities.

The main road took a dog-leg from the main street, beside and between the police station and the railway line for a few hundred yards before it crossed the line and headed for Kulgera. Across the railway line, adjacent to the police complex, was the railway singlemen's quarters and gangers' shed where the rail trolley was kept. Half a mile further south, east of the rail line were the cattle yards and rail loading facility and on the western side of the rail line, the airstrip.

The police residence itself was built in 1938 of steel, corrugated iron, flywire, canvas blinds and timber floor. There was no air-conditioning or overhead fans, consequently, it was as hot as hell in summer and freezing cold in winter, where morning temperatures several degrees below freezing were common. It had a small kitchen fitted with a combustion stove which doubled as the hot water service, although there was a copper to do washing, and a wood-chip heater to heat water for the bath. There was "town water" supplied by the railways but the pressure was pretty poor. The station had its own 240 volt lighting plant with back-up 32 volt lighting run from a bank of batteries charged up when the lighting plant was running.

The police office was a well set up single room, again with the radio taking pride of place. It joined the residence through an archway off the enclosed verandah of the house, so it was a simple matter to walk from the house to the office. You could almost listen to the radio from the house, particularly if you tuned it into the broadcast band and picked up either short-wave stations during the day or the likes of Adelaide or Melbourne AM stations at night.

The Finke police district actually ran from the Stuart Highway, 90 miles (145kms) to the west, right across to the NT/Queensland border, south about 30 miles (50kms) to the NT/South Australia border and 90 odd miles (145kms) to the north. Finke itself was bordered by New Crown station to the east and south and Lilla Creek to the west. Andado station was further east, while Horseshoe Bend, Idracowra and Umbearra stations were all in the district. Further east of Andado was the great Simpson Desert. All the cattle stations in the district were family owned and run.

The Ghan stopped at Finke for 10-30 minutes, depending on how late (or early) it was, whether or not the locomotives need to take on fuel (usually not) or the passenger carriages had to take on water. Finke was one of the few locations along the route where the water was acceptable to "take on", and more often than not, the train took on water at Finke. The large water tank at the southern end of the railway station was also a reminder of former years when steam trains took on water.

The time also allowed some passengers to make a quick trip to the hotel, to have one across the bar, or grab a couple of cans to take back on board. There was always plenty of warning before the train would pull out. The station master had a large hand bell which he would feverishly ring, calling out *"all aboard"* for a minute or so before waving the green flag to the head conductor and guard, a blast of the loco whistle and slowly the Ghan would move away.

The first news at Finke was that the police vehicle was unserviceable, the fuel pump, another common problem with that model of Toyota Landcruiser, had broken the day before I arrived! A replacement had been ordered but I'd have to wait for it to come down on the next train. That would be next Wednesday! The second piece of news was that it was clouding up and expected to rain. Sure enough, before the day was out, it was raining, as it did most of Monday, with some quite heavy showers. Laurie, his wife, Eileen, and two girls were booked to leave on the Wednesday Ghan, their holiday packed station sedan having left on Saturday's goods train to be ready in Port Augusta on their arrival on the Thursday.

Next came word that Tuesday's northbound Ghan was being held at Oodnadatta, 150 miles (240kms) south of Finke, with no prospect of moving north for several days due to wash-aways. In fact the railways were planning to airlift the north bound passengers out on chartered Fokker Friendship aircraft. Laurie decided to charter a light plane to come from Alice Springs and collect him and his family. He could then try to get on the charter back to Oodnadatta or he could change and fly to Adelaide, although it would mean him having to make a trip up to Port Augusta to get his car which by now was sitting there waiting for him.

The rain had been enough to close the Finke airstrip. Laurie, as the airport manager, one of the extra duties of the policeman at Finke, had closed the strip on Monday due to a soft surface, so when on Tuesday he re-opened it, and Brian Smith from the Alice Springs based air-charter company SATAAS, lodged a flight plan to fly to Finke, DCA officials in Alice Springs were immediately suspicious. They were quickly on the phone seeking re-assurances that the airstrip was in fact safe for landings. The airstrip actually was quite big, wide and long, and while the more northern, lower, end of the strip was a little soft, the southern, higher end, was very sound with sufficient length for any light aircraft. The $70 cost of the charter was the least of Laurie's worries, he was on leave and wanted to be out of Finke! He rang and booked the charter at 2.30pm; by 4.05pm he and his family were on board and on their way.

The tracker was "Brownie", an older man, who had been in the job for years. He was a loyal and helpful off-sider. There was no dog to look after but there was a big ginger cat "Mr Boob" and a calf, no doubt inherited from the railway trucking yards, too young to have travelled the 800 miles (1,280kms) to the Gepps Cross saleyards near Adelaide in South Australia and handled the two changes of rolling stock at Marree and Port Pirie. It was a job for the tracker to look after the calf to make sure it was tethered to feed and had water.

Ted Reeves was the PMG repeater station technician. He and his wife, Doreen, who ran the post office and telephone exchange, and their children, had been at the Finke some years. Don Burgess, a former NT police officer, and his wife, Joan, ran the hotel, which had a roadside inn licence, thus could sell liquor at any time. He could be quite a handy back-up if you found yourself in a spot. There was a young couple at the school with one child. Miss Margaret Bain was the Australian Inland Mission pastoral worker who mainly worked amongst the aboriginal people in the camp of 100 or so at Finke, and other smaller communities around the district. One of the fettlers, Bill Hanley and his wife, an English migrant couple, had 10 children, the eldest little more than 14 years old. The ganger and his wife, Kevin and Val Stephens, had seven children so between both the European population and the aboriginal community, there were quite a number of children to attend school.

The seasonal conditions had the side effect of helping a rabbit plague develop. What had been thousands of rabbits a year or so ago was now hundreds of thousands right across the border district. At night you could drive just a few mile out of town to a colony and 'spotlight' a number in minutes. A nice young fat roast rabbit made a pleasant change to steak and roast beef, especially when the other perishable supplies started to run low with the rail out of action.

It was 10 days before the Ghan ran again, its first journey north only six to seven hours late through Finke. Most of the freight trains seemed to pass through Finke at night. As the rail track was literally only 25 yards (22m) from the station, separated only by a roadway, the noise of the locomotives and the rolling stock always woke me. The first time I wondered what the hell the noise was. It was even worse when they needed to shunt a few trucks out of the train. Finke was also a popular passing location, thus the powerful throb of an idling southbound locomotive, virtually parked right outside the house, on the loop, waiting for the northbound to pass was a common and annoying interruption to sleep during the early hours of the morning.

It was a fortnight before the fuel pump arrived for the vehicle. At least it was accompanied by a diagram on how to fit it so with some mechanical wizardry on my part, I was able to get the vehicle running. At least I could move from foot patrols to a mobile patrol, and have a bit of a look around the town and surrounds, take a trip down to the Finke River itself and see that the recent rains were not going to flood the railway causeway. It was also handy as the wood supply was drying up, and Brownie and I needed to get a fresh supply to keep the fires burning on these cold nights.

It was great to be able to lie in bed in the morning, during the July/August frosty morning period, get up to find the stove alight and the kettle boiling, ready for that morning cuppa, to make some porridge and be ready for the Southern Division 9am radio sched. If it wasn't so cold and frosty in the mornings, I might have got up earlier to listen to the Royal Flying Doctor Service frequency where all the local gossip was exchanged in the "galah" session. It would start as soon as radio conditions would allow and continue until 8am when the first base call would be made. There was another "session" for about 30-40 minutes before 1pm and then again late afternoon, after the 5pm telegram sched. had been completed and the base closed. Ted Reeves listened, joined in the "sessions" and if anyone from one of the cattle stations wanted me for something, he would pass the message on.

Frankly, there wasn't much to do at Finke. The aboriginal camp was well behaved with no outward liquor problems, the railway fettlers knew their limits. If they misbehaved not only were they in trouble with the law they would find themselves out of a job. The cattle station staff were no problem either. There were not many young men in the aboriginal camp. To their credit, most were out working on cattle stations, particularly at this time of year when cattle could be worked without the fatigue of hot summer conditions. The cattle in the district were predominantly British breeds, Hereford, Angus, some Shorthorn and many crosses between the lot!

I had the airport to maintain so with the vehicle back on the road, and a new supply of steel arc-mesh on hand, it was opportune to spend some time "dragging" the strip and cleaning around the markers. The "dragging" job was what probably took the life out of the police vehicle. With the tray weighed down with a couple of bags of sand, and towing the 8 x 10 feet (2.4 x 3m) sheet of steel arc-mesh, itself weighed down with a couple of old tyres, which filled with sand as they 'dragged", giving some stability, the 1,200 yard (365m) "runs", in 4-wheel-drive, up and down the strip to ensure its smooth surface, not only ran up the miles but also put a good load on the motor. As well as the strip being 3,600 feet (1,100m) long, it was near 300 feet (90m) wide. Still, the strip had to be maintained. It was not just an important strip on the north-south route, it was important to the local community as a good airstrip to allow landings by the Royal Flying Doctor Service (RFDS) and the Department of Health Aerial Medical Service which made regular visits to the community. Only a few days earlier the RFDS had flown in to pick up a young girl who had caught her thumb in the pump-jack of a windmill, splitting it. Fortunately, her father had a light plane at their cattle station located to the south-east, over the border in South Australia, and could fly to Finke, rendezvous with the RFDS plane and allow both to return to home base before the last of the afternoon light. The job of maintaining the standard of the strip was made more difficult when non-thinking people, like a young jackeroo "tailing" some cattle awaiting loading at the cattle yards, walked the 200 or so head in the herd right across the strip, to greener pastures east of the strip!

Another regular task was issuing the aged and infirmed rations. The Welfare Branch kept a store of rations in a shed in the police station compound. It was part of my job to issue out, at my discretion, appropriate rations to the aged and infirm aboriginals in the local community. There was no shortage of tea, sugar, powdered milk, flour, salt, Weetbix, tinned rolled oats, tinned jam, tinned meats, canned fruit and so on. In addition, there were regular arrivals by train of cases of oranges, and on each Wednesday Ghan day, two flour bag packs of large sandwich loaf bread. So as not to waste much of the issued rations, I often gave a case of oranges to the school. Others in the community not necessarily aged or disabled, but certainly disadvantaged, got an issue too. After all, there was no real general store in the community so the Welfare Branch supply was a vital supply for many.

The first two dogs I registered for the new financial (dog registration) year were those of my parents - "Joe" a black and white cattle dog, and "Nick", a six-month old black and white fox terrier. At 50 cents each, it was a cheap novelty to send home to Mum - Finke district dog registration tags numbers 001 and 002. The next week I had a letter from my sister ... could I register her dog too?

Catalogues were a popular way for many folk to shop. The mailman must have dreaded the delivery of the likes of the David Jones, John Martins of Adelaide or Boans of Perth catalogues, not just the delivery of the 100 page plus catalogue but then the boxes and boxes of goods purchased and forwarded by mail. I think every woman in the Territory, at least outside Darwin and Alice Springs, looked through the latest catalogues to check the fashions, order up on new styles, see what was new for the kids. With the delivery of the latest catalogue, the women of the local community would be talking for days on what they thought of this and that, what they would order and so on. Of course, there were no credit cards then, it was a matter of sending off a cheque or money order. Oh yes, there were a few pages for the men but most interest was for the women even if it was to buy basics.

There was a greater "buzz" through the town when the Northern Territory Fire Service Chief, Peter Holten, accompanied by one of the Alice Springs firemen, both in full uniform, braid and brass buttons flashing, turned up as a follow-up to a fire which had razed one of the railway cottages eight months ago. Holten was tall and imposing with a very proper upper-crust English accent. Finke had never seen anyone quite like him. His job was to survey the town to see what fire equipment was needed. After all, the town of 20 buildings had none at present! Ideas came of a high pressure pump attached to the railway water tower with enough hose to reach all houses and buildings. Even a fire siren to alert everyone was suggested. Holten would have fitted in well in the far flung colonies of the Empire. At times I am sure he thought he was in an outpost of the Empire. When he visited the hotel, the bar quickly filled with inquisitive people, not only eager to provide their ideas on how to address the situation, but to gawk and see who these people in their braid and unfamiliar uniform actually were, if they were 'real'. All I knew was nothing would happen in the time I was relieving at Finke, it would be a long term project getting it through department budgets, especially with the Commonwealth Railways involved as well as the Department of Territories. I just wondered if the officer-in-charge of police would also have to act as the fire brigade captain too!

One thing about relieving was the ability to save money. My salary went into my bank account each fortnight; there was not much to spend it on at places like Finke, in particular when I didn't smoke or drink. Food costs were very reasonable despite the additional costs of getting perishables delivered, but as the reliever, as I had experienced at places like Larrimah and Elliott, I was often invited by the local hotel or one of the local cattle station owners to join them for a meal, not to mention the additional income from that great government institution "Travelling Allowance" which I was able to claim for the time I was away from my "home" station - presently Alice Springs.

I had developed an interest in the share market, buying a few hundred shares in companies such as Adelaide Steamship, South Australian and Swan breweries, and some of the regional television stations. I had paid off my car a year early so with free accommodation, uniforms and a well paid job with its perks like travelling allowance, I was feeling pretty comfortable financially.

My good mate in barracks, Bob Henfrey wasn't into the share market but he was looking for an investment too and on one of my visits to Alice Springs, no doubt for vehicle repairs, we talked over buying a block of land

and building some flats with a view to picking up on the shortage of accommodation in the town. We talked about it one night I was in Alice Springs, then next day set off to the Lands Branch office to make some enquires about the availability of suitable blocks, with planning authority to build flats. To our delight we found a suitable block owned by the wife of a former sergeant and within 48 hours of us talking about the idea, we had signed up to buy the block for $654, the same as she had paid for it at the land auction a year earlier. Like most land in the town, it was leasehold, a 99 year lease from the Government, with a current annual rental of $45 a year. The block was in Gap Road, on the corner of Gynolyia Street. It had a permit to build up to six units under one roof. When the conditions of the block were met, we could apply for the Title to be converted to Freehold. Our first idea was to build two units, the first of six on the block, but all that had to be planned, and financed, meaning I would sell all my shares, my block of land at Cape Paterson, perhaps even my car, if we were to meet our goal.

Over the next couple of months I sold my shares and the block of land at Cape Paterson. We had the plans drawn up and advertised for quotes to build the first two units. Then the stumbling block ... the bank manager ... he couldn't see the boom in Alice Springs continuing ... money was a bit tight ... no, he couldn't approve the loan. Bob Henfry had worked for the Commonwealth Bank before he joined the force. For him it was business with the Commonwealth Bank or not at all. I suggested we go and speak with the National Bank manager but his loyalty was with the Commonwealth. We shelved the plan and later sold the block, covered our outlays but for years later reflecting on what could have been.

Vehicle repairs at the Government garage never seemed to be speedy, they would always be waiting for a part or have some urgent job in hand, so it was nothing to spend a whole week in town waiting for the return of a vehicle from the workshop. Of course, the boss at Alice Springs would be reluctant to let you take one of his spare vehicles, he might never see it again! On the other hand, he didn't like to see a member in town not usefully deployed, so when the right job came along, a word in the Inspector's ear had you into the task.

A report had been made that near Rodinga, on the rail line some 60 miles (100kms) or so south of Alice Springs, there were two children, a youth and a girl, wandering about. Speculation was that they had eloped from Alice Springs, they had probably been "riding" one of the goods trains south. Technically, it was in my police district, so as I had my tracker with me, we were given a vehicle and sent off to investigate. We got to Deep Well or Rodinga, I don't remember which, but a rather excited, non-English speaking cook at the fettler's quarters, indicated through sign language that the two run-aways were headed south. We ended up spending the night at one of the fettler camps, and then early next morning began tracking. With the help of the vehicle, we could follow the tracks along the sandy track, which ran near parallel to the rail line as the two walked south. We just hoped we could catch up to them before they "jumped" another train, although the train crews had been alerted and would be watching too. Mid-morning we caught up with them, yes, they were in "love", they had a disagreement at home and had decided to run away.

Still, I am not sure if they were sorry or pleased to see us. We took them into care and returned them to town. *"You always get your man"* said a pleased Sergeant "Dave" Mofflin. I felt pretty pleased too. While in town, and unknown to some, in particular a storekeeper who earlier in the week had a charge of selling liquor outside his hours discharged on a technical point, (liquor/licensing convictions were very hard to obtain before Mr Hall SM), it was decided to use me as a decoy to try to buy liquor outside his hours. I wore a pair of glasses to add to the decoy image, but once bitten, he was twice shy and I didn't get to make a purchase, or have the excuse to come to town for court in a month or two!

It all made for a break from Finke, which continued to be uneventful. The most exciting thing was the delivery of another calf to be cared for and raised. I'd been relieving at Finke two months now and the time had gone by virtually incident free. The arrest of the odd drunk, the sorting out of a domestic dispute in the native camp or speaking to a lad who wanted to run away from home, a few games of Scrabble at the hotel and the monthly Sunday morning CWA of the Air meeting in the police office had been the sum excitement of the job.

The only time I have ever played golf was at Finke. To get a break from the hotel, Don Burgess and his wife organised a couple of Sunday afternoon picnics. When the southbound Ghan had left, usually shortly after noon, Don and his wife Joan, the school teacher and his wife, Rob and Jill Bourke, their baby daughter and I would drive down to the Goyder River, near the rail bridge which crossed the 100 yard (90m) wide sandy river bed, before it joined the Finke. We would light a fire, barbecue some meat, have some lunch and a drink, then Don and Rob both keen golfers, would mark out a three or four hole "course", up and down the river bed, under and over the rail bridge, then proceed to hit that little white ball up and down with a laugh and cry with the frustration of the game. I had a hit too, and certainly did no better, but it all was a great "get out of town" afternoon.

All this was to come to a sudden end. It was Tuesday evening, the Ghan had gone north, I'd cooked tea and was cleaning up when Ted Reeves, arrived on the doorstep. *"There's been a shooting accident at New Crown . . ."* New Crown Station was about 20 miles (32kms) south east of Finke. The station owner, Bob Smith, and his wife, were away in Adelaide, leaving his second son, Francis, and the jackaroos at the homestead. At dusk they had gone out to get a "killer", slaughtered and returned to the homestead to hang it. They then headed for the bathroom, to clean up, wash and shower. The .22 repeater rifle used to kill the beast was there. It was new, they had only had it four days. "Slim" counted out the remaining bullets in the rifle *"... 12, 13, 14, 15"* empty, pulled the trigger, "bang", the rifle discharged, the shot hitting 14 and a half year old Michael Hanley in the chest.

Francis Smith left immediately for Finke to seek medical assistance, but before Sister Cousin could leave, a second vehicle, conveying the injured lad arrived at Sister Bess Coulson's home. When I got there he was still lying in the back of the Landrover tray, being comforted by another of the jackaroos, Michael Morris. Hanley was unconscious and very pale but when Sister Bess checked his pulse she was satisfied with it and arranged for him to be lifted into her house.

With Ted Reeves, I set about contacting the Alice Springs hospital to make some arrangements to evacuate him. Our first thoughts were to light the airstrip in some way to allow the Flying Doctor to land. However, before we got anything organised, word tragically came that Michael was dead.

Michael was a likeable lad, he was the eldest of the family living in Finke with 10 children, his father working as a fettler for the railways. The lad was not at all academic and when given the opportunity to work at the cattle station only weeks earlier, he had been given Education Department exemption from school and took the job. In fact, most of the lads working at the cattle station were from a disadvantaged background, being given an opportunity to make good, make a new life in the Outback.

There was not only the grief of his death but the concern was what to do next. I had the investigation of the shooting to follow through and had to interview for want of a better word the "culprit", the lad who had let off the fateful shot. He was only a couple of years older than the deceased.

I made contact with my Divisional Inspector, Inspector Greg Ryall, in Alice Springs. He was still at the golf club; he had probably driven there after work, about 4.30pm-5pm. I don't think he had been playing golf in the couple of hours before I made contact with him. He ordered *"well, question and lock up the fellow who pulled the trigger, bring him up with the body!"* No other support, just an instruction to arrest "the offender" and bring him to Alice Springs.

It had also started to rain, with the forecast uncertain as to how heavy the overnight rain might be. At this hour, the last thing I wanted was to be driving to Alice Springs in the rain, in a hardly mechanically sound motor vehicle with a prisoner and a corpse. The Ghan "chaser" would be coming through in a couple of hours, so I thought the best thing would be to travel north on that. Don Burgess was a great help; he helped organised the body and the train for me while I formally questioned young "Slim" on how the shooting had occurred, then arrested him on a charge of being in possession of an unregistered firearm.

I had time to throw some clothes into a case, get a few papers together and be ready for the train. When next I saw Don Burgess he was fuming, ready to "snot" the station master, Bill Marjapau. In making the arrangements for me to travel on the train, with my prisoner and the corpse, the station master remarked *"Of course you realise, the carriage of corpses is payable in advance!"*. Here we had the son of a railway employee tragically killed and the station master was telling us that we would have to pay **"in advance"** for the conveyance of the body. *"Look"* I said *"When I get back from The Alice I'll give you a freight warrant ... here is the money for the two tickets"* (Second class was $2.80 each to Alice Springs).

It was after 11pm before we left. The corpse was in the guard's van, "Slim" and I had a "sit up" non-air conditioned, non-heated compartment in the adjoining carriage. I tried to keep awake and keep an eye on "Slim", I didn't want him to be doing anything 'stupid'. I also didn't want to be handcuffing a person who I held in custody only on a charge of being in possession of an unregistered firearm, a .22 rifle he had owned only a few days. The rail journey was slow, painfully slow, and cold. At times we both dozed off. In a way we both couldn't get to Alice Springs soon enough.

We got to The Alice sometime after 7am; it was daylight; the outward bound Ghan was waiting to head south with many eyes watching as the ambulance met our train, collected the body and took it to the mortuary. Guys from the station also met the train and took us back to the police station. As soon as the station sergeant, Sergeant First Class Cossons, arrived at work I had a chance to talk the matter through with him. *"It looks like more of an accident to me, I think you should bail out the lad. We'll let the Coroner decide if he wants to charge him with anything more"* Fortunately, New Crown had an Alice Springs "town house" where the owner's mother-in-law lived, so "Slim" was fingerprinted and bailed on his "own recognizance" and I dropped him at the house.

The rest of the morning was spent on preparing coronial paper work, reporting the death to the Coroner, obtaining an order for a postmortem examination and serving it on the medical superintendent at the hospital. Perhaps the most unpleasant aspect of the inquiry was to attend the post mortem the next afternoon, at the hospital mortuary, where Dr John Hawkins carried out the PM. It revealed the bullet had entered the body and hit the main vessels around the root of the left lung causing it to collapse and causing internal bleeding which resulted in his death. An inch or so either way and it would not have been as severe.

By now the whole family of the deceased was in town, generally being cared for by the Catholic Church although Margaret Bain, the Inland Missionary, based at Finke, was also a great help. In fact, I think she drove them to town. The funeral was on the Friday afternoon. I not only attended at church but was also a pall bearer.

I returned to Finke on the Saturday morning freight train, leaving Alice Springs at 6.45am. I think I was the only non-aboriginal passenger on the train. I spent most of the trip talking with the guard or hanging out the open door window of the carriage as the train rumbled though country, admiring the countryside which was a picture after the recent rains. The wildflowers were really coming into their own with a carpet of small white daisies and yellow buttons. The guard was good enough to provide me with a cup of tea along the way.

The train pulled into Finke with the guard's van virtually outside the station master's office. I had not reached the ground when I heard the station master's voice *"I still haven't got that freight warrant!"* I walked to the police station, wrote it out and took it straight back, slapped it on his counter and walked out. Ironically, a fortnight or so later I had a phone call from the accounts clerk at police headquarters, Darwin. *"I've got a freight warrant here for the conveyance of a body from Finke to Alice Springs ... it's twenty-odd* *dollars ... it only cost $2.80 for you ... what's the go?".* The answer was simple ... the carriage of corpses was at a set rate per mile! Bureaucracy in action.

As soon as I got back to Finke I set about getting the whole coronial file together; I had to gather statements from all the witnesses, take photos, make some sketches of the scene, gather information for the death certificate and so on, all ready for submission to the Coroner to allow him to decide if he wished to conduct an Inquest or not.

I no sooner got the file complete and ready to mail off when I was awoken in the middle of the night by the roar of not just the four-wheel tractor used by the station master to shunt carriages, but the bellowing of the station master himself. *"You there Dave? ... there's trouble on a southbound train ... the guard wants you to meet the train!"* It was 2am. I dressed and went to the railway station office to await the arrival of a southbound freight train. The story was that in the freight section of the guard's van there was the fresh food orders for the various railway camps en route. It had become obvious some of these had been tampered with and items, likely to be bread and other perishables, were missing. It was likely the culprits were passengers in the adjoining passenger carriage, mainly people who had been employed by the railways to work at some of the railway camps along the track. Hans Voigt, the railway road master at Alice Springs was also on the train, heading south to inspect track work and help organise rail gangs.

So into the passenger carriage I went, checking a few cabins until I came to one with three rough looking characters, the prime suspects, all having had a drink or three along the way but sitting so innocent with a *"what is going on?"* look on their faces. The breadcrumbs on the compartment floor sort of gave the game away as I asked if they knew anything about the matter. Oh no, they knew nothing *"Have a look in our gear"* they offered. Just as I was beginning to think this was a lost cause, I opened the wash basin, the typical standard stainless steel basin that folded into the wall of every railway compartment ... and there, hanging over the tap was a string of red saveloys! *"And where do these come from?"* I asked. In almost a chorus they answered *"Ah ... ah, the fellow that got off at the last siding . . . it was him . . . we had nothing to do with it ... that's true, really, it was him, we told him not to, but ..."* I looked at Hans, he looked at me, he looked at the three of them *"You are sacked, get your gear and get off the train here"* he said as he turned to the next and the third and repeated the words. So here at 2.30am I had three total itinerants dumped at Finke.

I thought, "what the hell am I going to do with this trio? ... they will be broke, they obviously will 'have form', (a criminal record) they are trouble waiting to happen" ... perhaps the best thing might be to see if I can arrest them for being idle and disorderly with no visible means of support, and at least get them out of town, out of my hair. So later in the morning off I went and rounded them up, to question them about their "means of support". In moments, I was shot down in flames as one of them produced a bank pass-book showing a credit of more than $1,000.

As the day went on, they became more intoxicated from a flagon of wine they bought with the little cash they had between them. When by mid-afternoon they had made no attempt to secure money from the passbook I began to wonder about it and decided to re-visit the trio and have a second look at the book. Using a little mental arithmetic I quickly realised that the last half dozen or so entries were forged, they had been altered to give the impression of a bottom line substantial credit when in fact the bottom line was that there was no money in the account at all. *"Game's up lads, I'm detaining you as 'idle and disorderly persons, without sufficient means of support' get in the back of the truck"* which they did, renewing their protests of innocence.

It was a short drive back to the police station yard. I pulled up outside the cell, a single, stand-alone unit built of re-inforced timber, corrugated iron and cement, with a half-moon roof, not that well lit, a bench and a portable pan. There was no point taking them inside the station office, I already had their names, date and places of birth, I thought it would be best to search them, get them into the cell and sort out the formalities a little later when they were sober and likely to be a little less antagonistic. The leader of the pack was Irish born with that accent of typical resistance, getting more and more vocal. *"Get that rifle out of the bag and shoot the bastard"* he repeated several times. I had no concern as none of the bags was big enough to conceal a rifle, but he had the aggression in his system to turn nasty as he did when I went to search him. The search was to remove anything of value, anything that could be harmful, like a belt, pocket knife, matches, leaving them with nothing but their bare clothes and footwear.

As I went to check his pockets, he flung his arms in resistance. What he hadn't realised was that Don Burgess had quietly walked into the background, so when he resisted Don stepped forward, put a head-lock on him in such a flash that he wondered what the hell had struck him! The search was completed and he was promptly put into the cell with no follow up resistance from the other pair. The thing now was, I had three prisoners, what was I going to do with them next? I phoned "the boss", Inspector Ryall, in Alice Springs and asked if he could send someone down to help me escort them into Alice Springs for court; could he send me some spare hand-cuffs, I only had the one pair, with an open vehicle I'd need to hand-cuff them for security.

A little later he rang me back to say Constable Jeff Allen was coming down on the evening's goods train and he would help me take the trio up to Alice Springs on the Thursday so I could front them up to a court on Friday morning. It was a windy, dusty, bouncing trip for the three of them, each handcuffed, sitting on their swags in the back of the Toyota tray. We stopped and gave them a break and lunch at Kulgera before heading on to Alice Springs. By this time, they were a very quiet, sober, you could even say, a timid trio.

Ironically, the Magistrate, in his indeterminable "wisdom" decided that rather than jail them for a month, which was the common "idle and disorderly, insufficient means of support" sentence, he would fine them and give them a couple of months to find work and pay the fines! Perhaps he took pity on them knowing what they had gone through over the past few days. After all, they had gone out and gained a job. In his eyes it seemed he believed they deserved some good fortune. Still, as I recall, the fines were never paid, and in turn, at a later time, each ended up in jail, "in default" of payment.

After court I returned to Kulgera in readiness for the gymkayna on the Saturday. It was an annual get-together of the district's stockmen to provide the opportunity for some racing and horse skills not to mention a ball in the evening. Half the proceeds of the day went to the Royal Flying Doctor Service while the entire proceeds of the "Calcutta" auction race, which raised $1,518 in itself, went to the RFDS, a great effort. One horse alone sold for $600; the prize money was only $40, but it was a great way to be seen making a donation to the RFDS.

With John White and his wife, Ruth, active organisers of the day, I got roped into participating in one of the late afternoon events - the "Galloping Darts". The idea was to gallop a horse past three dart boards, throwing a dart at each board as you rode past, the highest score winning the event. I had no claim to fame as a horseman but they provided me with a quiet horse so I had a go. I got one dart to hit the board, scoring four! - certainly not a winning score, but some fun. The day was also a great opportunity to meet many of the people from the Kulgera district. Within a couple of weeks I would be

The flood-wrecked railway bridge at the Finke River crossing, Finke, after the February-March, 1967 floods

transferring to Kulgera as officer-in-charge of that police district.

Next morning there was a Uniting Church service and the christening of five local children before people 'broke camp' and went home to their stations. I headed for Finke but only got 30 miles (50kms) before the Toyota again broke down, and ended by being towed the next 70 miles (110kms) back to Finke by a Landrover, a slow and dusty trip. A couple of days later I loaded it on the train to be sent back to the Alice Springs workshops yet again!

It was ironic that while without a vehicle, an aboriginal owner of a couple of camels passed through Finke. I was able to have a ride on one, and in uniform positioned the camel in front of the Ghan train at the water tower, getting one of the fettler's wives to take a couple of photos - three modes of transport - the camel, the modern day diesel Ghan locomotive and the relic of the steam days - the water tower and water filling turret to the old steam locomotives. Fortunately, a couple of the photos came up well and I was able to use one on my Christmas card later in the year.

Just as I got the paper-work ready for Laurie to return and takeover his station again, a quiet Saturday afternoon listening on the ABC short-wave broadcast to an Essendon winning game, the peace was shattered by word that an aged aboriginal, who had been unwell for some time, had died in the aboriginal camp. After speaking with the Coroner in Alice Springs, I was able to get a local Justice of the Peace, a deputy Coroner, to sign an authority to bury. The question I then asked Tracker Brownie was *"Where do you bury him?"* followed by an animated conversation in language amongst the aboriginal people. *"What's the matter?"* I asked *"They are deciding where they are going to go rabbiting in the next few weeks, they will not be able to go rabbiting anywhere near where they bury him for a while"* he responded. *"Well, where did you bury the last one?"* I asked. *"Over there on the sandhill"* he responded *"Well, that's where we will bury this one, right beside the last one"* I said thinking that the last thing we wanted in years to come was old bones around half a dozen sites.

So the village was mustered, the grave was dug, and we carried the body to the sandhill where it was lowered into the grave. The aboriginal missionary assistant Toby Ginger read a service mainly in aboriginal tongue, the grave was filled and a makeshift wooden cross put at the head of the grave. As we walked away, Brownie, with a sense of concern in his voice came to me *"Boss, boss, we forgot to put the sheet of tin on top of him!"* I looked at him, wondering *"What do you mean?"* . . . *"well, without the sheet of tin he might come up again!"* The grave had not been a standard "6 feet down"; it was shallower, so there was a risk that in the decomposition process, the body could rise. In a very shallow grave the body would end up on top of the grave a week or two later. *"Too late now"* I said hoping that between the weight of his swag and the depth of the grave would be enough. It was ... and the rabbiting sorties were not interrupted!

CHAPTER 11

Kulgera ... an extended stay

Saturday morning ... VFL grand final day in fact, but I hardly had time for that to cross my mind. I'd come up to Alice Springs on the Friday night Ghan and now had only a little time to do some last minute shopping before I was off to Kulgera. I was getting to know the road well.

There was special excitement at the White household ... John and Ruth, and their two boys, were virtually all packed, much of their effects already gone, some sold locally, some given away, the rest waiting to be picked up by a carrier coming through. They were not just going on leave, they were leaving Kulgera, the Territory, planning not to return. The only thing was, everybody knew except the Divisional Inspector. He would find out when John's resignation arrived in the mail a month or so before he was due to return from leave.

I'd known of John's plan for some time. It had given me time to make sure I had all the equipment for "home" I would need. I had my own sheets, blankets and towels. I knew the beds would be bare, the kitchen would be empty, even the drapes were all gone. There was plenty of furniture as like most bush stations, all the furniture was government issue and rented by the married officer. When he went on leave the rent would be suspended. The rent was very reasonable for what was basic, practical furniture featuring plenty of chrome and vinyl, tubular stainless steel and laminex.

Then again, I wouldn't have to do too much cooking as the Taylors at the local roadside inn had already given me an open invitation, as "the reliever", to eat with them, as their guest, during the time of my stay. They just liked to know when I wouldn't be there for a meal so they didn't have to save one if I was out on the road coming in late or away at one of the nearby cattle stations where I was also warmly welcomed for a meal.

Kulgera was one of the newer police stations of the Territory, the complex being less than 10 years old. It was on the eastern side of the Stuart Highway, set back a little from the highway itself. About 250 yards (220m) to the north, on the opposite side of the highway was the Kulgera store and another 100 yards (90m) north the Kulgera homestead. Opposite it was the road to Finke.

The home was of modern design, although of timber and fibro construction and featuring plenty of flywire around a good enclosed verandah. The complex had a 240v power plant and 32v battery back-up system, the standard combustion stove to supply hot water, plus a gas stove, two large kerosene refrigerators and a good tank supply of drinking water. There was bore water pumped by a windmill and a second supply with a motor pump a few hundred yards (metres) east of the complex. There was an office and court room (never used to my knowledge) about 25 yards (22m) from the home, with a two-room free standing tracker's quarters. The rather large cell block was also free standing with a garage/storeroom attached.

To the rear of the police block was the water tower which doubled as usual as a radio aerial point. There was a short hedge along the front fence, a row of cedars and some well grassed lawns in front of the house to help keep the dust down, but there was no vegetable garden. To the west the country was flat. The sunsets on an uninterrupted horizon were spectacular. About half-a-mile (880m) to the north-east of the station was a rocky outcrop within which was a rock formation in a series of pools. Legend says the pools were the tears of a weeping eye and would never dry up.

The area was alive with rabbits, predominantly the traditional grey rabbit but amongst them were black, ginger and multi-coloured ones. There were about 15 professional rabbit trappers and shooters working the area, most of then delivering up to 1,000 pair of rabbits a week. The trappers checked their traps at dawn, gutting the rabbits as they went, but not skinning them. They put them in portable freezers and each week sent them across to Finke where they went south in freezer containers for further processing. The trappers were being paid about 40c a pair for the rabbits which helped put a few extra dollars through the local store.

In the late afternoon it was quite easy to drive a mile or two away from the station and within minutes shoot half a dozen rabbits. The tracker loved them. Even the store cooked up a lovely baked rabbit, (underground mutton), now and then for dinner.

The police district was probably the largest I relieved at. While perhaps no bigger than the Finke district, it was more widely populated. It ran from the Stuart Highway, where the station was located right across to the Northern Territory-Western Australia border with the South Australia border to the south and north of the station about 100 miles (160kms). As well as the cattle station to the south, Mt Cavanagh, south west of Victory Downs and Mulga Park, the district took in Erldunda, Mt Ebenezer, Angus Downs, Curtin Springs, Palmer River, Henbury cattle stations, Kings Canyon, Ayers Rock and The Olgas and the large aboriginal reserve between The Olgas and

Kulgera Store with proprietors Jim and Nord Taylor, February, 1969

Kulgera Police Station with the power house and water tower to the left

the Western Australia border where a new aboriginal settlement had been established at Docker River, just a few miles (kms) inside the Northern Territory border. In all, the police district was about 45,000 square miles (116,550sqkms), half the size of my home state, Victoria. The Finke and Kulgera districts together were probably as big as Victoria!

There was a bit more routine work at Kulgera than Finke. With nearly a dozen licensed premises within the district and the annual licensing reports to be completed and submitted to the Licensing Court there was a fair bit of work ahead. As well, there was no telephone. It was the first location I worked where I was totally reliant on short-wave, two way radio for communications, either through the police network or the RFDS network. At both the store, and at Victory Downs they kept a list of all motor vehicles passing through - the vehicle registration number, make, type, the number of passengers and whether it was towing a caravan or trailer as well as the direction of travel. I had to drive over to Victory Downs, 10 miles (16kms) to the south of Kulgera and then 15 miles (24kms) west, to collect the list, type it up and pass it on to the CIB in Alice Springs. At both locations, virtually all vehicles had to stop for fuel, so it was easy for the store keepers to keep the lists. They not only served to track wanted vehicles but the movement of travellers reported overdue or people often wanted just to pass on an urgent family message. Mrs Nord Taylor at the Kulgera store had a 'nose' for trouble amongst travellers. She had noted the passing of several serious offenders, her evidence helping in the conviction of more than one murderer.

Apart from the store at Victory Downs there was also a large motel which could cater for about 125 people a night, in particular bus parties travelling through to Ayers Rock. On most trips to Victory Downs I would stop either coming or going at Mt Cavanagh station and more often than not, join them for lunch or sometimes an evening meal.

Again, all the cattle stations in the district were family owned and operated with a great sense of community between them all Although they might be miles apart, they spoke daily in the "galah" sessions on the RFDS network and were always ready to help each other out at a time of trouble.

I'd only been at Kulgera a fortnight and I had to travel to Alice Springs for the Inquest into the young Hanley death at Finke. One thing that was consistent at Kulgera was the unreliability of the ageing police vehicle. As I made the trip to Alice, through a bit of mud and water from a good spring shower, the engine cut out several times with water in the distributor and a jamming accelerator. The Inquest went well, the Magistrate, acting as the Coroner, at his passionate best and fully accepting the accidental nature of the incident. I was also pleased with the 'pat on the back' from the Inspector *"a good file and report lad"* he told me. I was more than pleased as I had completed the whole file myself without any CIB input or take-over of the matter.

The mail-run to Kulgera was weekly, the Connair mail plane landing at Mt Cavanagh airstrip about 1 o'clock, just long enough to exchange mail bags and take delivery of any parcels sent by air. I usually went to meet the mail plane taking the store and station mail bags. However, if any of us from the store, Mt Cavanagh, De Rose Hill station (over the border in South Australia) went to town, we would invariably pick up the mail, fresh bread and any other perishable goods needed and bring them back for the others.

Being on the main north-south road, and on the border without a telephone, radio communication with Alice Springs was even more important with up to four radio schedules a day. There was a constant look-out for undesirable characters moving both north and south. The police vehicle was you might say an unmarked vehicle, it didn't have a POLICE sign or a blue flashing light on top; I'm sure they would have shaken or broken off with vibration on the local roads, even if it was called a highway. Around the station I dressed pretty casually but whenever I went on a patrol to places like Victory Downs, I went out in uniform.

Of course, when I knew the Inspector was coming to make his annual visit, I was in uniform to meet him. Looking back, it was good to have his visit, even if he was critical about a few small matters, it was a good learning process. After all I had worked at one-man stations for more time than I'd worked at centres like Alice Springs. Kulgera was the fifth station where I'd acted as officer-in-charge and I hadn't been in the force three years yet.

Inspector Ryall stayed a night with me before going over to carry out his annual inspection, six months late, at Finke, then came back to spend a second night with me. After all accommodation at Kulgera was free, yet he would be able to claim full travelling allowance. Although he had never worked the area himself, he knew many of the local people and we went to Mt Cavanagh station for dinner. I also got out with the tracker and we shot him some nice rabbits to take back to Alice Springs. On Monday, the day of his inspection, there was no rifle on the inventory at Kulgera. Only the tracker owned a .22 rifle. Before the end of the week, there was a brand new 10-shot automatic .22 rifle on the books!

He also arranged for a new 12v battery to be sent down for the station base radio, a back-up for the ageing battery presently in use. With the 9am police radio sched out of the way, and a message that the battery should be over at the store, I drove over to collect the battery wearing my casual shirt, shorts and probably thongs (known commonly as 'Japanese riding boots'). As I walked into the store I exchanged a *"hello"* with a young lad, about 17, just leaving. He had just filled his vehicle with petrol. Nord and Jim Taylor were standing at the counter, Nord had just recorded the details of the vehicle on the running sheet. She remarked *"There's something fishy about that one ..."* with Jim retorting *"Don't be so bloody ridiculous, you are at it again, what's the matter with him?"* Before she could respond he re-entered the store and asked me if I could give his car a push to help start it, so out we walked to try.

However, as we walked to the car I identified myself and asked that before we tried to start the car, could he show me his licence and satisfy me of the ownership. After all, he was about 17-18 years of age, travelling south by himself. He rummaged through the glove box and gave the excuse that in cleaning out the car, his younger brother must have taken the papers out of the car. *"We better go over to the station and call up Alice Springs and get some confirmation the vehicle is yours ... "*

The police radio sched had finished so I had to cut into the RFDS system and ask them to phone the police station and request them to "come up" on the police frequency. Unbeknown to me, the Alice Springs CIB were asking the radio operator at Alice Springs to try to contact me as they were anxious to speak to the young fellow I was speaking with. As the radio operator was trying to explain to the CIB that I would be "off the air" until at least 11am, the front counter officer, who had taken the call from the RFDS, was trying to interject "Kulgera want you to 'come -up' on the network" *"Yes, the Todd Driveway was broken into last night, stolen were cigarettes, aboriginal paintings ... the suspect is a young fellow who worked there until yesterday ... "* the CIB rattled off with the young fellow standing there beside me in the station office. I turned and looked at him *"Don't look at me, I don't know anything about it"* he said.

So we drove back to his vehicle to have a bit of a look. As I pulled up beside his station sedan he quietly said *"It's all there . . ."* ... and it was. He worked at the service station but the evening before had a disagreement at home, decided to 'run away' to Adelaide, broke into his work-place and took a radio, flashlight, some cigarettes, a plastic funnel, a car headrest and 28 water colour paintings which he hid in the back of his station sedan under a blanket. He was licensed and the vehicle was his, it was just that it didn't run too well. He later admitted to me that when we went to the station the first time he deliberately looked to see if I took the keys out of the police vehicle when I pulled up. He had thought that if I'd left the keys in the vehicle, he would have tried to escape, taking the Toyota.

I formally took a record of interview, arrested and fingerprinted him and later in the day took him to Alice Springs for court next morning on a charge of break enter and steal, where after the evidence, and committal to the Supreme Court, he entered a guilty plea. The next month the Judge sentenced him to a month's jail. *"Seems you have to learn the hard way"* the Judge told him.

I was a little miffed ... the report in the *Centralian Advocate* on the day of the arrest, had a late front page report *"On instructions from the CIB, Kulgera police detained a man who is being brought to Alice Springs for questioning"* I'd already 'detained' him before I even knew of the robbery, then I did the questioning and made the arrest. All CIB did was gain a credit for a crime "clear-up", yet they claimed the public credit. As a uniform man, we had become used to that. The lad continued to live in Alice Springs. He learnt his lesson, became a very good citizen and years later when he married, we were neighbours, and always friends.

The weather continued to be warm, days around 100F (37.8C) were common. There were attempts to rain. Cloud would build up from the west, there would be some lightning but nothing more than a cool change before more warm weather. The days were longer too, I seemed to be rising early to listen to and to join in the galah sessions. One afternoon a couple of the local cattle station "barons" Dick Morphett, from Horseshoe Bend station, (his two sons owned Kulgera station) and Bill Coulthard, from Lilla Creek station, both in the Finke police district, came through on their way to Kenmore Park, a South Australian station, which bordered on to Victory Downs, about a 75 miles (120kms) drive south-west of Kulgera. Dick was going over to look at a couple of hundred head of cows and calves they had for sale. He was taking Bill along as his "adviser" to give a second opinion. The deal was going to be worth about $15,000. They asked me if I'd like to go. At the risk of it being a boozy afternoon, I guess they knew if I went along, they would have a sober driver for the trip back. Bill was known never not to have a bottle of rum and some good water too far from his reach. We looked at the cattle and

Preparing dinner - Tracker Peter singes the body of the emu while George, from the store, holds a "drumstick". The emu was then put into the coals of the fire, covered and allowed to cook

the deal was done as Bill Coulthard quietly said to me, *"Well, if he doesn't take them, I bloody well will!"* We ended up having dinner at Kenmore before returning home toward midnight. Needless to say, Bill didn't do any of the return driving, but he could tell a good yarn and some great stories about former identities of the district.

The first Tuesday in November is as well recognised in the Territory as it is anywhere else in Australia, if not more so. While large Melbourne Cup sweeps organised by the likes of Rotary in Alice Springs and Darwin were legal, those organised by the local store for the locals were not quite so legal. But who cared?

Next day I was getting the mail ready at the office, with the RFDS radio operating in the background when the general session was interrupted a couple of times by a lad giving just his call sign - Sierra - Echo -X-Ray. After the third or fourth time, the RFDS base operator responded *"S-E-X, do you have an urgent medical?"* remembering that urgent medical call had precedence over all other traffic on the network, telegrams, School-of-the-Air, even the galah session. By this time I had recognised the called as young Tim Lander, a jackeroo, at Angus Downs station. *"Yes, Mr Barney is here and he's dead."* There was a silence, then a response. *"Just a moment, I'll transfer you to Sister"* ... *"Sister speaking, what is your problem?"* ... *"Mr Barney is here and he is dead"* ... *"Are you sure?"* asked Sister. In a firm but sombre voice Tim replied *"I'm positive"*. Fact was, Mr Barney had been dead more than a day! *"Well"* said Sister *"you will need to send a telegram to the Coroner and advise him and get further instructions"* At this stage I cut in, I identified myself and asked for a moment to speak with young Tim, who I knew was at Angus Downs station, within my police district, but a good couple of hours drive to the north and then west, in all about 120 miles.(190kms) *"Don't worry about a telegram, I will come over in a couple of hours and pick him up and take the body into Alice Springs"*.

Alexander Barney was the caretaker at the Angus Downs station homestead. He, like the owners of the station, the Liddle family, was part aboriginal. He was about 71, and 18 stone (115kgs) in weight, a big fellow. He loved a drop of brandy, in fact the house was scattered with a number of empty 40 oz brandy bottles and the odd VB "Stubby". It appeared that, probably in an intoxicated condition he had either tripped and fallen, hitting his head on the concrete floor and fracturing his skull, or he had a heart turn, fallen and hit his head hard on the concrete floor. There was uneaten food. A thermos flask of tea was still warm, and he had his Melbourne Cup bets written out and sitting beside his radio ready to telegram them to his Alice Springs bookmaker. The wireless beside his bed was still on. He was in the house by himself as the rest of the "family", the Liddles, and Tim Lander, a lad of about 16 or 17, from Alice Springs, but a great mate of the Liddle boys, were out mustering cattle. One of the aboriginals had walked past the house and seen Mr Barney laying on the floor, and gone to the stock camp to raise the alarm. Tim rode back to the homestead, found him dead, and got on to the radio; this is when I heard his call.

Fortunately, the weather was cool, and although all the evidence was that he had been dead about 24 hours, his body was still sound The job now was to remove the body from the house and load it on to the back of the Toyota. Tim had already returned to the stock camp and the few aboriginals at the cattle station didn't really want to have anything to do with the body. However, when I wrapped it and got it into a body-bag I had, one helped me load it on to the Toyota for the near 200 miles (320kms) trip into town. My troubles were not over. Suddenly as I drove along the Stuart Highway there was a shudder. I stopped to find one of the rear wheels loose, it had sheered off two wheel nuts. At least there were three more still in place. So with some tightening, and slower travel, it was a late night arrival at the Alice Springs morgue.

Another chore at Kulgera was the occasional wide load escort usually a piece of mining equipment on its way north. This time it was a load 14ft 6in (4.5m) wide, on its way to Peko Mine near Tennant Creek. Although it had its own escort in the outback sections of South Australia, Territory regulations required a police escort for such a wide vehicle. Fortunately, the timing on this occasion was to leave about 6am and with a little luck, get to the southern outskirts of Alice Springs mid-afternoon and pass it over to a traffic section patrol.

It was getting on to the end of November so I decided to get stuck into the licensing inspection reports and have as many, if not all, done before Christmas. Between the travel and physical inspection of each premises, then the typing up of the actual report, there was the best of a day's work in each. I started with Victory Downs. When I made the arrangement to carry out the inspection, they suggested I come over and stay on for dinner, which I did. Victory Downs was run by Colin and Pat Morton. During the severe drought years they took the opportunity to capitalise on the tourist industry developing a large motel and camping ground facility as an adjunct to the cattle station.

They held a roadside inn licence, which entitled them to sell liquor at any time, but required them to provide meals at certain times, snacks at other times and a minimum of six beds for accommodation. They had brought in a whole group of demountable, accommodation units, some self contained, others using communal facilities. They had a large dining hall and bar area as well as more intimate dining facilities for times of small numbers. In all, they could accommodate some 125 people in beds.

Pat was the main driving force and worker associated with the motel, and the small store and petrol outlet, while Colin took care of the cattle and under his breath, ran down the tourists. They had good home help which they certainly needed in the kitchen and motel during the busy winter tourist months. I got all the details together for the licensing inspection report, before and after dinner, played some cards and headed home. Normally on a patrol to Victory Downs I would have taken my tracker, Peter Amadarra, but as I was staying on, I'd left him home.

That was an unfortunate and untimely fatal mistake.

I had no sooner got home when a couple of aboriginal women arrived at the house seeking medical treatment for cuts to their heads arising from fights in the aboriginal camp. John White's wife, Ruth, was a nursing sister. He had met her when she was working at the Alice Springs hospital when he first came to Alice Springs to work in the police force. She was the local nurse. Like so many other places the medical chest was held at the police station. Although Ruth had left, they still knew to come to the police station for first aid. Before I had time to set about treating them, several more men and women, all sporting cuts and wounds, arrived at the back door of the house. They said there had been a "big fight" in the native camp involving tracker Peter and his wife and most of those who had turned up at the station. Next thing tracker Peter arrived on the scene complete with a substantial cut to his forehead above an eye, blood, mainly dried, all over his face and down his clothes, intoxicated, shouting and wanting to renew the fighting.

I knew it would be pointless, in deed very risky, even dangerous, for me to try to detain him by myself. I feared his supporters in the fight could also turn on me. The best thing was to get some assistance to help put him away, drunk, in the cells, and then get on with treating the wounded. So I quickly jumped into the Toyota and drove across to the store and the cattle station, where I knew some men were, Richard from the store and Peter and Dick Morphett at the cattle station. They were well in bed but quickly dressed, jumped into the Toyota, and back to the station we drove.

As we arrived in the driveway, my worst fears were realised. There was Peter, shirt off, blood over his body from the cut above his eye, walking around carrying his .22 rifle. He had his own rifle, which he kept in his own quarters. The thing was, I did not know if he had any ammunition, I always "rationed" the ammunition and tried to ensure that on a rabbit shooting expedition, he would use all the ammunition I gave him. But I knew he was cunning enough to have had at least one, if not more bullets "up his sleeve" so to speak.

He wasn't threatening anyone with the rifle, rather he was walking around with the gun butt to the ground, held in a way that the barrel was pointing at himself, under his chin. I pulled the Toyota up at the back door of the station and while the men got out, I quickly darted into the house and pocketed the station revolver which I had in my bedroom. I had taken it to Victory Downs, and put it inside the house when I'd got back, before the commotion started.

Then I approached Peter and started to try to reason with him. As he walked around, the rifle still pointed under his chin, he began to say *"I take myself, I take myself"*. Everyone else kept their ground while I got closer and closer trying to reason with him. Then without warning, he crossed himself and pulled the trigger. He fell to the ground dead, six to eight feet (2m) from me. There was a silence, the first thing I said was *"What's the time?"* The aboriginals scattered leaving just the four of us with Peter's body. As I recall, it was near 1am.

I got my camera and took some photos of the scene before I got a blanket and a body bag and with the help of the men, put him first in the bag, and then on the back of the Toyota. I took them back to the store and cattle station, then went home, had a couple of hours sleep before I got up and at dawn headed for town. Along the way, I radioed ahead with advice of the incident but of course it had already been over the "galah" session. Everyone in the district knew.

The trip to Alice Springs was not made any easier by a failing vehicle; the normal 4 hour trip took me nearly eight hours. In fact I had to be towed the last 25 miles (40kms), towed right to the mortuary and then on to the government garage where I was nearly at my wits ends with the continual breakdown and malfunction of the vehicle.

Two members of the Alice Springs CIB were sent down to Kulgera to carry out further enquiries and prepare the report for the Coroner.

Immediately, there was a "swearing off" of liquor by all the local aboriginals. *"Proper bad thing"* was how George, the store keeper's labourer described it. In the local community there was the traditional "singing" and "sorry" gatherings.

It was a couple of weeks to the Inquest. It transpired that Peter was known to go "silly in the head" after drinking liquor, the effects of a horse kick to the head years earlier. The afternoon I went to Victory Downs, the aboriginal stockmen at Kulgera Station, who had been mustering over recent days, had been "paid -up", they went to the store and bought liquor for a grog session which Peter joined in. Intoxicated he became amorous with a young woman and got "caught". The girl's mother became angry and struck Peter's wife across the head with a billycan. She also struck another woman as well as Peter himself. He ended up with a cut above the eye, opening up a wound which bled quite a bit. The injured women, with cuts and abrasions then sought treatment at the police station.

Peter was a talented tracker but like so many of his race, whether carrying a hidden injury or not, he could not handle liquor. The Coroner's finding *"The wound was self-inflicted by the deceased and the deceased committed suicide"* was a sad ending to his career. To me it was a relief that my actions were accepted as all I could have done in the circumstances.

In the meantime, I had the task of carrying on the duties of the tracker such as mowing the lawns, feeding the fowls - all the "fatigues" around the station he would normally carry out. I had to arrange for a widow's pension for Peter's wife and in time recruit a new tracker, Sambo Williams, not from "this country" but a jolly fellow who had worked some of the area and was more than pleased to accept the job.

The routine of the place was also disrupted by the attendance of the painting contactors. All the buildings were on an external maintenance and paint programme every three years, internal; every six years. As I at the station by myself, the contractors actually stayed at the station and ate across at the store. It was known that at some remote localities, they would contract with the officer's wife to feed them, or they would have to take caravan facilities to the site during renovation periods

Still work had to be done. The Welfare branch reported to the Divisional Inspector that there had been a fight amongst some aboriginals at Docker River, the newly established aboriginal community just inside the Northern Territory border. They believed the attendance of the police would 'show the flag' on the need for law and order and thought it would be a good idea if police attended. So, being in my district, I was given the job. At least I had a nice new police vehicle for the trip - a 6-cylinder Landrover, equipped with long-range fuel tanks, water tank and short-wave radio.

It ended up a quick four-day, 748 miles, (1,198kms) patrol to and from Docker River. The first day I travelled up the Stuart Highway to Erldunda and then across the Ayers Rock road to Mt. Ebenezer station-roadside inn, Victory Downs station-roadside inn and Ayers Rock where I stayed the night. Next morning I headed for Docker River, 155 miles (250kms) beyond Ayers Rock, past Mt Olga and then into "Lasseter's Country" toward Docker River, just seven miles (11kms) inside the Territory border with Western Australia.

The road past The Olgas was virtually only wheel tracks through some hills, sand dunes, several big sandy rivers and across plains, through mulga forest and a lot of spinifex grass. It took near-on seven hours for the trip, with the road twisting and winding, even taking a bend as it crossed the river beds. I passed Lasseter's Cave, where the prospector had spent weeks hoping for rescue after his camels had run off while he was setting up camp in his 1930 solo attempt to locate a reef of gold he claimed to have first discovered in 1900 during an expedition across Central Australia. Despite many expeditions since, even in more recent years, there has been no trace of the reef.

At Docker River there were about 170 aboriginals and one European family, Max Cartwright and his wife, and their four children, all home from college or school. At this stage of development, there were no permanent buildings. There were a series of large caravan type buildings, on wheels, for the house, the office, the school (closed for the holidays) and so on. Several shade-houses had been built. On arrival I set up "office" under one of them, with a tea chest as my desk, and registered several dogs, 11 rifles and carried out some enquiries about the fight which it transpired happened a month ago. An upset father "Big Foot Harry" had taken offence at the name of his daughter and a male being linked together in a carving on a tree trunk. A fight ensued, the various parties took sides and several were injured. Soon after, Big Foot Harry took his daughter away to Jay Creek, on the western outskirts of Alice Springs. I considered it all quite domestic. Yes, it should not have happened. Yes, they had been disorderly on a reserve within the meaning of the regulations. But what was going to be achieved by arresting them and taking them to Alice Springs for court (only half the parties were still at Docker River anyway) or by issuing summonses for a court appearance. That was the way I reported the incident back to my divisional headquarters but Acting

Inspector Len Cossons didn't quite see it that way, resulting in a 'red ink' note back to me on my report of the incident.

I stayed the night at Docker; I would have liked to have stayed on the next day and had a good look around the country. It was a very picturesque spot where very few white people had ever travelled. But I didn't trust the weather, a wise decision as rain soon followed my departure on the Wednesday morning, back to Ayers Rock. While the country was new for tracker Sambo, he was surprised to find people he knew at Docker River and had spent his time there catching up with friends and being given the task of taking several mineral samples back to Alice Springs for submission to the government mineral analyst for assay. The region had a reputation for being mineral rich but nothing of substance had ever been found.

On the trip back we stopped to "boil the billy" and have a break in the driving. Tracker Sambo showed me several of the mineral specimens he had been given and asked to take to the government assay office. In turn he looked at them *"what do you think about this one boss?"* he asked. Before I could answer he remarked *"looks rubbish to me ... don't see anything in this one"* and in turn, threw the specimens into the scrub. After all, Sambo had come from the mineral-rich Harts Range area, he had an eye for what might have had some mineral potential and what didn't have any potential. I was just left to wonder what would happen in future years if a prospector passing by picked up one of the samples and indeed found it was of value, then started to hunt for the real mineral field. It sounded like Lasseter all over again to me!

We made better time on the trip back, and had good time to have a look around The Olgas before reaching The Rock for another over-night stay. I came on home through Curtin Springs, then south around Mount Connor, Mulga Park station, Victory Downs and Mt Cavanagh before an early evening return to Kulgera. Of importance, I was home in good time for the local Christmas party, this year on the Saturday afternoon/evening at Victory Downs.

Once again, a local committee of the station owner wives and others had planned the Christmas party for months. There was not just the food to be organised for the spread but also the children's gifts, the drinks and so on. At least being at Victory Downs there were no hassles about the drinks and there was ample space to prepare food for the 100 or so locals who would get together for the party. Much of the food was ordered-in from Adelaide. It came up by train to Finke, was collected and brought the 135 miles (220kms) on to Victory Downs. There were precious once-a-year items like ice cream, the new season fresh stone fruits - cherries and apricots for example - hams, salad vegetables, the lot. The children's Christmas presents were also "ordered-in" from an Adelaide or Alice Springs supplier, pre-wrapped, pre-labelled with the child's name. A month or so earlier a list of names, sex and age group had been sent off to a firm which specialised in preparing gifts for such functions in remote areas.

The plan was for Father Christmas to arrive sitting on the bonnet of the police vehicle, but the man expected to wear the red-suit was a last minute "no-show" - so eyes turned to me. When I arrived sitting on the bonnet of the police vehicle being driven by someone else the children were told I was back minding Santa's reindeer.

My mother decided she would like to visit me over the Christmas-New Year period, so on Boxing Day she flew to Alice Springs. She had to make the Adelaide-Alice Springs section of the flight on a F27 Fokker Friendship which did a "milk-run", stopping at Leigh Creek and Oodnadatta before arriving in Alice Springs, and more than likely continuing on to Tennant Creek, Daly Waters, Katherine and Darwin.

I got a lift up to The Alice, picked up my car at the barracks and went to the airport to meet her. We had a late afternoon look around town, met a couple of friends, including the Watts, then booked her in to stay the night at the Mt Gillen Motel where we had dinner. Next morning we made a quick trip to Simpson's Gap, 25 miles (40kms) west of Alice Springs, and Standley Chasm, another 20 (35kms) or so on, then collected the mail, some bread and provisions for the store, and headed back to Kulgera. For my mother it was a bit of an eye-opener; not just the road, but the remoteness. She wrote home ..."*It is a hell of a long drive, 168 miles without a shop or a farmhouse or dwelling in sight, as we got well out we saw a few cattle, 4 young bulls fighting in the middle of the road - we did a detour ... we then went up a bush track filled high with 'tumble weed' (like in the Westerns) to a Homestead called Erldunda. Mrs Stanes was home and invited us in to this lovely room. Antiques galore!, but there had been a burst water pipe in the shower off the main bedroom and had flooded nearly all that side of the house 'and right through the Cedar Room'! We had an ice cold drink, a talk about radio troubles and delivered the mail, then set out for the highway and Kulgera. We had one fright when David hit the edge of an abandoned shovel and it got stuck in the works under the passenger side. But all is well.*"

We got to Kulgera about 6pm, had time to shower and go to the store for dinner. Mum couldn't get over the film of fine red dust over everything, it was part of the life at Kulgera. She was also concerned about the lack of curtains in the house, after all, John and Ruth had taken all their curtains when they left so she rigged up some sheets to not only give her room some additional privacy, but also keep it a little cooler as the sun rose in the east and shone into her room first thing in the morning. I tended to sleep on the western verandah, catching any cool breeze that came by.

We made the most of the couple of weeks she had in Kulgera. One day we set out early, at 6.30am and headed for Ayers Rock, taking the "help" from the store, Roslyn, with us. It was also her first visit to The Rock. We stopped at Mt Ebenezer for fuel and then continued on through Curtin Springs for morning tea before reaching The Rock. We stopped at the hotel for a few minutes before driving on around the circuit road, stopping to admire formations at 'Maggie Springs' and 'The Brain'. We went to 'the climb' but in the mid-day heat of summer, a climb of The Rock was out of the question. We went on out to The Olgas which in their own way are as remarkable as Ayers Rock.

Before leaving I made another call at one of the motels before we headed off toward home, stopping for a restful dinner at Mt. Ebenezer where I got word that the folks at Erldunda *"have been looking for you"*. There was no getting away, someone always knew where I was. We called at Erldunda but all they wanted to tell me was an aged aboriginal woman had died there earlier in the day; they had buried her before sunset, we could attend to the death report next time I visited.

We got back to Kulgera in good time for New Year. They had a small party going on at the store; then toward midnight, the north-bound Redline Express bus pulled in. Everyone piled out, there was time for a quick drink, even a little dancing as the mid-night hour passed and 1969 was with us. Some even took advantage of the shower, for 20c, at the store, to freshen up and make the last hour hours on the road that little bit more comfortable.

Being holiday time there was a fair amount of passing traffic, 20-30 cars a day. This kept me a little busier than normal with travellers wanting to register their low powered rifles, like .22's, and shotguns, and gain a visitor's permit for the high powered .303 rifle, or even bigger, that they might also be carrying. The permit didn't allow them to use the rifle, it only allowed them to keep it in their possession while in the Territory. I wondered why so many people carried so many firearms? What were they going to shoot? Rabbits were common in most of the places the travellers had come from, all the

Territory's wildlife was protected, there weren't any other feral animals about, except if you went right to the Top End and could get permission to go on to a property to shoot wild pigs. All that they could do much closer to home anyway. It's probably why so many roadside signs and other features were "shot-up" in sheer frustration. Personally, I never owned a firearm, a rifle or a sidearm. If I needed one I had access to one at the station, like I had a new .22 now after the recent Inspector's visit.

I took Mum out to most of the local stations, usually for lunch or afternoon tea. *"We are really made welcome everywhere we go and all the people speak well of David"* Mum wrote home ... *"but I am really looking forward to a cream cake, they only have tinned cream here and ... "* Sorry Mum! The other thing she missed was a radio in the house. The only opportunity to listen to a radio broadcast was on the broadcast bands of the police radio, in the office, and that just wasn't practical.

Mum even had a stint or two at the store, either serving groceries or a stubby in the bar. I often helped on the petrol bowser. In my "plain clothes" I could chat away and find out a lot about what was happening along the way, without them knowing just who they were telling. One afternoon Mum was in the store serving a young fellow who asked if the police station was the local Flying Doctor Base. She told him it was the local police station ... *"huh, what's the local copper like here, tough bastard?"* ... *"He's my son, he's out there filling your car with petrol"*. His jaw dropped.

After Mum had been with me a couple of weeks I took her across to Finke to catch the Sunday southbound Ghan. In one sense, she was pleased to be leaving the heat but underneath, she had enjoyed her adventure with me and took home many stories of her son "Davie in the Northern Territory".

Into the second week of January it was still not clear what was happening about my replacement. One of the Justices of the Peace from Tennant Creek, stopping at Kulgera for petrol could tell me more than I'd been told officially - that was that Dean Symonds was being "up-lifted" (a term for his furniture being picked up by the government removalist contractor) then he was going on leave. Word came the furniture would be delivered to Kulgera on 13 January but of course for Dean to have any insurance claim on any damage, that had to be reported within days of delivery which meant he would have to physically come to Kulgera, check the unloading, and then go on leave, which transpired. Then when I received a letter from the Victorian Amateur Athletic Association asking if I was likely to be in Melbourne in late

March *"we need some experienced officials for the Australian Championships"* ... *"We have tentatively selected you as an anemometer observer, a position of considerable responsibility"* I jumped at the excuse to apply for leave commencing in early March rather than wait until May when I was currently rostered. This would let me finish at Kulgera, get back to The Alice, then go on leave and come back ready for some town work before going bush again. After all, after such a request, how could I not try to be available for the Championships. The next question was, would my VAAA blazer still fit? My grey trousers certainly would not.

The only worry about taking leave in March was the uncertainty of the weather, whether or not the Ghan would be operating, if the road would be good enough to travel or would it be an opportunity to travel down through Queensland. However, a quick look at the mileage soon put that thought out of my mind. Although it continued hot, there were some storms around but little general rain, in fact the country was in its own way getting a bit dry. The lack of wind kept cattle station people at home rather than head off for a break. Finally, myxomatosis had hit the rabbit population, badly effecting the trappers and even putting the aboriginals off catching and eating them. One thing the 'myxo' provided was plenty of easy food for the hawks and eagles, not to mention the dingoes; at least they would not be chasing any calves that were around. And still the days were 110-112F (43-44C) in the shade.

One thing about the hot weather was that it was great for a sunset BBQ. At this time of year, in the late afternoon, when Mt Cavanagh went out and got a killer, they had a BBQ for the rib-bones. The rest of the meat was a little too fresh to eat, but the rib-bones tasted great. We had just got the BBQ going well when a car pulled into the station (a half-mile or so off the highway) *"wonder if you know where there is a policeman? ... a car has rolled over about 35 mile south,* (in South Australia), *there are three people hurt, in fact one of the injured, a woman, is still partly stuck under the car ... she is in a pretty bad way!"*

It was getting dark and short wave radio reception was always difficult at this time of day. We tried to contact the Flying Doctor base without success, we blew the whistle, listened, called, but no response. So Dave and Mona Major from Mt Cavanagh and a couple of the others headed for the crash site. I headed for Victory Downs to try to get through on the radio telephone they had. If that was unsuccessful, then I would go back to Kulgera and try the police network. As it turned out, I was able to get through to the Alice Springs hospital and arrange dispatch of an ambulance, even that would take a good four hours, in all probability, longer, to reach us.

Just as I had that arranged, the officer-in-charge of police at Oodnadatta, South Australia, Sergeant Lloyd Bevan, Constable Romans and Cadet Constable Aitkin arrived in their Landrover with eight aboriginal prisoners on board, along with a couple of kangaroos they had shot on the road, to take back as some bush tucker for their prisoners. They had been on a patrol to Musgrave Park, in the North West South Australian Aboriginal Reserve. The best access to and from the reserve was through the Northern Territory and although they had patrolled through other South Australian localities to reach Musgrave Park, the quickest way back to Oodnadatta was to come into the Territory west of Victory Downs, travel that access road east to the Stuart Highway and head south into South Australia.

So in convoy we headed for the crash site. We had crossed into South Australia when we met Dave and Mona Major bringing the crash victims back to Mt Cavanagh. We then realised that one of the passengers in the car, Janet Shelton, 23, of Darwin, who had been partly crushed in the roll-over, had died. Although the young police cadet applied mouth-to-mouth resuscitation for some time, there was no response.

We all went back to Mt Cavanagh to wait for the ambulance. My reaction was to take the body on to Alice Springs but Sergeant Bevan wouldn't have it ... *"we have just had a recent directive that all road accident victims have to be submitted to post-mortem; I have to take the body for post-mortem."* he insisted. *"Well, I can arrange that in Alice Springs for you"* I said. *"No, she died in South Australia, I have to keep the body in South Australian jurisdiction"* (although at this moment the body was in the NT) he responded. Of course, the problem was, how was he going to get the body to Oodnadatta? He had eight prisoners (and the kangaroos) not to mention the three police crammed in the front of the Landrover. It became obvious I would have to take the body to Oodnadatta but before I could do that, I should gain permission from my Divisional Inspector.

Constable Romans tried to activate the South Australia Police radio system, which had a large extension whip aerial. The idea was to contact Port Augusta or another SA base station and get them to phone through to Alice Springs and get the authority. As much as they tried, things became more muddled than ever as the radio message got garbled and confused. They made contact with Mount Gambier, in the lower south-east of South Australia and before we knew it

Mount Gambier had the 'story' that the Oodnadatta police vehicle, with eight prisoners on board, had rolled over and they had all been killed! I went back to Kulgera and again struck trouble; Alice Springs could understand that I was requesting permission to travel to Oodnadatta but they could not pick up why. In the finish, in exasperation, they replied *"The Inspector says if you need to go, then go and we will sort out the details tomorrow".*

I had a little sleep, some breakfast and then left Kulgera at 7am for Oodnadatta. The police cadet came with me. We got to Oodnadatta at 12.30pm. It was 113F (45C). There were no mortuary facilities at Oodnadatta and the best that could be arranged was the use of a fly-wired meat house like a large scale Coolgardie safe. I spoke with Alice Springs by phone and cleared up what had happened, then stayed the night and went back to Kulgera next morning. It was a good 250 miles (400kms) trip, again in stifling heat.

Ironically, later that day the Alice Springs undertaker, Jack Maskell, took a chartered plane to Oodnadatta and collected the body. As far as I know, a post-mortem was never undertaken. I was angry and upset that the young woman had been treated in such a way. It was a typical border power-struggle bureaucratic stuff-up where common sense, and decency and dignity failed to prevail.

I had yet another trip to Ayers Rock to execute a few debtors warrants and with one eye continually on the weather, generally prepared for the return of the new officer-in-charge at Kulgera. I got a couple of the store's "helps", Mavis and Kitty, over to clean out the house, and had everything in place for the handover-takeover. The Symonds got back to Kulgera without trouble but in the finish, I couldn't leave for a couple of days after the handover as the road was impassable to my conventional drive car.

I only had to work four nights before starting leave myself. This included 28 February, the third anniversary of my joining the Force. I could not only look forward to leave, but also a $1 a week pay increase. It also qualified me to sit for the Sergeant Third Class promotional examinations which were advertised to be held in July. I lodged my application to sit for the exams with the resolve I would get stuck into study when I returned from leave.

Giles Waterhole on the Northern
Territory/Western Australia border

Mum, Mrs Daphne Pollock, at the
Northern Territory/South Australian
border, Stuart Highway, south of Kulgera

Entrance to the Anthony Lagoon residence and police station

CHAPTER 12

I finally get to Anthony Lagoon

In Melbourne there had been a long-running locally produced television programme on HSV-7 called *"Tell the Truth"*. There was a panel of three personalities and three characters, one playing him/herself and the other two claiming the same identity. The three would be questioned by the panel of personalities, then the personalities were asked to identify who was telling the truth ... *would the real ... stand up"* with all three making a few shuffles before the real character stood up. There were a few dollars for the real person plus a few extra dollars for each mis-identification. When I was still working at Wonthaggi I sent in an application to participate in the show, goodness knows why, but I did. I heard nothing of it until one day a brown envelope, re-addressed in Mrs Featherston's writing, (my land-lady at Wonthaggi) arrived in the mail at Kulgera.

It was from the producers of the show asking me to contact them to participate as a "blind" in a forthcoming programme. I wrote back and explained my present situation, more than three years after I'd originally applied. However, I mentioned I expected to be coming down on leave in March-April and if they wanted to contact me, they could at my parent's address.

Soon after I arrived home on leave they did contact me, not to play the part of a "blind" but to be the truthful one! So one Saturday afternoon I went into the HSV-7 studios in South Melbourne, was briefed about the show, had half an hour or so with the two young fellows playing the "blinds", had the make-up applied and the show was recorded.

We didn't do a very good job. Well perhaps it was the other two who didn't do a good job, as all three panellists correctly identified me! I didn't get to see the show on TV as it was recorded and shown some weeks later. The folks of course watched closely and said it went well, despite our poor showing of deception. Of course virtually nobody from the Territory saw the show except one Alice Springs chap, Tom Cole, the Works department bore foreman was in Melbourne on holidays. He watched and was able to tell his grandchildren just who the real David Pollock was!

It was an uneventful trip back to Alice Springs at the end of leave, which seemed to pass ever so quickly. I'd only been on duty a few hours when I was told that next day I was to accompany the District Welfare Officer, Jack Cooke, to Docker River to assist in investigating a report that prospectors operating in Western Australia had unlawfully crossed into the Northern Territory's Petermann Reserve and carried out illegal prospecting, interfereing with aboriginal sacred or tribal sites.

Welfare branch had a charter flight organised to fly us the 300 miles (480kms) to Docker. The manager had changed but many of the aboriginals who had been there when I visited from Kulgera were still there. They were quite upset that some of "their land" had been travelled by a team of prospectors, chipping away at rocks here and there and interfering with several aboriginal tribal or sacred sites along the way. This had in part been made worse by the aboriginals themselves having recently travelled some of the land and dug from traditional custody spots to retrieve, then rebury sacred stones. The prospectors seeing the fresh digging, had inquisitively dug the spot to see what was there. What made it worse was, on at least one occasion, they had swung the prospecting hammer into a sacred stone, chipping it, which caused considerable offence.

Some of the prospecting party was still at Docker River, waiting for another charter to arrive and fly them out, which gave me the opportunity to speak with them. It became pretty clear that the prospecting party leaders at least knew they were quite unlawfully in the Northern Territory and had absolutely no right to be prospecting in the area. The problem for them was not only that they found nothing of interest but they got found out.

For me the best part of the trip was to travel along the Gunbarrel Highway into Western Australia to the junction of the road, well, track really, leading back into the Territory and the headwaters of the Giles Creek – the Giles water hole, discovered in the 1870's by pioneer explorer Ernest Giles. His mark of the water level and his presence at the hole was still distinguishable on the rock face.

When we arrived at the freshly abandoned campsite it was obvious the prospecting party had been camped there for days. There was also plenty of evidence of prospecting around the area, the keen eye of the aboriginals with us could show us many an example. Nearby there was also a freshly dug mine shaft 6ft x 4ft and 10 feet deep, a couple of outcrops of freshly blasted rock plus innumerable vehicle tracks.

We ventured further to a rocky outcrop where the aboriginals stored their most sacred "churingas", their "land titles". Unlike the churingas I had seen around Alice Springs, the ones here were not made of stone but wood, six to eight inches (15-20cm) wide and perhaps eight to 10 feet (3m) long.

We went to the location to check and ensure that the churingas had not been interfered with or stolen. They had been used in recent weeks in ceremonial activities and there was a real fear amongst some of the aboriginals that they might have been stolen. The churingas were stored in a cleft in the rock, with the entrance to their hiding place camouflaged. I felt not only honoured to be shown the churingas but also to be allowed to photograph them. Fortunately, the churingas had not been interfered with or damaged. We ended up camping out the night before getting back to Docker River in time for the weekly supply plane arrival, and a ride back to Alice Springs.

It was a real hitch-hike job by air back to The Alice. The supply plane only had the pilot and front passenger seat, the rest of the cabin of the single engine plane having been cleared out for perishable goods. Of course, Jack Cooke took the seat and I had to sit on the floor of the plane. I had a seat belt of sorts but it was a hard seat. In one respect, to make it worse, we had to stop at Ayers Rock on the way back to take on fuel, but at least that gave me the opportunity to stretch my legs.

A week or so later I got to interview the leader of the prospecting party, when he was passing through Alice Springs. I ended up proceeding by summons against him for being unlawfully on an aboriginal reserve and in turn he got fined the grand sum of $10.

I was back only a few days when I got a "please explain" from headquarters, through the officer-in- charge as to why my name was on a list of unregistered motor vehicles issued by the Registrar of Motor Vehicles. Fortunately, I had the papers to show I had re-registered the vehicle two weeks before it was due for renewal. When the next list appeared, it had both the officer-in-charge of the traffic section and the officer-in-charge of the station on the list, showing up that the registrar's list wasn't that reliable. I don't recall receiving an apology from headquarters either.

The next few weeks were fairly routine, on day shift I usually ended up court orderly. This could be quite interesting, even entertaining, when orderly at the Supreme Court listening to workers compensation claims. I recall one matter was centred around a motor on a concrete mixer which back-fired when a man was attempting to start it. He hurt his thumb and could no longer do his same job as his hand hurts every time he tried!

I had a few licensing applications for stores or merchants to handle and the routine run of enquires, service of interstate summonses and the like. The "boss" knew they wouldn't last long in my folder. There were the usual incidents on evening shift, an assault or two in the beer garden of the Hotel Alice Springs and on night shift, the normal "Miss Pink" calls about people shooting on her reserve or dogs barking! Another night we had some concern when a woman rang to say someone was shooting a purple ray gun on her bedroom wall complete with smoke haze. We advised her to go back to bed and have a good sleep, hoping like hell she wasn't going to develop into another Miss Pink. Fortunately, we never heard from her again.

I also got out on another mission patrol which had become more frequent for a couple of reasons. First, we had a few more men in The Alice, and second, there was a need to 'show the flag' more around the aboriginal communities.

I lashed out and bought a new stereogram and moved rooms at the barracks, into a bigger room, to enjoy its sound better. I easily sold my old player through the tracker to see out the rest of its days playing Slim Dusty records.

Night shift didn't escape me before the promotional exams and my next relief job. It not only disrupted my studies but it turned out quite a hectic shift over the Alice Springs Show weekend (a holiday on the Friday) plus there was word of an attempted gaol break at the prison over the weekend. To add to that, I was working the night shift with a fairly new recruit, not the brightest of the bunch, young Stan, who had come to the force from a stock camp. Apart from having a pretty full cell block (126 prisoners for the weekend including 63 on Friday night) the tip about trouble at the prison meant a half-hourly patrol of the area. To add to that drama, an off-duty member came to the station to say he had just noticed a car parked in the side street beside the gaol. He recalled seeing the car some time earlier over the weekend with a couple of "louts in it". So a quick trip to check out the vehicle revealed the two "louts" in the car were railway employees from one of the ganger camps along the line, in town for the weekend, who thought they had found a quiet spot to stop and sleep. It also turned out one of the lads was the son of a policeman at Belgrave, at the station opposite where my parents lived!

Next night, Sunday, or actually the early hours of Monday morning, when things were generally quiet, Stan "the Ringer" went out on the first patrol. An hour later he came back and said there was something suspicious on the doorstep of the local electrical mechanic, perhaps the place had been broken into. So I went to have a look. Yes, it was unusual, but everything seemed in order at the premises. As it transpired, the owners had left a piece of machinery on the front door step for someone to collect later in the morning as they left for the bush ... that's how trusting Centralians were. But the excitement did not end there. As I drove back from the north east corner of town, across the streets to the south I could see what first I thought was a fog ... or was it? A few moments later I had tracked the "fog" to smoke coming from the dining room of the La Tosca Restaurant in Hartley Street. The fire brigade was called but the inside of the building was completely gutted. The fire had obviously been burning an hour or so, it was at flash-point when the brigade arrived. The boss was quite pleased that a patrolling policeman *"had seen something".*

Late June and into July I got stuck into the study for the Sergeant Third Class exams. There were nearly 30 sitting for the exam, many for the second, even third or fourth time, no doubt spurred on by the fact that with the expansion of the force, there were nine immediate vacancies in the rank. A promotion was worth an extra $1,200pa, better than a yearly increment of $50 for a constable. Some were sitting for only one section of the exams, a pass in either of the two sections carried forward for two further exams, so if you passed the written at one attempt, you could just sit for the practical the next time around, or vice-versa. However, the first time you sat, you were required to sit for all parts of the exam. There were four of us in barracks planning to sit for the exam, but in the end I think only three of us did – Bob Henfry, Bruce Wyatt and myself. We had the use of past exam papers as a guide to the likely questions, but really, the questions could come from anywhere, especially as this year the exam papers were being set by someone new – Sergeant First Class Cronshaw who had been my recruit school instructor.

There were three exam papers. First up was the written (law) examination of three hours, on the morning of the first day, in all nine questions ranging from treason under the Crimes Act to the provisions of the Traffic Ordinance on dipping of headlights. Prostitutes, unlawful games, auctions, neglected children, dogs and firearms all got a mention in questions.

The written (practical) examination was in two parts, first an education paper of two hours in the afternoon of the first day, this time eight questions ranging from a 250 word essay on either "Moral Standards in 1969" or "Statehood for the Northern Territory" to mathematical questions, correct meanings of words and a precis of an article, in all for 80 marks.

The third paper, on the second morning, was the second half of the practical exam, a three hour general paper with 11 questions for 100 marks. A percentage was then taken of the combined papers to reach a pass which had to be 60%. As indicated in its name, the questions in this paper were about day-to-day practical matters, some common, others not so common, such as instructions to police under the standing orders surrounding boxing contests, mistaken arrest, nomination and appointment of justices of the peace, police messages on the police radio network and with payment of accounts by valueless cheque. Legislative questions surrounded the difference between "dying declarations" and "dying depositions", powers of entry and seizure under the Brands Ordinance, exemptions for a hawker's licence and unroadworthy motor vehicles. A gift question for me was a question *"Detail the obligations of the incoming officer-in-charge under the standing order on handover/takeover of police stations"*. As well, the question was worth 14 marks, more than any other question in the paper.

I hardly had time to dwell on the exams, compare notes and say to myself *"why didn't I think of that?"* On past performance it would be a month, even two months, before the results would be published, so there was no point worrying about anything now. I had to pack and ready for my next relief – Anthony Lagoon.

It was a two-day trip to Anthony Lagoon, in the centre of the Barkly Tablelands. On the Friday I drove north to Tennant Creek where I stayed overnight. I took the opportunity to go to the movies, the open air theatre, and being July it was still cool at night. I saw *"Guess who's coming to Dinner?"* and really enjoyed it. For some reason, it is a movie that always stuck in my mind. Next morning, just as I was getting ready to leave, my folks rang to say "hello" before I headed out bush. After all, there was no telephone within a hundred miles of Anthony Lagoon. There was the last minute perishable shopping before the 15 miles (24kms) drive north to Threeways, then east along the Barkly Highway for 116 miles (185kms) to the "Beef Road", another 137 miles (220kms) north to the Anthony Lagoon turn-off and seven miles (11kms) of dirt road across a black soil plain to the station.

I really looked forward to going to Anthony Lagoon, there was something about the place and the tablelands. I'd seen it marked on maps when I first became interested in joining the force, I'd seen the "town" of Anthony Lagoon in the film *"The Sundowners",* my first shift sergeant in Alice Springs, George Simpson, had worked at Anthony Lagoon before being promoted and transferred to The Alice, the former Divisional Inspector, Greg Ryall, had worked there too in his younger days as a constable. And of course, there was the chance I was going to Anthony Lagoon to relieve back in early 1967, in my probationary days.

The Barkly Tablelands was basically flat country with wide open grassy plains and short scrubby areas. It was black soil country which made it practically impassable in wet weather. I arrived in the midst of the dry season, just as the weather was getting warmer. Already the days were in the low 90's (32-34C). The past wet season had basically failed which made the whole area dry, needing stock reductions and in some cases, supplementary feeding, like molasses, which was taken around in tanker trailers and left in feeders at watering holes. There was good underground water but it had to be pumped. This meant virtual daily rounds of the bores/waters to make sure the windmills were working, the troughs had not been damaged and the water wasted, that stock had not become bogged and so on, keeping the staff at the cattle station busy as they also tried to muster, brand and 'mark' young cattle, and send a few truck loads away to the meatworks. At least there was usually plenty of wind on the Tablelands to keep the windmills working.

There was no town at Anthony Lagoon, just the police complex and half a mile (800m) or so further to the north, the Anthony Lagoon station homestead and associated station buildings. There was a large lagoon, a few hundred yards wide and a good mile (1.6km) or so long at this time of year. There were about 10 whites and 50 odd aboriginals at the cattle station. It was a company owned station, an Australian Pastoral Co property with a resident manager who had been at the property about 6 months.

The police station and residence were quite old, they had been at the location many years, but the building was well maintained and quite comfortable. There was a good lighting plant with both 240v power and 32v lights with a good bank of batteries, a combustion stove, hot water service, sewerage and tank water for drinking. There was a windmill to supply other water pumped from the Lagoon, about 500 yards (150m) to the west. The house had a well enclosed verandah around more than three quarters of the living area. The yard was well fenced with a nice front gate and path which came to the police station office entrance as well as the house entrance. The police station office was its rugged self, a painted concrete floor with a 16-18 inch (40-45cm) diameter tree stump, cut off at floor level, also painted over green, a centre piece. The tracker's quarters were to the back of the complex, basically corrugated iron with concrete floors with cooking facilities and showers. They were really quite big as some years earlier, when there was an active horse plant at the station, there had been two trackers.

Again, after my arrival at Anthony Lagoon, there was time for a cuppa, some late lunch, and the chance to catch up on the police gossip before we got into the work of the handover-takeover. There was hardly time to show me around, give me the drum on all the local happenings and get settled in. Basil "Bluey" Smith was a Constable First Class, he had been in the Force 10-12 years, a gruff and good hearted guy. Unfortunately, he did not get along with the cattle station manager, a Mr Stewart, not that anyone else in the district did either. It made life that bit harder not to have good relations with your closest neighbour. Mind you, the fault was probably as much with the station manager who appeared quite an anti-social character. In the three months at Anthony Lagoon, only once was I invited into the station homestead. It was for afternoon tea with him, his wife and the matronly bookkeeper, cum companion for the wife. Even then I had to "sing for my supper". They presented me with a batch of motor vehicle re-registrations. I could have been a real bastard and knocked the vehicles back on some technical unroadworthiness, but in the long run, I didn't think that would do me any good. It didn't do me any good either attending to the matters efficiently!

Before Sunday was out we had everything attended to, the handover complete, a run down on how the district ticked, what to do *"if so and so ... happens while I am away"*, leaving "Bluey" time for some last minute packing. His plan was to leave at dawn next morning, and they did.

The tracker was Dashwood. He and his wife, Salad, had four children. They were a happy family and were staying while their "boss" was on leave. Again, I had a dog to look after, along with two caged finches. There were fowls, thus plenty of fresh eggs, the remains of a vegetable garden (from which I got some fresh peas before the bush rats did) and the goats ... yes, a herd of more than 150 or so goats of all shapes, sizes and colours. They were kept yarded at night but by day they roamed the open land around the station, returning by themselves at sundown. It was one of Dashwood's main tasks to look after the goats and each morning, before releasing them, to milk enough to get about a gallon of milk, most of which he and his family got to use. With so many goats, there were always kids, and it seemed more so than ever at this time of the year. They were kept yarded all day so that they didn't get tired out walking during the day, become weak and be a target for dingoes. When a drover coming through a few days later dropped off a calf abandoned by its mother, we yarded it too in the goat yard, and fed it goat's milk.

The goats were not just handy for milk. They were a meat supply too, not that I was fond of goat meat but Dashwood and his family enjoyed it. Often we would sell one to a Works department gang operating in the area; they would cook it up, as if it was lamb. Each time I went into Tennant Creek, Dashwood would kill two or three and pack them into a couple of Esky boxes. There the station sergeant would use the meat for prisoner's meals. I don't remember cooking goat at all at Anthony's, I had too good a supply of beef. "Cookie" at nearby Brunette Downs always made sure I left there on my weekly visit with some steak, a roll roast of beef and some fresh bread.

The season had brought a plague of bush rats and although they were not so bad yet around Anthony Lagoon at Brunette Downs the rats were everywhere. They were so bad that at the stock camps they had to get steel framed, wire mattress beds to lift the ringers' swags off the ground so that the rats could not get into the swags, or as they had on more than one occasion during the night, bitten a piece out of someone's nose! However, the real danger of the area was snakes . . . king brown snakes. Not only were they highly venomous, they were usually big, 5-6 feet plus (1.25-1.85m) with a reputation of "having a go" ... they would stand up and fight! At night you just would not walk outside without a torch for fear of standing on one. The result would have been a bite and an uncertain prospect of seeing the next morning.

George Simpson always told the story of his days at Anthony Lagoon when at New Year, as the wet season began, thinking of not just his three children at the time but also the tracker's, he decided to see how long it would take him to kill 100 snakes. He had the two trackers rake the yard and surrounds, then each morning they would trace the fresh snake tracks until they found and killed the snake. He said it took him only 20 odd days to reach the 100. Of course, as the wet season set in, the lagoon to the west of the station, would start to rise. As it rose, the water forced the snakes to higher ground with the station buildings being right in the path of the snakes from the lagoon to the highest ground.

Brunette Downs station was 60 miles (100kms) to the south, seven miles (10kms) out to the Beef Road, 50 odd miles (80kms) along the bitumen and then three-four miles (5-6kms) into the homestead. The busiest part of being at Anthony Lagoon was servicing Brunette Downs station. There was a real community there. It was a King Ranch property of 4,730 square miles (12,250 sq kms), near double the size of Anthony Lagoon, 2,416 square miles (6,257 sq kms). Brunette was intensely managed, well stocked, and carried better than average blood-lines of bulls. Writing home after my first visit I described it as the *"most modern, well set up and equipped cattle station I have seen"*. The manager was a Mr Ray Green who lived with his family in the homestead.

Then there were guest houses, homes for all the married staff, the jackaroos' quarters and office block with the dinning area and cookhouse, plus the single men's quarters. There were about 20 in the single men's quarters and a dozen or so in the jackaroos' quarters. There was a substantial general store and of course all the associated building like garages, workshops and so on.

I made a patrol to Brunette Downs at least once a week, usually on a Thursday, arriving before lunch and staying through until after afternoon smoko. They operated on Eastern Standard Time, half an hour ahead of Central Standard Time as did most of the cattle stations between Brunette and the Queensland border. They also looked after the local policeman. I remember the first time I visited, I was hardly out of the vehicle before someone was standing there to welcome me and invite me to stay for lunch. I ate with the staff, that is the overseer, the accountant and the pilot and other staff single officers. Those accommodated in the single men's quarters, if in residence at the station, ate in an adjoining dining room.

On my first visit to Brunette Downs I found a couple of hawkers there. There were two or three who regularly worked the Barkly Tablelands selling everything from clothing to pots and pans, usually not groceries, but general everyday items. It was amazing what they could pack into their van and how they could set up and display their wares wherever they went. Of course, hawkers were licensed – or at least supposed to be. A good way of spreading the word that there was a new copper in the district was to visit the hawker and ask to inspect his licence, which I did. It was the first time they had their licences checked for some time and it also looked good in my weekly journal report back to the Divisional Inspector.

Brunette Downs was a hive of activity getting ready for a Royal Visit. The Duke and Duchess of Kent were to stay a night during their official visit to the Northern Territory. After spending a few days in Darwin, the couple were to fly by RAAF VIP aircraft, a prop-jet HS 748, to Brunette Downs arriving late one afternoon, and remaining until after lunch the next day before flying on to Alice Springs. This allowed the tour organisers the time to get the VIP fleet of motor vehicles, like the Rolls Royce, from Darwin to Alice Springs. As soon as the couple had boarded their plane in Darwin, the vehicles set out on the 950 miles (1,500kms) trip to The Alice to be ready there in time for their arrival next afternoon.

There were painters, carpenters and plumbers all getting everything spic and span. Even the yards of the stud bulls were getting a coat of paint. The biggest problem was the bush rat plague. In what seemed a futile effort every night for a couple of weeks special traps were rigged up. The base was half a 44-gal. drum with a plank running from the ground to the edge of the drum. At that point there was a wire across the drum on which was a large tin, like a Sunshine powered milk tin. It revolved freely on the wire. Meat fat, dripping or something the rat might like to eat was smothered on the tin so that when the rat attempted to get from the plank on the edge of the drum across to the rolling tin, the rat would fall into the drum which was half full of water, and thus the rat would drown. Hundreds of bush rats a night were caught in the lead-up to the visit.

Back at Anthony Lagoon, my regular contact with the cattle station was on Fridays ... mail day ... when the mail plane came in from Mt Isa. I would pick up the station bookkeeper and take her to the airstrip, wait for the plane, pick up the mail and any freight and then return. I even arranged for the Brisbane *"Courier Mail"* and the *"Sunday Mail"* to be sent to me from the newsagent in Mt Isa as getting Melbourne papers was out of the question. It was not only the cost but by the time I'd get the paper, the news would be history. The Connair flight was pretty regular but the mail did take that bit extra, all having to go through Mt Isa. There was a weekly each-way TAA flight through Brunette Downs from Mt Isa to Tennant Creek so if anyone was going through and could drop off mail to be posted at Brunette Downs for the Monday morning flight, it was a good back-up.

I'd been at Anthony Lagoon a week. I was back into the routine of the radio sched times, after all, at Anthony Lagoon, it was only two a day – 9am and 3pm, except Sundays it was 10am. I also had radio contact with the Royal Flying Doctor Service for telegrams. On the Saturday morning I forgot to check the RFDS traffic list so failed to hear there was a telegram waiting for me, so it was the next morning, Sunday, before Bob Henfry came on the 10am sched to tell me I'd passed my Sergeant Third Class exams. To everyone's surprise the results were out in little over a week. I was floating on air. Although I'd been happy with my effort and quietly confident I was still surprised with the result. I gained 66 per cent for the written section and 63 for the practical section, good pass marks. Bob had also passed gaining percentages of 74 and 63. We were the only two of the seven to pass both sections, and what's more, at our first attempt. I was the only one from my recruit school to pass although one chap, Chris Crellin, by now the plain clothes constable at Tennant Creek, gained a pass in the written section.

Bruce Wyatt gained a pass in the practical section while Norm Wright and Colin Eckert were amongst those to also pass the written section. One of those to pass was Constable M. J. (Mick) Palmer, who had a 1967 credit for the written section and gained 78 for the practical section. Mick went on to become Commissioner of the Northern Territory Police and later Commissioner of the Australian Federal Police.

The telegram that was waiting for me, which I went on to receive on Monday morning, was congratulations from George Simpson, now in Darwin. He recalled he was at Anthony Lagoon when he passed the exams and went on to be promoted out of the station. First there were all sorts of rumours and stories that I would be pulled out of Anthony Lagoon and moved into a position although it would be more than 6 months before I was eligible to be promoted. They might even have another set of exams in that time, and anyone senior to me gaining a pass, could jump over me. Even a fortnight later, when the Duke and Duchess of Kent came to stay-over at Brunette Downs, in my District, I was not the senior man. That was something Constable First Class Harry Cox, officer-in-charge at Avon Downs, on the Barkly Highway near the Northern Territory-Queensland border, who came over to assist, could not help himself but to tell me. He was probably 10 years senior in service to me. I knew that. I didn't need reminding. But then I also knew that in six months time, when I was promoted, I would become senior to him.

You never knew what the mail bag was going to bring. One day there was a warrant for payment, or arrest in default, for an unpaid City of Sydney parking fine, the defendant's last known address being Long Bay Gaol but now understood to be employed at Mallapunyah Springs cattle station, 80 odd miles (130kms) to the north. Mallapunyah Springs was run by the Darcy family, half a dozen or so brothers, bred rough and tough, with a reputation across the whole district. You didn't mix it with the Darcy boys; you might knock down one but there were three or four more behind him. I set off to Mallapunyah with the thought of getting there just before lunch, getting the matter fixed as I only had to collect $10-$15, and coming home again. What I didn't take account of was they also worked on Eastern Standard Time, so when I pulled up at the home, a large, double storey place, they had all just sat down for lunch.

I was met at the vehicle by one of "the boys". I hardly had time to introduce myself, let alone explain the reason for my visit before I was escorted into the dining room, given a place at the table and invited to join in lunch. No introductions, hardly a word, just a plate, knife and fork and into the fresh damper,

Barkly Stock Route, near Brunette Downs

"My" goat herd at Anthony Lagoon

The Duke of Kent films the marking and branding of young cattle at Brunette Downs

cold meat and whatever else was on offer for lunch. There must have been 20 of the family sitting around the long rectangular table. The meal over, a cuppa, and then time for business. Yes, the guy I wanted was working at the station. He quickly came up with the cash to settle the warrant *"but please don't tell them where I've been!"*. He didn't seem a bad sort of bloke, he was able to settle the warrant, he had a job, I knew where he was and I left it at that. It was one of the strangest cattle station visits I made the whole time I was in the force.

One thing the trip did was shake up the vehicle a little, causing a petrol leak between the two tanks under the seats in the main cabin. Not only were the fumes a worry but there was the risk of fire also. With the Royal Visit coming up, a quick word on the radio to the Inspector and it was into Tennant Creek to get the problem fixed and a good vehicle service, completed. While there I got the chance to go on a gold escort, accompanying officers from the ANZ Bank out to Peko Mine, witnessing the gold pour, the weighing (1,000 oz ingot, worth about $40,000 at the time) and escorting it back to the bank. Later we would escort the "gold box" from the bank to the airport and witness its loading onto the aircraft, bound for the Perth Mint. The strange thing was, once on the aircraft, the gold went unescorted.

When returning to Anthony's on the Saturday morning, I was asked if I would take with me a blind aboriginal woman who had been in Tennant Creek hospital but was now well and needed to be returned to her community family at Anthony Lagoon. At least I had company but she was not a talker. I also returned to Anthony Lagoon through one of the other cattle stations in my district, Rockhampton Downs, calling in to attend to some routine matters. From there the road to Anthony Lagoon wasn't signposted, I'd been given a mud map of the route and had to hope for the best ... a real case of the blind leading the blind . . . but we made it safely and there was a happy reunion on our arrival at Anthony Lagoon.

———>•◦•<———

The Royal Visit to Brunette Downs was pretty straight forward. Apart from Harry Cox coming over from Avon Downs to assist, young Constable Paul Kauter, stationed at Borroloola, to my north, also came for the visit. The three of us were told to keep things low-key.

For the arrival of the VIP aircraft, the fire trailer was hooked up to one of the police vehicles and two of us had to man the unit! As the aircraft didn't stay overnight, we didn't have to guard it; we could just keep in the background "in case". The Duke and Duchess were accompanied by their aides and a couple of protocol officials from Government House, along with a detective from New Scotland Yard, Inspector David Coleman. David's normal job was body guard to Princess Anne but he was taking a break and had been sent on the tour with the Duke and Duchess. He spent quite a bit of his time talking with us and exchanging police stories as policemen do when they get together. His visit to Australia so impressed him that when Princess Anne married in late 1973 he resigned his position as her personal bodyguard and migrated to Australia, taking up a job as an inspector for the Royal Queensland Society for the Prevention of Cruelty to Animals. Sadly, a few years later he was stricken with cancer and died.

We stayed the night at Brunette at the single men's/jackaroos' quarters. Next morning Paul and I went along with the entourage that went to the stock camp and watched the young cattle being branded. Both the Duke and the Duchess had a try at bringing a young beast, roped, to the crush. The Duke rode his horse unaided but someone led the horse that the Duchess chose to ride as she brought her beast to the crush. I kept my fingers crossed as one of the ringers said quietly *"last time I got on that horse it threw me off"*. The next day there was a photo in the Melbourne *"Sun"* captioned *"A ride in the dusty north"* with Ray Green, the station manager, holding a horse before the Duchess had a short ride. *"The picture shows a stockman . . . ".* Stockman indeed!

The Duke remarked that Harry Cox was *"the biggest policeman I've ever seen"*. Well, Harry was a good 6ft plus and how many stone, I dared not ask a senior member! The visitors less than 24 hour visit to Brunette soon came to an end, but before it did, the Duke and Duchess asked to meet the three of us, and to personally thank us for our work. So we "paraded" near the aircraft as they readied to board, shook hands with them both and then took up our fire drill positions ready for take-off.

Another event came up soon after – the Borroloola races. Borroloola was 185 miles (300kms) to the north of Anthony Lagoon, through Mallapunyah Springs and McArthur River stations and then toward the Gulf of Carpentaria. The Borroloola township was near the bar of the McArthur River. This was not only a vehicle crossing place in the dry season but also the point where the tidal influence, about 80 miles (130kms) upstream from the Gulf, ceased. The local community had resurrected the annual Borroloola Picnic Races with a sports day on the Sunday so I was sent north to help out.

The Borroloola police station was still a temporary facility, two large shiny aluminium covered caravans, 10-12 feet (3-3.6m) wide and about 30 feet (9m) long, one the officer's home, the other serving as office, lock-up and storeroom. I drove up on the Saturday morning, leaving Anthony Lagoon about 7.45am for a good four hour drive, only 10 miles (16kms) of bitumen, then some secondary road before meeting the Daly River-Borroloola Beef Road, another good road, but still unsealed from the Barkly junction.

There were four police in attendance; Constable John Francis based at Wollogorang, on the NT/Qld border close to the Gulf, Constable Dave Swift from Daly Waters, Paul Kauter and myself. There was a good crowd, the best part of 500, and even better still, a well behaved crowd. At one stage there were nine light aircraft on the airstrip at Borroloola, many flying in from Darwin, Katherine and even Alice Springs. The Northern Territory *"News"* had a reporter there and even an Assistant Administrator was in attendance. He stopped me, introduced himself and had a five minute talk.

Over the whole weekend we only had three arrests for drunkenness one of them was from Brunette Downs. We bailed the three, the two we felt sure would not turn up, for $5 cash bail, to a court at Brunette Downs on the Tuesday morning. There were two Justice of the Peace at Brunette Downs, which made that job simple. On the whole the organisers, and in particular the pub, were pretty pleased with the crowd, not just for the races on the Saturday but also the sports day on the Sunday as well.

There were eight races including a race for women jockeys, and like Renner Springs, two bookmakers, more interested in betting on Sydney and Melbourne races than on the local hacks. The races were followed by a big BBQ at the Borroloola Inn, which I believe went to near dawn. There was no doubt the odd game of "two-up" and other gaming activities common at such bush gatherings were carried on somewhere. The main thing was if you didn't see it, you didn't know about it, and it was the last thing I wanted to know about. It went a bit against my grain, but that was part of a bush race meeting. I called it a day about 1am on Sunday morning; it had been a pretty full day.

The morning twilight was shattered by the husband of one of the women we had arrested for drunkenness arriving, himself intoxicated, to bail her out. We hunted him but at 7am got up to provide the three prisoners with break-fast. Then we fingerprinted and bailed them before we had some breakfast ourselves. If we thought we were in for a quiet Sunday morning our thoughts were soon upset. About 8am the local Welfare officer arrived to report two deaths in the native camp, a combination of old age, ill health and a flu epidemic which had hit the local aboriginal community quite severely. Before we could start to make arrangements for these two, another aboriginal arrived from the native camp to tell of a third death in the same circumstances.

There wasn't a resident Justice of the Peace, who could act as a deputy Coroner, at Borroloola but I remembered that one of the chaps on the light aircraft from Alice Springs was Mr Len Kittle, a Justice of the Peace who regularly "sat" when the magistrate was out of town. We caught up with him a few minutes before he was to fly out. Yes, he would sign the Authority to Bury documents but he would like to view the bodies to assure himself there had been no violence and that the deaths at least appeared natural. So we quickly escorted him to the aboriginal village and the death beds of each of the three victims. He was satisfied there were no suspicious circumstances and signed the authorities, then flew out.

Some from the aboriginal camp proceeded to the burial grounds, a couple of miles downstream of the township, on a high bank of the river, to prepare the graves. Others wrapped the bodies in their swags and we took them to the river where we loaded them in two aluminium boats and with a missionary and two of his linguist assistants, we took them to the burial ground. It was a moving sight, looking down the water of a magnificent river, overhung by trees, the water blue and still. At the burial site we pulled to the river bank, lifted the bodies up to the burial ground and lowered them into their graves.

The missionary was a "hell fire and brimstone" character, giving a sermon (more of a lecture) on the evils of intoxicating liquor and its effect on a man's health, an effect which had no doubt, at least in his mind, contributed to the deaths of the three we were burying. He knew the three of them and also knew that only two of them had accepted the Christian faith. For them he gave a joint Christian graveside service. For the third, it was a non-religious service. After all, he could not be buried as a Christian if he had *"not accepted the Faith"*.

During the Saturday evening BBQ at the inn, there was an auction of a rather large trevally fish, freshly caught in the river. It was 25-30lb (11-13.5kgs) in weight and would not quite fit into a bran bag. It was a "Dutch" auction, that is, they started the bidding at a high price – $100 – and came down until someone bid and bought it at the bid price. Well, the price kept on coming down and down, then at $5 I bought it!

The inn kept it chilled for me and on the Monday morning I packed it in a couple of wet bags, and got it back to Anthony Lagoon. I had to take all the shelves out of one of the refrigerators to store the fish overnight. Then on Tuesday morning, when I went down to Brunette Downs to hold court I took it to "Cookie". He prepared it for lunch in several ways – grilled, fried and mornayed. The "big house", and I think even some of the staff houses and the quarters all had fresh fish for lunch, quite a novelty.

It was the first time for 10 years court had been held in the Anthony Lagoon district; the local lass got a lecture for getting drunk at the races; the other two failed to appear and forfeited their $5 bail.

At Anthony Lagoon I was rarely out for dinner. There was no local road-side inn. The closest was a good 150 miles (240kms) away, which also contributed to a lack of any liquor inspired "incidents" in the district. I was never invited to dinner at the cattle station. So I became a little more adventurous with cooking. Sometimes I would do a roll roast of beef, which provided a hot meal, then a nice supply of cold meat for a day or so. I remembered Mum's trick of warming the cold meat in a gravy mix, and that worked too. Fresh potato was a little rare but again the likes of "Deb" whipped up a good substitute. There were no frozen vegetables as although these were available in town, like ice cream, they were more than thawed by the time you got them back to the station. Going to the bother of dry ice and special boxes wasn't worth it for the level of my needs, but there were now "Surprise" peas, again dehydrated but which when soaked and boiled came up well. Even in the bush, I refused to eat tinned peas, the memories of disputes with Mum at the dinner table as a kid still vivid in my mind.

Another significant cattle station in the district was Creswell Downs, about 27 miles (43kms) to the east of Anthony Lagoon. It had recently come under new management, with a new resident manager, Bob Wing, only too happy to invite you in for a cuppa and get the cookhouse to knock up a fresh batch of scones on the odd occasion. Again visits were pretty routine, dogs, firearms and vehicles to be registered. One Saturday just as the RFDS network was closing down, I received a message, could I attend as there had been a death. I arrived to find an aged, frail aboriginal woman had died just as the Flying Doctor aircraft, which had flown a good 450 miles (720kms) from Alice Springs to evacuate her, was landing. They flew back to The Alice. I was left with the job to see to her burial. I had her formally identified to me then wrapped in her swag and we went to the burial site where a grave had been prepared. There were a handful of relations and other aboriginals from the station work force there, I said a few words and we lowered her down and the men back-filled the grave. It made me think *"just what should I say in the circumstances ... police in outback locations are required to assist with burials . . .we have never been told what we should say or given a set of words"* Probably today the situation is the same. Around their campfires later in the day the aboriginals would sing "sorry".

The local cattle stations, except Anthony Lagoon, had regular film/picture nights, usually on a Saturday. The station would have a 16mm projector and have prints of various films flown in for a showing. I had the brain wave to ask the Road Safety Council for a couple of short road safety films, then I could take these along to the film nights and have them shown. Then I could travel to the stations officially in the police vehicle, and take the tracker and his family along. It also broke the loneliness the weekends tended to bring.

Some of the cattle stations also had a practice of registering all their motor vehicles to a common day. They did this at Brunette Downs, where they had more than 30 vehicles, nearly a day's work in itself checking all the paper work let alone casting my mechanical eye over the vehicles. It was a bit of a joke really, here was I, with no real mechanical knowledge "inspecting" vehicles to vouch for their roadworthiness. However, again at Brunette Downs, where they had a full time motor mechanic, they were very professional in their approach and had the motor mechanic check everything before it was submitted for registration. Yes, some of the vehicles would probably never leave the station but they would travel roads within the property and carry people, so there was a need to show some 'duty of care'.

I was about to leave for Brunette Downs for a day of registering vehicles when I got a radio message from Tennant Creek concerning a vehicle which had been left at the Frewena roadhouse, on the Barkly Highway, back in May, when it had broken down. When the owner returned to pick it up, three months later, it was no longer there! I don't recall all the story but for some reason I went to Alroy Downs, about 50 miles (80kms) south of Brunette Downs, and located the car, then went another 25 miles (40kms) out to a stock camp where I found the new "owner", an aboriginal who had "bought" the car for $120. I had a chuckle later in the day when I went back to Brunette Downs and told the vehicle's real owner that I'd located the vehicle and the story as I knew it to that time ... his boss, a fencing contactor, quipped *"that was quick work, they'll make you a Sergeant soon at that rate"* I reported progress to the Tennant Creek CIB and they followed the matter through but proving just who did what and why was going to be a real puzzle.

Meantime at Anthony Lagoon, the number of new baby kids – goats – had run up to 20, with problems with abandoned kids, but at least it kept Dashwood and the family occupied. The fowls were also laying well, with up to a dozen eggs a day. The problem was what to do with them all, as there was a limit to scrambled eggs for a meal. The weather was getting warmer, days constantly about the 100F (38C) mark and even the nights keeping warm. Next the government stocktaker arrived, checking from the lighting plant to the office scales that every piece of government property listed on the inventory was present. His only difficulty was the horses ... there were still horses listed on the inventory ... *"they are out grazing"* ... that's what "Bluey" had told me when I took over. It was good enough for the stocktaker too!

He ended up staying two nights, he was a bit ahead of his schedule, so he went with me on a patrol up to the road works gang a couple of hours north, where I had a few civil debt summons to serve on a couple of workers in the camp. I no sooner got rid of the stocktaker than two Works department chaps arrived, one to fix the windmill, on which the "stop" arm had broken and thus it continually pumped and overflowed the storage tank. This caused a flood across the roadway in front of the police station, not to mention attracting thousands of birds – finches, budgerigars and galahs along with corellas each morning and evening. The other came to "measure up" for a new gas stove and a solar hot water service to replace the slow combustion stove; and for a bank of eight 2,000 gallon (9,000 litres) rain water tanks. The real question now was, would the tanks be installed in time for the wet season or would fate be that the tanks would roll up at the end of the wet season, and most of the water in the current, ageing tanks, be lost in the installation process?. They also planned to tile the floor of the police office; "Bluey" wouldn't know himself!

I did my normal Thursday patrol to Brunette Downs, a routine visit. I had no sooner arrived home than the Brunette Downs station aircraft began to circle the police station, and then flew over to the airstrip to land which could only meant they wanted me. So over to the airstrip I drove to be told that soon after my departure the single men's quarters and the general store had been burnt to the ground. So I went straight back to Brunette Downs. Sure enough, there was only a smouldering remains of the single men's quarters and the general store, while the nearby jackaroos' quarters, office block, dining rooms and kitchen block was pretty paint blistered with many louvres broken from the heat of the flames, which fortunately had been fanned away from the jackeroo quarters block.

Nothing had been saved from the single men's quarters and although quite a lot was got out of the store, there was still a considerable loss of goods. The old safe, which only weeks earlier had held the jewels of the Duchess of Kent during her visit, said to have been worth about half a million dollars, was burnt too. Everything in it had been removed except the storekeeper's gold watch, which he had hidden in there for safe keeping! One of the masts for the radio telephone service had buckled in the heat, thus losing the radio telephone service. There were 19 men in the singlemen's quarters who were left with what they were standing in. Not only did they have to be re-accommodated, arrangements had to be made for clean clothes and new work gear. The fire also threw out the whole electrical supply of the station so there was virtually no power or lighting which made things more difficult.

By the time I had arrived, everyone seemed to be satisfied the fire had started from an electrical fault although the possibility of it starting from a cigarette butt could not be eliminated. The fire had been so intense that the fuse box and the associated wiring had all been well burnt. Although the pole fuse on the pole supplying the building had blown the station electrician was unable to confirm if this was because of an electrical fault when the fire started or as a result of the fire itself. We could come to no other conclusion than that the fire was "electrical". Even the bush rats were being blamed, the thought being they had got into the wall cavity and started to eat the electrical wiring. They were known to eat at electrical wiring on vehicles around the station so there was no reason why they could not have also eaten electrical wiring in the building walls. I spoke with several of those living in the quarters, in particular those who found the fire, and one who had left his room only 10-15 minutes before the fire was discovered in the general vicinity of a power point in the wall of his room. Next day I belted away on the typewriter taking statements.

The personal losses upset a couple of the lads in the quarters, especially one, a young Austrian guy, about 25, who had been left only with what he wore at the time – a pair of shorts, thongs and a handkerchief. He said he had not only lost his personal effects but also $700 cash he had hidden in the room. There was an undercurrent of "blame" and without wanting to say or do anything which might inflame the unease, the station manager asked me if I would "hang around" for a day or so. Because the single men had to be re-located into the jackaroos' quarters, the usual room I would have stayed in had been taken up. Instead it was felt I would be better staying in one of the guest houses, and ended up in number 1 guest house. The only problem on the first night was that the place was completely dark, with no power, but a kerosene lamp was found and I was at least able to find my way around. With everything settled down, I went home on the Saturday afternoon to complete my file for the Coroner and take it to Alice Springs the following week when I was going down for court.

Before I could even present my file to the Coroner, it was all cut and dried that he and the prosecuting sergeant, Sergeant Second Class Tim Egan, the man who would "assist the Coroner" at a hearing, would travel to Brunette Downs and conduct an Inquest. Tim Egan had worked at Anthony Lagoon, he too had passed his sergeant's exams while stationed there, so an Inquest at Brunette Downs was a good opportunity for a trip back to the area. For "Scrubby" Hall, it was a great way to see another part of the Territory at tax-payers expense. Still, an Inquest would "clear the air", everybody would get a chance to have their say on the fire and if everything went to plan, the Coroner would deliver a pretty open finding, blaming nobody, congratulating all those who had fought the fire, and cleared the way for all insurance claims to be met. That's precisely what happened.

I was now in my last couple of weeks at Anthony Lagoon and I was hoping as much as would happen while I was there had already happened. I'd been so busy I really hadn't had the chance to look around any of the stations. At Anthony's there was an agriculture degree student doing a stage of his practical, hands-on work experience. He was one person at the cattle station who would at least stop and have a yarn. We had arranged that one Saturday morning, when he went out to do his "bore run", and drop off some of the molasses, he would pick me up and I would go along for the ride. It was about 8am when I heard the Landrover pull up at the gate, I dashed out the office locking it behind me to go with him. However, it wasn't him ... it was the station manager ... *"My cook's son has gone missing at Benmarra, he wandered away from a camp about 3 o'clock yesterday afternoon, they want you to go over there and help get a search organised ... "*

Benmarra was about 100 miles (160kms) east of Anthony Lagoon, a new holding, not even on the Pastoral Map, with a couple of Americans as share-holders. They had a station manager and a crew of about 18 station hands, all whites. The property was actually in the Wollogorang police district, although I was much closer and had better road access. The only trouble was, my vehicle was broken down, so the Anthony Lagoon manager loaned me a Landrover to get there.

I was anxious to get to the scene as soon as possible, not just to get the search going quickly but also as all the indications were for another 100F plus (38C) day. The lost person was a young 20 year old, Hans Lipinski, a German migrant. He had only been at Benmarra five days. He would have no bush skills and when he realised he was lost, he was likely to panic not only exhausting himself but likely to generate quite a gap between the first of the searchers and himself before he slowed down. My radio sched time with Alice Springs was not until 9am but being within range of the Northern Division network, which had an 8.30am sched, I could pass on a message, including a message to Constable Bob Kucharzewski, now officer-in-charge at Wollogorang, to come down and join the search.

I loaded my tucker-box and swag which were always at the ready and Tracker Dashwood got his gear loaded too. The station manager also got his mustering contractor's horse plant organised to move across so that later in the day we would have about 10 aboriginal men on horseback to help. Benmarra was known to have a light plane, but it was away in Mt Isa. A message had been sent asking for it to return to Benmarra to join the search.

On the Friday afternoon, about 4.30pm, young Hans had been in a station work gang gathering sand from a dry creek bed about 10 miles (16kms) further north east of Benmarra homestead along the road to Wollogorang, the sand being gathered for construction work at the new station. A team had taken a load back to the homestead leaving Hans and another young worker at the creek crossing to await their return for another load. While waiting, the other young chap decided to go for a walk along the creek bed. When he returned to the road crossing, Hans had disappeared. A late afternoon search had not found him and as there were no aboriginals at the station none was available to try to track him.

It was towards mid-day before I arrived at the spot where he had gone missing. The first thing was to try to find the exact circumstances of his disappearance. The assumption was that he had also headed west along the dry creek bed. The job then was to prove that. Dashwood and a couple of other aboriginals I took along with me as "honorary trackers" then made a circuit search from the road, through the bush, crossing the creek and rejoining the road, in a half moon movement you might say. This was to satisfy them-selves, and me, that Hans had not walked off in the opposite direction to our thoughts. They also checked the road to the north-east and the south-west to again satisfy themselves that he had not walked in either direction, and then walked off the road into the bush. We had just satisfied ourselves of this when Bob Kucharzewski arrived with his tracker.

It was another hour or so before we were satisfied that a set tracks, of a person in boots, were those of "our man", first moving along the creek bed and then out of the creek bed into country, roughly heading west. The track-ers were satisfied they found a place where he had sat and rested. Then we found his hat band, he went through a fence and into open bushland. The sta-tion plane arrived and made a circuit or two but we had no means of com-municating with it.

Nightfall came but we were probably still 24 hours behind him. I remem-ber I slept the night on the ground, just with a blanket, a canister of water and a tin of meat. Bob went to meet up with the horse plant with the idea of try-ing to move in front of or across the tracks of Hans further to the west. From first light next morning we continued to track Hans, so slowly, as whenever possible, he would move to rocky ground which made tracking very difficult. At one stage we lost his tracks for a couple of hours before moving on again.

As darkness approached on the second day, I retreated to the search start point. My intention was to go to the Benmarra homestead, not just for a meal but to re-assess just where to go next morning. As I arrived there was a jubi-lant air. Hans had been found just on dusk by the horse plant team with the aid of a grader. Having been satisfied with his general sense of direction, Bob and the horse plant team, had successfully cut across his path, just ahead of him. At the same time they took the silencer off a grader and drove it through the bush, with a fan of riders either side moving roughly north-south, the idea being the noise of the grader would attract Hans, the fan of horsemen would see his tracks, if they cut across them, or with the extra height of the horse, would see him if he came toward the grader. Just on dusk he staggered toward them, very sunburnt, suffering exposure and barely still on his feet.

They took him to the nursing sister at the station; he was safe, he survived. I was relieved, then headed home to Anthony Lagoon to pass on the good news to his very relieved mother.

I think the official embarrassment of having an unserviceable vehicle just when life was in danger prompted action to have my vehicle towed into

Tennant Creek. It was a long slow tow. There was no sign of the vehicle being quickly fixed either so I was given a relief vehicle to return to Anthony Lagoon and prepare to leave on the return of Basil and his family.

One thing I had hardly had time to pay any attention to while at Anthony Lagoon was to collect some good specimens of ribbon stone which abounded in the area. While in Tennant Creek, one of the supermarkets had canned soft drink on an extra special, so I bought a box, and took it back to Anthony Lagoon making the offer to the children of the tracker that I'd exchange a can of drink for a nice piece of ribbon stone. Before the afternoon was out, I had nearly half a ton (well a couple of buckets fulls) of reasonable specimens brought to me. The soft drink was gone, but I had some nice stone as a reminder of Anthony Lagoon. When "Bluey" returned he picked out a couple of the better specimens and said he would cut and polish them, which he did.

I left Anthony Lagoon with very mixed feelings. I was happy in myself that I'd carried out a good "relief", I'd done the job well for my three months at the station. I also left knowing it was likely to be the last time I'd be a Constable, officer-in-charge, of a "bush station". With two Sergeant Third Class positions vacant in Alice Springs, I wouldn't have to wait long to slip into one of those positions.

A typical envelope and note from Miss Pink, usually personally hand delivered to the police station

CHAPTER 13

My Sergeant's stripes

I had a new and strange feeling on my return to Alice Springs this time round. As I talked with Sergeant Cossons, the officer-in-charge, I sensed he had a new respect for me having passed my promotional exams. It was the same with the Divisional Inspector and I knew life ahead wouldn't be the same. There wouldn't be any more bush station relieving, I'd have a new supervisory role, there would be greater demands on me from within the force, and from the community.

Being not only young in age and still junior within the ranks of the force, my promotion would lift me in seniority above many I had worked under. I had to make sure the promotion that awaited didn't *"go to my head"*, that I kept everything in perspective. As I wrote home to my mother a day or two after arriving back . . .*"I had a good trip back from Anthony Lagoon. I stopped the night at Tennant Creek before coming on to Alice ... when I got back to Alice I was told that on November 17 I am to be made an Acting Sergeant Third Class. I don't know why they picked that date, it's a Monday and I think a new recruit school starts duty then. It is my birthday too so will be a good present. I will get Sergeant's pay; I'm not sure if I'll be able to wear the "hooks" – three stripes on the right arm . . .I worked last night 4-12midnight, first night on duty and ended up in charge of the shift so am right back into it"*

"I have the weekend off. I went and voted early today and went shopping. Next thing someone in a police car was yelling at me – I was called on duty – an aboriginal had gone berserk with a rifle at a station (Milton Park) *about 75 mile out. To cut a long story short an aboriginal shot another twice over a row about a woman. The shot aboriginal is in hospital and is very ill - naturally! I, two Detective Sergeants and a photographer rushed out to find the offender sitting in the camp waiting for us! I got 6 hours ($14) overtime!*

I went and saw a young solicitor, Paul Everingham, now getting well established in Alice Springs, to have my will prepared. Paul first came to Alice Springs to practice much the same time as I arrived in town. As a partner in a firm operating from Mt Isa, he came to Alice Springs for a few days a month but quickly saw the opportunity of establishing a second law firm in the town (the other being Barker and Martin). He wasn't regarded as a good court lawyer but he quickly established a reputation for civil and document work. In the time I had been out of town relieving, he had established a significant practice and had taken in at least one other solicitor more suited for the court business. It was my first will but I was impressed by the sincere manner in which he addressed the matter. It cost me $16.

I now had to wait just three weeks for the acting position promotion. In the meantime, it was back into the routine of day and evening shifts, the street brawls and hotel disturbances and court. I also had to put on my keg, a tradition for those passing their exams. It went a little against my grain, but it was best I was one of the boys and on a Friday evening arranged for an "18" to be set up on the barracks lawn with everyone at the station, off duty of course, invited to help demolish it. It was usual to also invite some friends from around town, but as I had so little time in town over the past two years, I didn't have a big circle of friends to invite. It was also traditional for Joyce Giles, who had the prisoner meal contract but also ran a general catering service, to provide some eats to help keep everyone that little more sober. Still, there were a couple with thick heads for most of the weekend!

I was rostered on to another mission patrol. The patrols had now been stretched to six days giving extra time to spend at settlements and provide time to visit some of the out-stations the aboriginal communities were establishing. This time I wasn't taking a tracker, instead one of the new chaps in barracks, Keith Colebrook, an ex-Queensland police officer who had joined the NT force in recent months was going with me. His experience made the job just that little easier, but being his first mission patrol, most of the job of preparing the vehicle, the stores, the paper work and making sure we had our swags and provisions fell to me.

It was a fairly routine patrol, again out to Yuendumu, and back across Central Mount Wedge station to Papunya, some of its out-stations, Haasts Bluff, Areyonga and then Hermannsburg. I was very keen to camp out the Friday night at Palm Valley, 12 miles or so (20kms) south of Hermannsburg, and next morning take the short walk to have a good look at the famed *Livestona* palms which gave the locality its name. However, other people had other ideas, especially a young Pamela Beckmann, the clerical assistant in the superintendent's office at Hermannsburg Mission. She had an eye on Keith and before I knew it the plans to travel on to Palm Valley were scrapped! Instead, a bed had been arranged for both of us at Hermannsburg, dinner and an evening playing Monopoly until the power plant was shut down at 10.30pm. It was the beginning of a romance that had us in church two years later, and still endures today.

We had no sooner arrived back at the Alice Springs station when there was a radio call from the Traffic Section for assistance to apprehend a suspected drunk driver. I didn't even have time to read the circular from the Superintendent, pinned to the notice board, advising of my promotion to Acting Sergeant. All dusty and gritty from six days on mission patrol, Keith and I jumped into one of the vans and took off to assist. It was the first time I'd used the flashing blue lights and siren for ages ... almost a novelty, if it wasn't so serious. Fortunately, just as we arrived in the vicinity, Traffic had successfully pulled over the offending vehicle and the excitement was over. Still, we also had to check-out the driver, form our own opinion of his sobriety, a sort of insurance, first to back up the arresting officer, but of equal importance, to qualify for some court overtime if the need arose.

Ironically, I was rostered off duty the first two days of my new acting rank, then had a day or two on the job before another series of off duty days and the start of a night shift. I took the opportunity to go down to Kulgera, staying a couple of nights with the Taylors at the store. However, I cut my stay a day short to come back for a late afternoon funeral of a young local lad, Paul Sabadin, a keen sportsman and likeable lad, tragically killed in a car accident on the outskirts of town. It was normal to have funerals in Alice Springs, particularly at the Catholic church, at 5pm. It was one of the first big funerals at the new Roman Catholic church, so to see it three-quarter full was in itself a reflection of the community's grief. I also found it strange not having a hymn as part of the service, in fact, like many non-Catholics at the service, I had some difficulty in following the Mass.

One thing about Sergeant First Class Len Cossons as station sergeant was you never knew when he would call at the station during his off duty hours, to check the evening mail, to see "how things are going", or to make sure everyone was on their toes all the time! He had called at the station one evening, about 8 o'clock, when there was a report that a man appeared to be attempting to break into motor vehicles further down the street. He was checking the vehicles to see if they were locked, checking windows and the like. With no plain clothes officers on duty, rather than approach in a police vehicle, which would give the game away immediately, we quickly decided I would travel as a passenger in Sergeant Cosson's private vehicle (with him driving) try to spot the culprit and apprehend him. We travelled east along Parsons Street (the street where the police station was located) and just crossed Todd Street (the main street) where outside the ANZ Bank we saw a chap still walking along checking car doors, trying to gain entry to a car. We pulled up along side, I alighted quickly and immediately spoke to the suspect. He was denying everything until another aboriginal spoke-up dobbing in the suspect. His response was to punch me in the stomach and attempt to run off but I quickly grabbed and restrained him. As we wrestled to the ground he bit me on the shoulder blade, taking a piece clean out of my shirt. At this point assistance arrived and the apprehension was complete.

I went to the hospital to have the large blood blister and bruise on my shoulder blade checked. Fortunately, he barely broke the skin, but I can tell you, it was sore for a few days. Next morning the culprit was fined $32.75 including the cost of a new shirt!

The night shift, being the second week of the roster, was quiet although we knew the weather was getting warmer – Miss Pink was back on the phone. Early in the week she had rung during evening shift inquiring if dogs could have sex *"tail to tail as there are two dogs running around here tail to tail"*. Keith Van Rangleroy, reported in the journal that he quietly explained a few facts to her before he went to the reserve to chase the dogs away, only to find none in sight. However, last morning of night shift we struck a real "jackpot". She rang at 7.40am, just while a couple of us were on the final patrol of the shift, to complain *"There are people on the hill behind my house"*. Jeff Allen and I were on patrol; we went to the Reserve and just as we pulled up at the house, we could see there really were some people just going over the top of the hill behind the house.

I told Jeff to drive back around, over the Todd River and north along the river bank to where they could be expected to come down the other side of the hill. In the meantime, I walked up the hill behind them. I reached the top of the hill to see about half a dozen 16-18 year old part aboriginal youths crouched down behind rocks, all watching Jeff drive in from the other side. I snuck down behind them until I was only a few yards from their hiding places, then in an authoritative voice, which startled the daylights out of them, *" ... game's up boys, all stand up and stand still . . .".* I then walked them down to the patrol van and asked them what were they doing. Some of the lads were locals, a couple were relations or friends from out of town; they had just gone for a morning walk, from one home of relatives across town to another. They had not taken the wisest of short cuts and had now ended up in the hands of the police!

We loaded them into the van and drove back to Miss Pink. As we pulled up, her first reaction was an expectation we would be empty-handed as on every previous occasion over the years. But she became quite excited when we told her that we had indeed apprehended the culprits, then opened up the back of the patrol van, and they all stepped out and stood in line. *"Take them away, lock them up"* she barked. Well, really they had not done anything wrong. There was no charge we could lay against any of them but there was a need to satisfy her that justice had been done.

"Look Miss Pink, these boys are not from Alice Springs (my tongue in my cheek), they are from out of town and got a little bit lost, they didn't really mean to come on to your reserve, they are very sorry and I think if they said 'sorry' we should warn them not to come back again, I am sure they will not" I said to her. *"Well, alright, if they say sorry and that they will not come back on the reserve again, I am prepared to give them a chance"* she responded. *"Well boys, you heard Miss Pink. Say you are sorry and you won't come back onto the reserve again"* I said to them, to which, in unison they said *"Sorry, we won't come back"* ... *"Oh no"* interrupted Miss Pink, *"They have to each individually say 'sorry for coming on to your reserve and promise I will not come back again'"* she said.

So in turn, each said their "sorry" lines. By the fifth or sixth they were all trying to keep a straight face. So were Jeff and I, but we got through it, loaded them into the van and headed back to the town centre. *"Please don't drop us off in Todd Street, take us around a corner please Sergeant"* came from the back of the van. I took pity on them and we pulled around a corner and dropped them off. The rascals thought the police were not bad fellows altogether. Miss Pink rang the Inspector to say we had done *"a real good job"*. I was back in the good books but in the sure knowledge it would not be for long.

The night shift out of the way, I would normally look forward to a day or two off duty, but Christmas was approaching and the pre-school year about to end. I was nominated to make a round of the three pre-schools in town, each having a morning and afternoon attendance, and give the children a talk on road safety. With up to 35 children in each session, it was quite a handful. My weekend again got disrupted when Sergeant Cossons got it into his head that the local speedway, which was opening on the Sunday, didn't have the proper authorities under the Public Entertainment Ordinance and Sunday Observance Ordinance to operate. So I was called on duty to attend the speedway and check that they did indeed have the correct authorisations. As it turned out, they had everything covered; I ended up with three-and-a-half hours overtime and the boss with egg on his face.

The week before Christmas, word came from Papunya settlement that an elderly aboriginal, Paddy Nuguta, had gone missing. Paddy, about 50, had only

The new Alice Springs Police Station, August, 1970

Getting served at Richard and Carol Morphett's wedding during my meal break

one arm and was a light frail Pintubi tribesman, who lived with about 200 of his fellow Pintubi tribesmen at Alumbra bore outstation, about 20 miles (32kms) west of Papunya. He had wandered away into waterless sandhill country to the north of the bore. Locals had searched for two days but had been unable to locate him. There were reports he was "*silly-along-a-head*" and a belief that he had deliberately wandered into sandhill country "*to do away with himself*", a traditional act of aged aboriginals who felt they were becoming a burden on family and tribe. So Bronte Savage, another recent recruit in barracks, a former member of the Victoria police, and I were sent to coordinate a search.

As we arrived at Papunya, the superintendent, Warren Smith, who I had known at Elliott, had just returned from the search area. He was satisfied Paddy had not wandered north as there were no fresh tracks at all to be found. It had rained the day before he had wandered away so tracks should have been easy to find. He agreed we should start to look more westerly and southerly, so we headed to the Alumbra bore and spoke with others at the camp site. Several of Paddy's friends believed he was all right, that rather than "do away with himself", he had left the camp to get some peace and quiet from the women and children. The trouble was that we had to be satisfied, had to have some evidence that in fact he was safe, indeed had wandered off under these circumstances rather than to perish. With the assistance of a group of expert trackers from the local tribes, we scoured the area until late afternoon, when we stumbled on tracks heading roughly west of the camp. But still we had no evidence that he had gone to water at the many rock-holes and watering spots across the area.

Next morning we were out at sun-up, being taken from known water hole to water hole, four in fact, with still no sign of him being to water. Using horses, some of the men made sweeps to the west and south, then finally his tracks were found at a rock-hole where they believed he had rested. Then his tracks were followed with considerable difficulty, the trackers believing he was trying to avoid being followed as he moved from grass tussock to grass tussock rather than walk on the sand. They found where he had caught, and presumably eaten, a goanna, and where he had gathered the native drug Pitcheri and other bush tucker.

Next day we continued to search, increasingly satisfied that he had been to water, had gathered food, was walking briskly, and we were probably a couple of days behind him. Already his tracks were about 15 miles (24kms) west of Alumbra bore. In the weather conditions, hot and humid, it had to happen. First there was a wind storm followed by a sharp rain storm over the whole area, followed later in the evening by a heavy soaking, obliterating any tracks we might hope to follow.

There was a noticeable change in the concerns of the searchers, from despair and concern when we first arrived to one of *"he must be all right boss"* after we had found he had been to water. And then the rains came. We did a last sweep of the area, driving about 30 miles (50kms) west of Alumbra bore, our only sight the beautiful Mt Liebig range.

On Christmas Day, fit and well, he walked back into his camp, had a meal and 'disappeared' again.

I worked Christmas Day on night shift but that would give me New Year's Eve off. There was a party organised at the Barracks which seemed to go off pretty well. I went to bed at 3am while the last left at about 5am. One thing I did adapt to was being able to sleep above the noise of partying colleagues.

Early 1970 saw the stock market, in particular surrounding mineral exploration companies, running "hot". The Poseidon roller coaster was in full swing; there were stock market reports in virtually every news bulletin and the financial pages were filled with speculation. Everybody seemed to know somebody who knew somebody who was "in the know". I had previously held shares too, but they had all been in industrial stocks. Five of us at the station, all Sergeants or Acting Sergeants, started a share syndicate, each putting in $50 to start with, with the idea of putting in $5 each a week and building up an investment. As others joined in, we named the syndicate "Lawmen Eight". We started our adventure with a 500 share purchase in Target Petroleum at 45c each! – a "hot tip" was the word! We never made our fortune. Interest quickly wained, especially when the "calls" came on the shares!

The days slipped by closer to 28 February, 1970, the fourth anniversary of my joining the force. I'd been told to stop using the title "Acting" Sergeant, to just refer to myself in reports and journal entries as Sergeant Pollock. Although the Inspector told me my promotion had been recommended, regulations prescribed the procedures. First, on 28 February, 1970, the fourth anniversary of my joining the force and having passed the promotional examinations for the rank of Sergeant Third Class I would be automatically promoted to Senior

Constable. That was a Saturday; so it wasn't until Monday I received formal notification. It was another three days before the notice arrived in Alice Springs that the Commissioner had approved my provisional promotion to Sergeant Third Class on 1 March, 1970. Again, the police regulations provided a system for provisional promotion, then allowing 30 days for any aggrieved member to appeal. The fact was there was nobody eligible to appeal against my promotion, it was a matter of sitting out the 30 days for confirmation. I then took my shirts to the contract tailor and she sewed on the three "hooks" on the right arm sleeve, smart new, white-as-white they looked the real thing. I wore them with pride.

I also lashed out and bought a new suit. Over recent weeks I'd received a couple of wedding invitations and knew that with Bob Henfry's engagement, there was a chance I would go to New Zealand mid-year to attend his wedding. There were only three men's wear stores in town, the main two run by the same fellow, Jack Graves. Fortunately, he had a suit in stock that I not only liked, but near fitted me, just an alteration or two and it would be perfect, for a mere $49 too.

However, the first wedding I expected to wear the suit to (Richard Morphett from Kulgera station who married an Alice Springs girl, Carol Griffiths) I could not attend as I was rostered on duty that Saturday evening. With one of the other Sergeants from the shift on leave, I had no one to swap with. However, I arranged to have my 40 minute meal break (which I slightly extended to close on an hour) to attend the reception in the Commonwealth Railway Institute, just in time for the speeches and toasts. While most had eaten, the chef carved me a meal from the buffet. Without realising it, I broke regulations as I joined the toast, taking a rare sip of champagne, a toast at a wedding or similar event being a rare exception to me ever drinking liquor.

The patrol collected me from the reception. Just as we drove away, down Railway Terrace, a radio call came *"there is a report of a train coming into town running over an aboriginal laying across the rail lines beside Telegraph Terrace, just inside The Gap"!* We went immediately to the scene to find the train crew had "separated" part of the train. Sure enough, there were the remains of a person spread fifty or more yards along the rail tracks, a thousand human body pieces for the CIB to photograph and pick up. It was never determined if the dead man had stumbled and fallen across the tracks, had gone to sleep on the railway line or had been deliberately placed on the tracks. But tests showed he was well intoxicated and the first theory prevailed.

The buzz within the force was a series of pay rises, some involving basic wage increases which went back 18 months. My new salary as a Sergeant Third

Haasts Bluff is the backdrop for a radio check while on patrol west of Alice Springs

The ladies race at the Yuendumu Sports Carnival

Class was $5,005 p.a. plus a district allowance of $300 (for a single person) and shift allowance of $249, a total of $5,554 p.a., or a few cents under $107 per week, plus overtime. I calculated my back-pay would be in the vicinity of $400, enough to pay for a trip to New Zealand if I decided to go. A surprise when the increases were finally signed up was a 25% loading for working night shift, never a popular shift but now made a little more bearable.

I also renewed my association with Australian Rules football. In a week I was approached and asked if I would consider being secretary of one of the clubs in town, a job I had no desire for at all while a few days later I was approached and asked if I would be interested in joining the Central Australian Football League executive. I went along to the annual general meeting and before the evening was out, I was elected a vice president. The local Department of Works Regional Engineer, Kevin Sweet, was president of the league and a young journalist at the *Centralian Advocate*, Phil Stone, was secretary/treasurer. The second league meeting I attended, where the forthcoming season's arrangements were thrashed out, I ended up in the chair with the president on one of his regular bush trips. It was the beginning of a great interest for the rest of my time in Alice Springs. At times it was most frustrating but at the same time a happy release from work and I believe in many ways a real bridge-builder between many footballers, youth of the town and the police. I like to think that through football I had a special relationship with many people in town which I would not have had if it had not been for my association and work with the game. This was something most higher ranked officers failed to see.

My role at the station also changed when Sergeant First Class Cossons returned to the job of station sergeant after a stint as Acting Inspector. He decided to appoint me as his assistant, the daily reserve officer, working Monday to Friday 8am to 4pm, making sure the station 'ticked', vehicles were cleaned, maintained and serviced, those in custody were properly conveyed to and from court and if need be, to the gaol, the cell block was properly cleaned, the day-to-day paper work around the station was attended to. It was quite a task with many a day my lunch meal break not coming before 2 o'clock

I'd been doing the new job only a few days when a telex came from the South Australia police asking us to notify Alice Springs relatives of the death in Adelaide of a member of their family. The dead man was Sam Griffiths, the father of the lass whose wedding I had attended only a fortnight earlier. He had been found dead in his room at the Grosvenor Hotel, Adelaide, the traditional hotel of Territory visitors to Adelaide. Rather than go to the home and tell the family alone, I found his business partner and the parish priest and the three of us went together to the home for what was always one of the most difficult jobs in the force.

It was 20 April, 1970, before I received formal advice that my promotion was confirmed; the next job was to find me a gazetted position. I really expected a transfer out of Alice Springs, to a Darwin based position. I was finally gazetted to the logical position of Sergeant Third Class, Relieving, Alice Springs. This was to cover the other sergeants of similar rank in Alice Springs who might be on leave, or doing higher duties while more senior officers were themselves on leave. One thing I had to get used to was fellows I had worked with, both those I had worked with when I first arrived in Alice Springs near four years ago and those who had more recently joined the force, calling me "Sarg" rather than "Dave" or "Polly". I think I coped.

A phone call from my parents early on the morning of 28 April was to tell me my sister had earlier in the day given birth to twin boys, Grant and Andrew. I was now also an uncle.

I decided to go to Bob Henfry's wedding in Blenheim, New Zealand and took three weeks' leave. I flew down to Melbourne and had four days at home before flying on to Christchurch, on an "Electra", a four engine prop-jet, the only international flights out of Melbourne's old Essendon airport. It was a 12.45am departure, an all-night flight to arrive in a very frosty Christchurch where I spent the day and night before travelling north by bus to Blenheim where Bob and Sally met me. My most vivid memory still is the *"Welcome to sunny Blenheim"* sign reflected in a flood of water!

It was a lovely wedding. Bob's mother and father had travelled from Perth; I think I was the only other Australian there. We were well outnumbered by Sally's relatives, who seemed only to be able to recall bad joke Australian stories such as the four sea-sick days involved in crossing the Tasman on visits to Australia in earlier days

---

When I returned to Alice Springs it was back to day reserve with the big job in hand to move office. The new police station at Alice Springs was rapidly nearing completion. It was to be a new era of police office accommodation. My contribution was to suggest a change in the police station telephone number, to try to remove some of the confusion with the hospital phone number, typified by an incident one Monday morning where Constable Terry O'Brien, who'd played rugby league on Sunday, went to hospital Monday morning for treatment and had an injection in his leg. It must have struck a nerve as minutes after returning to the station his leg paralysed. He phoned the hospital. The station phone rang and as reserve officer I answered *". . . oh ... ah ... I'm in agony . . ."*. The voice came to me in stereo as I listened to him on the phone and could hear him speaking in the adjoining muster room. Even he had rung 2 1966 (the police station) instead of 2 1699 (the hospital)!

Sadly, I also returned to learn that while I'd been away, Colin Eckert, who I had relieved at Maranboy, my first bush relief, recently promoted to Sergeant Third Class, had been killed in a road accident between his police vehicle and a transport on the highway between Katherine and Maranboy only days before he was to transfer to Darwin.

I continued to be more involved with the football, especially when I went to Tregear Park early one Sunday to be told by the league secretary that owing to illness and injury, there wasn't an umpire for the second league game of the afternoon – Rovers v. Melenka. So off I went to find Frank Bird, who ran a men's wear cum sports store. He kindly went to his shop, opened and sold me a new pair of sandshoes, a pair of black socks and a pair of white shorts. With a white shirt I had at the barracks, I was in business. Although there was a perfect ground surface, I dare not try to bounce the ball, nor let on that I had never umpired a game of football in my life! Perhaps the scores helped – Rovers 24.30 (174) defeated Melenka 1.6 (12). At the end of the match, there were not too many complaints, and several remarked *"I didn't know you umpired!"* There were quite a few gasps when I responded *"well, that was my first match"*.

I was pretty stiff for a day or two afterwards but found relief in the bath at the barracks, and half a packet of Radox! I took up training and did a few more matches before the end of the season. It was a bit of fun, good exercise, and although forbidden by regulation to accept any fee for the job, the $8 in a plain envelope was good spending money.

A big sports weekend was developing on the August Picnic Day long weekend at Yuendumu. Aboriginals from all over Central Australia gathered to play Australian Rules, softball and athletics along with traditional sports of spear and boomerang throwing for the older men of the tribes. The Inspector's Clerk and I were each rostered on duty for the three days overtime to drive out Saturday

Spear throwing at the Yuendumu Sports Carnival. Rev. Tom Fleming acts as steward

Two C.A.F.L. field umpires Shane Wolfe (left) and Ian Reid along with the goal umpires and teams for the Yuendumu Sports Carnival football team final. There was not a blade of grass on the oval, freshly graded for the carnival

228

morning and stay there until Monday in a show-the-flag and keep-the-peace mission. It was in fact a pretty uneventful weekend, right up until we were about to leave. Then it was reported that a young lass from the Warrabri contingent had gone missing, believed to have run away with a local lad. This had the potential to cause considerable tribal conflict. We put out the word and within half-an-hour she had been located, a few words of counsel and she was on her way with the rest of the Warrabri crew.

—⊶⊷—

The move into the new police station went better than I expected and we all settled in well. We got some new furniture which helped, and a new automatic telephone system with half a dozen direct lines through a central switchboard, plus direct lines for the Inspector, officer-in-charge of both the station and the CIB. We could also ring internally, and through to the watchhouse/cell block. We also had a new phone number – 2 2777. The new station was a double storey building with a fascia of natural stone laid against what was virtually a reinforced concrete building. There was a smart central entry with reception and the switch with the radio room adjoining reception. Traffic Section was to the left and General Duties to the right and rear of the ground floor. The Divisional Inspector was upstairs as was the CIB, Information Section, the photographic dark room and associated facilities.

For the first time there was a locker room which doubled as a meeting room. The shift sergeants had their own office next to the constables' muster room. The Prosecutor and the Licensing Inspector each had an office. There were offices galore. All the town's dignitaries were invited to the official opening by the Commissioner on Friday, 28 August, 1970, but none of us at the station were initially invited. The immediate reaction amongst us was for nobody off duty on the day to attend; there was a real feeling of being let-down, that the men, and women, who would make the facility work, felt unrecognised. Morale was shattered. This feeling quickly filtered through. Then, just days before the official opening, after the official RSVP date, a formal invitation from the Commissioner, envelopes individually addressed, appeared on the notice board. The response was a full turnout for the function.

Although I had unsuccessfully applied for the Tennant Creek Sergeant Third

Class position which came up in the shake-out after the last round of promotions, what I didn't count on was being sent to Tennant Creek to relieve; it was something that had never happened before. Then again, there had not been a single officer with the rank of Sergeant Third Class in recent memory either. Nor had a personality like Sergeant First Class E. A. A. (Andy) McNeill been officer-in-charge at Tennant Creek. It was a case of his nom-de-plume *"Big deal McNeill"* showing to the fore. He just had that knack of making a fuss out of nothing, particularly if it held him in good light.

When it appeared he would lose his Sergeant Third Class for a month between the departure of the present officer on promotional transfer and the arrival of the new officer, you could almost hear him in Alice Springs crying for a relief officer *" . . . you have a single Sergeant Third Class down there in Alice Springs . . . why can't he come up to relieve? ..."* and of course there was no defence, that is why there was a position of Sergeant Third Class Relieving at Alice Springs filled by a single officer.

At least the move got me off the day reserve job. After the best part of six months at the task, my patience was wearing thin. This had been noticed, Sergeant First Class Cossons asking one of the other chaps *"Why's Polly so short lately?"* ... *"well, wouldn't you be too after six months as day reserve!"* Still, there was time to get me on roster for a night shift before flying up to Tennant Creek.

The move firmed my decision to sell my car and arrange to pick up a new one when I went on leave myself on 1 December. The new HG Holden had just been released and I quite liked it. In fact I took a particular shine to the Premier sedan with the V8 253 engine. I could have arranged the deal through the local Holden dealer, Kittle Brothers, but decided to obtain a few quotes for a no-trade-in-cash-deal from one of the dealers in the vicinity of my parents. The best offer came from Peter Robinson Motors at Lilydale, the bottom line for a 2-tone, bucket seats, radio, sunvisor, locking petrol cap, mudflaps front and rear, 253 manual Premier sedan was $3,490.23 with a $250.23 discount for a no trade in, cash deal. I sold my HD Premier sedan to Winston "Lofty" Moffat in a deal that was good for us both.

There were seven police at Tennant Creek, the Sergeant First Class officer-in-charge, a Sergeant Third Class, four constables and a plain clothes CIB man. The Tennant Creek complex was still relatively new, the station building was standard grey cement brick. The sergeants shared the front office, then there was the reception/general office, a muster room and the CIB cum radio room.

Behind the police station was the cell block and to the north of the station, the clerk of court's office and the court house. To the rear of the block was the barracks, again grey cement brick, four single bedrooms, a kitchen area and large lounge along with showers, toilet and laundry. The other feature was that all the buildings were air-conditioned using the evaporative-cooler system, which worked well in the dry-air heat.

The station faced the Stuart Highway, on the southern edge of the town business area. Next to the station was the officer-in-charge's residence and next to him the post office and telephone exchange. The barracks had access to the rear street, in fact there was a dusty drive through the police block, allowing access either way. But there was no shade for the vehicles which could become unbearably hot.

The town had a fairly steady population just under the 3,000 mark, but within a few mile there was the Peko and Nobles Knob mines, then 30 miles (50kms) to the north west, the newly developed Warrego mine and copper smelter were under construction.

One of my main tasks at Tennant Creek was to act as Prosecutor. There was at least a monthly visit from the Alice Springs based Magistrate, Mr G. F. (Scrubby) Hall SM, with local Justices of the Peace sitting most Mondays and any other day they might be needed. My first court was before local justices with 18 defendants, two of whom pleaded not guilty, but I successfully gained convictions. I was a little nervous the first time before Mr Hall. He and I were not members of a mutual admiration club, at least on the surface. Perhaps his recent clash in court with the Alice Springs Police Prosecutor, Sergeant Second Class Kirian McCarthy, after which two Attorney-General's department inspectors were reputed to have visited and counselled him, had tempered his manner. Then again I tried my utmost to present the matters to him in the best and clearest way I could. He could help or he could destroy you. I managed to survive.

A fortnight later he returned for a run of Magistrate's Court, Coroner's Court and Children's Court sittings. Only a Magistrate could handle Children's Court matters, and where possible, not in a court house situation. The Coroner's Court was an inquest into a fire which had burnt out a tourist bus, the insurance company asking for the inquest, but not finding out any new information. For me it was all good experience, and to my relief, the Magistrate continued to be polite towards me. At the inquest he raised his tone a bit with an insurance investigator talking of contempt of court when the insurance guy came on a bit strong. He also had a habit of raising his voice toward Welfare branch officers during

Site of the former Arltunga Police Station. All that remains in 1971 was the concrete slab and stone chimney and the cell block

Children's Court hearings which as I recall, we held in the Magistrate's room rather than the court room.

Another quirk I recall was when after finding an offender guilty, Mr Hall would look down from the bench, over his half-moon glasses and say *"You are sentenced to a month's imprisonment with hard labour"*, then continue to write. As the realisation of his words started to hit the offender Mr Hall would put down his pen and quietly say *"suspended on entering a good behaviour bond of . . . for a period of ... ".* I'm sure it had the right effect on many. What was little more than 15 seconds was the longest 15 seconds of their life.

There was no night shift worked at Tennant Creek, when the evening shift finished work, they switched the phone through to the barracks, so an early morning call-out, and overtime, were frequently on the cards. There was no two-way radio communications at the station but the town still had a manual telephone exchange which had its advantages. It was possible to check in with the exchange to see if anyone was looking for you when on patrol and the station was unattended.

The Tennant Creek police cells served as a seven-day police prison. In other words, anyone sentenced up to seven days gaol could be kept at Tennant Creek, but someone sentenced to a longer period, or in default for more than seven days, needed to be transferred to Alice Springs gaol. This meant quite a bit of escort work up and down the highway.

My four weeks in Tennant Creek flashed by. I worked right up until flying out, prosecuting at a special court on the Friday morning, walking out the court house to hear the southbound Fokker aircraft circling to land.

In the dry Centre, drowning was virtually unheard of and sadly there was a contempt for the water that sat in gorges and waterholes like Ellery Gorge, about 58 miles (90kms) to the west of The Alice. It was an expanse of water of about 40 yards (35m) through the Gorge, narrowing to perhaps 10 yards (9m) in the jaw of the gorge, and said to be 60-100 feet (18m-30m) deep. The deeper water in the near continual shadow of the Gorge was bone-chillingly cold. This, combined with beer, food and skylarking was a recipe for disaster when a group of local bank boys organised a Saturday outing to the gorge. I'd just hung my washing on the line when I was called on duty to go to the gorge after a report that one of the lads had jumped from a cliff face into a deep section and disappeared. I spent all next day at the gorge as well, in a hopeless attempt to locate the body. We had virtually no equipment for such a situation – a borrowed aluminium row boat, some long line and hooks, rowing back and forth, dragging in a futile attempt to locate the body, on duty at 6am and not back to barracks until near 10pm.

On the Monday I had another 6am start to drive to Tennant Creek, taking up prisoners for court, prosecuting and returning on the Tuesday the first Tuesday in November. I was all ready to leave Tennant Creek when I got a phone call from Geoff Shervill at Ti Tree asking me to put on a series of bets for the Melbourne Cup for him and the Ti Tree storekeeper; they would pay me when I got there!

So I went to one of the betting shops and put on the bets, writing out a cheque to pay for them! I decided to round it off and put a couple of dollars each way myself on Baghdad Note, then headed to Ti Tree. I missed the running of the Cup but had the biggest smile when learning Baghdad Note had won at 25/1 – the winnings would pay my new car insurance! I didn't learn for another couple of weeks that I also won a sweep at the Tennant Creek Memorial Club – another $32, which probably paid for the registration!

I got back to Alice Springs to learn I was to go back out searching for the drowned swimmer again next day. It was yet another early start, a very frustrating day, finding nothing. In the evening when I returned and rang the Inspector to advise him, he wasn't concerned so much about not finding the body – someone had told him I was a virtual non-swimmer, and here I was, no safety gear, rowing up and down Ellery Gorge, a likely drowning victim myself if anything had gone wrong! I didn't go back to the search scene again. It was a week before the body was located, recovered using scuba diving gear provided by some American personnel from the Joint Defence Space Research Facility (JDSRF).

Details of my new car engine number arrived so I registered it, recovered my Northern Territory plates, 9-988 and mailed them to the dealer at Lilydale, near Melbourne. I worked right up to the evening of starting leave, had all day to pack, then fly out, first class and all, home to Melbourne, to Belgrave. Next morning David Read, the sales manager from Robinson's arrived with the car. I gave him the bank cheque and drove him back to Lilydale. Of course he was pleased with the sale but said the effect of the car, with NT plates, being prepared in the workshop caused real interest and a buzz for the staff. It was a great car.

CHAPTER 14

Tangling with Regulations

As my leave again came to an end, it was a routine drive back to Adelaide, over-nighting with Jim and Pearl and then heading north to Port Augusta and putting the new car on the train. At least it had become a little more civilised. They now loaded the cars in the afternoon, which meant you could drive to Port Augusta in the morning, load and depart all on the same day. There were 35 cars to be loaded so I was sure to know someone on the train. The railways head locomotive engineer, "Snow" Andrewartha was a passenger on the train, heading up to Alice Springs on a job. It was good to see him again after the time we had spent at Elliott when he had been moving locomotives from Alice Springs to the North Australia Railway. When we got on the north side of Oodnadatta, he arranged for me to spend an hour in the driver's cab, a hot and cramped position with the locomotive throbbing away as it rumbled over track which made you wonder how on earth the train stayed on the line.

I'd left mild conditions in Melbourne to strike a heat wave when I arrived back in Alice Springs. A day or two after I returned it was 109F (43C) and only down to 82F (28C) overnight. The barracks were quiet, only half a dozen chaps in residence with one of them, Bronte Savage, in hospital with recurring lung collapse problems. There were a few new faces around town but the main interest was the approaching centenary celebrations. Many men around town had started to grow beards, even the bank managers getting into the spirit of the celebrations. The banks and business houses had printed signs in their windows, or on the door, *"Our beards are being grown for the Alice Springs Centenary Celebrations".* Nobody at the station was growing a beard, that was against regulations!

The other talking point of town was whether or not to accept an offer of Local Government for Alice Springs made by the Department of Territories through the Northern Territory Administration. It would mean a mayor and nine councillors, and municipal rates. Presently, the only other area in the Territory with local government was the City of Darwin. There was a "for" and "against" campaign in full swing but the referendum was decisive, people in the town, including myself, voting 2-1 in favour.

Some business people in town had also got together to establish a commercial broadcasting station, 8HA – *Heart of Australia.* The station manager, Renton Kelly, had been in radio in Darwin and was busy getting his team of announcers and presenters together. He was looking for a sports commentator and first approached Ron Thomas, the Clerk of Courts, to see if he was interested. He wasn't, but had a word with me to see if I was interested, suggesting I contact the station manager and sound him out. However, before I could do that Ron Thomas had spoken with Paul Everingham, the solicitor, and secretary of the company, and the radio station manager, giving him a run down on my sporting background. Then Ren Kelly rang me, had a chat and felt that subject to an audition tape to make sure my voice was suitable, I sounded the right person for the job.

Ren knew the Commissioner personally and suggested that I could avoid starting a paper war which would inevitably follow if I applied for permission to take on the task. Ren said he would phone the Commissioner, tell him he was considering approaching me, and gauge his reaction. The response was a blunt *"NO"*. It was disappointing. Apart from the enjoyment I would have got from the job, I believe it would have been another stepping stone between the community and the police, particularly amongst the younger and part-coloured communities. That was always needed.

The radio station was officially opened on the afternoon of Tuesday, 2 March, 1971, by Hon. Ralph Hunt MHR, the Territories Minister. The most memorable part of the opening was, in typical Ralph Hunt style, he declared officially open H8A!

The people in the Finke district still remembered me and included me on the invitation list for parties and weddings, this time for young Phillip Clarke's 21st birthday to be held at Andado Station homestead, on the fringe of the Simpson Desert. I had the chance to fly out to the party on the Saturday with Brian Smith, the pilot/manager of the local charter company, SAATAS. We were taking the birthday cake and a few other essential perishables. We took off shortly before lunch, into low cloud, with Brian well in command. Fifteen minutes or so out he turned to me and said *"did you feel that?"* ... *"no"* ... *"I think we will go back"* So we turned and headed direct for the main airstrip with a request *"request direct approach"* ... *"direct approach permission granted"* from the control tower. We landed and taxied toward the hanger *"Tower to ... could you explain your request for a 'direct approach'"?* ... as quick as a flash ... *"one passenger violently ill"* Brian responded. The aircraft engine had just been overhauled. He thought he felt an abnormal shudder or vibration and took the precaution of returning rather than experience engine trouble mid-air. He also knew that by reporting the real reason would have been an air safety incident which would have resulted in all sorts of inspectors visiting the workshop. We reloaded into another plane, this time a twin engine model, and got to Andado in good time to join in a great night.

Many of the people attending had come from Kulgera, Finke and New Crown. On the Sunday morning we all left more or less together. The people driving back travelled in convoy as they had to negotiate a series of sandhills not too far from the homestead. Brian held back a little before take-off, then flew on to make sure they had all negotiated the sandhills. Well, that was his excuse. He flew low, at little more than 100 feet, (30m) if that, above the dunes, coming in behind the convoy, frightening the hell out of them all as cars pulled off the road, all doors flew open and we lifted to climb in salute.

March of 1971 saw a major political crisis in Canberra with the fall of John Gorton as prime minister and succession to the position of William McMahon. This threw the Alice Springs Centenary celebrations, and all the planning for the motorcade to town of the Governor General, Sir Paul Hasluck, and Lady Hasluck, into disarray. Their planned arrival Wednesday afternoon was postponed until next morning, until he could swear in the new prime minister and cabinet. Then when they arrived, the visit went as planned. It was only on the Wednesday afternoon, for Commonwealth public servants, and the Thursday morning for NT public servants – the police, fire brigade and prisons – that the Thursday was declared a public holiday. The only difference for us was, we would get extra pay.

One of the features of the centenary was the building of a fountain, at the northern end of Todd Street, just inside the Anzac Oval reserve. It had been built with sandstone the same as used as a fascia for the new police station; it was to be the first fountain in town. The Governor General was to turn it on. This was to be followed by the first Camel Cup race, a race of camels along the dry sandy bed of the Todd River before he returned to the Residency for lunch. Later in the day Sir Paul and Lady Hasluck visited the Old Telegraph Station for a re-enactment of the discovery of the "spring", in fact a waterhole in the Todd River. It was discovered on 11 March, 1871, by William Mills, surveyor in charge of constructing the central portion of the overland telegraph line. He named the waterhole 'The Alice Springs' after the wife of Charles Todd, the South Australian Superintendent of Telegraphs, and named the watercourse, the 'Todd River' The following year the telegraph repeater station was built at the site of 'The Alice Spring'. The telegraph station was part of the first landline link between Adelaide and Darwin, and the rest of the world from 1872 to 1932.

My task was first to be in the oval grounds near the fountain and near the official party, then later to be a sector commander for traffic control for the Governor General's trip to and from the Telegraph Station. I think the whole town turned out for the switch-on of the fountain and camel race. I'd never seen so many people of the town all together. At the fountain opening, I was standing right beside it, keeping children out of the water. When it was turned on, it went full bore, the breeze catching the water so everyone standing on one side, including myself, got wet. It was also quite a job trying to keep the traffic flowing. People were not used to a police officer putting up his hand to stop them from crossing the road. We didn't have a whistle to blast, so to get some attention and pull up people wandering across the road I pulled the cap off my pen and blew across it to give a shrill whistle. It worked.

There was more traffic control when the Governor General left town on the Friday morning, and even more for a large funeral later in the day, and on the Saturday morning for a sports parade in the main street. For me the side effect of the traffic control came a couple of days later – aching shoulders.

After a couple of weeks of on-again, off-again dithering it was finally decided I would go to Tennant Creek to relieve again for a couple of months while the Sergeant Third Class took leave. Now with the local radio station, there was some company along the way, for nearly 200 miles (320kms) of the trip. I had a late lunch at Wauchope. Don and Joan Burgess, who were at the hotel at Finke when I relieved there had now taken over the Wauchope Hotel, about 75 miles (120kms) south of Tennant Creek. They took the opportunity to send their banking, some $2,000, to town with me. There was only one bank in Tennant Creek, a branch of the ANZ Bank.

I was the only one living in barracks. One of the single chaps at the station was away relieving and a couple were on leave, so for a couple of weeks barracks life would be quiet, the duty roster busy and the prospect of overtime seemed pretty good.

I was on duty only a couple of days before the first visit of the Magistrate, and quite a long court list with three defended cases. One was an assault between two chaps who worked at the local weather bureau office; another was a chap who had shot a cat. He was the luckier of the trio, having one charge dismissed, but overall, at the end of the day, I felt very pleased with myself having obtained convictions in all the other matters. I enjoyed the change and the challenge, although you never really knew if you had the Magistrate with you or set against you. We knew only too well how he could take a set on an arresting officer or turn against a defendant or his solicitor.

Things were fairly routine although one evening we had a little excitement – a resident in the new estate on the south eastern outskirts of the town rang to say he had trapped a dingo in his chicken house ... for some nights he had noticed a fowl or two disappearing, so he had set a trap. The dingo was now in his chicken house and could not get out. So over we went to see. Sure enough there was a fully grown dingo in the chicken house and under the lights and with all the attention it was receiving it was too scared to attack any of the fowls. I had one of the station Smith and Wesson .38 cal. revolvers, a World War II relic, but still police issue. It was one of the rare occasions I fired a shot in anger, and despatched the dingo chicken thief.

Next day the *Northern Territory News* made its normal police rounds phone call to find out what was happening in Tennant Creek ... the incident not only made a few paragraphs in the *NT News* but also made the Adelaide *Advertiser.*

Hitchhiking was a regular feature on territory roads. Many were genuine international or interstate tourists while others were little more than migrating criminals. Still, there were the community minded hitch-hikers as I found out one Sunday evening I was working. It wasn't long after tea, we had been away from the station for an hour or so, returned to the station and checked in with the telephone exchange ... *"Anyone been looking for us? ... "yes, Frewena roadhouse was wanting you half an hour or so ago" ... "could you put us through then" ... "Police, Tennant Creek here, what's the problem Fred?" ... "Oh, an hour or so ago a car refuelled here, the driver was speaking with an American accent, he had a hitch-hiker with him, the hitch-hiker got me on the side and said 'there is something funny about this bloke, he is speaking with a fake American accent, I think you should let the police know' so I thought I'd ring and tell you"*

We took a few more details and then headed out to Threeways, the junction of the Barkly and Stuart Highways. By the time we reached there, we learnt the car had already refuelled and had headed into Tennant Creek; it must have been one of the cars we passed on the way out but did not recognise it from the description we had been given.

As we arrived back in Tennant Creek, just 15 miles (24kms) from Threeways we saw the car at the petrol bowser outside the newsagency. The driver had refuelled again and was about to drive off. While my patrol partner spoke to him I got to talk with the hitch-hiker for a minute or so and then spoke with the driver. His American accent certainly didn't ring true, especially when he was effected by liquor he had bought at Frewena and most likely elsewhere as well.

There was something 'wrong' about the guy, an athletic 29 year old. I spoke with him long enough to satisfy myself I could sustain a charge of driving under the influence of liquor against him and formally arrested him, and took him back to the station, along with the vehicle. At the station he gave nothing away apart from the fact he had flown from Brisbane to Mt Isa earlier in the day, hired the car and was driving through to Darwin. The fact he had driven south of Threeways to Tennant Creek, instead of his stated intention of heading north, supported my belief he was affected by liquor.

He was also travelling light, only one small bag with a few clothes ... then the surprise, as we searched through the bag ... $780 in cash. I got the boss, still Sergeant First Class Andy McNeill, over from his house. He couldn't get any 'make sense' information out of the fellow either. Finally, I convinced the boss that we should phone Brisbane and ask if they knew anything about the fellow. *"Yes, we want that bloke ... "*

He was no American, he was a 29 year old Australian soldier, David White, based at Enoggera, just out of Brisbane. The previous day two of his fellow soldiers had a flutter on the newly introduced Queensland TAB treble and won $1,935.35 on the Doomben race meeting. They had partied on, then split the money. One put nearly $1,000 in his locker, in the room he shared with White. Early next morning, while his room-mate was still sleeping, White removed the money and took his room-mate's car keys, drove the car to Brisbane's Eagle Farm airport and bought a ticket for the flight to Mt Isa. In Mt Isa he hired the car. After further questioning he finally told us he was heading for Darwin with the intention of trying to get on a trawler working out of Darwin, with the hope of getting to Indonesia.

The arrest was all too much for Sergeant McNeill. He was now right in his element and he took over. Next day we had White remanded in custody on a charge of being unlawfully in possession of the $780, as well as the driving under the influence charge. The Queensland police wanted him back in Brisbane but they could also see the costs involved. Then the army stepped in and declared White absent without leave with the offer to take him back to Brisbane for court martial, and in turn, hand him over to the Queensland police. This was seen as an easy way out of the situation. An army officer duly arrived with a warrant, we fronted the soldier before the Magistrate, withdrew the charge of being unlawfully in possession of the money and handed him over to the army officer. While initially peeved that the matter had been taken out of my hands, I was later pleased when Sergeant McNeill had to respond to the please explain from the Commissioner who considered the action an improper circumvention of correct extradition proceedings.

A change in hotel trading hours, allowing them to stay open until 11.30pm Monday to Saturday and noon until 10pm Sundays, forced some changes in our work roster, working through until 1am most nights instead of 12 midnight, and rostering two staff on duty on Sunday evenings. The hotels were not obliged to stay open the additional hours but the Swan Brewery-owned Tennant Creek Hotel stayed open, the Goldfields Hotel initially only staying open late at weekends and to 6pm on Sundays. It was extra drinking time we could have done without. Well, at least I thought so anyway. We seemed to have managed pretty well with the previous late night licence arrangements. Of course it was our job to cope rather than wonder why.

Before going up to Tennant Creek to relieve, I'd been to the annual general meeting of the Central Australian Football League and been re-elected vice-president for the coming season. As the first round of matches got under way, I was able to drive down to The Alice for a couple of days, see the start of the season and even scored an invitation to the officer-in-charge, Sergeant Len Cossons', home for dinner. When I arrived back I felt quite off-colour, I thought I was in for a bout of flu, but that didn't happen. A couple of days later, still feeling off colour, I went to the hospital and saw the Sister on duty, who cheered me up no end telling me she thought I had hepatitis ... *"it doesn't appear serious, in fact, it might have already passed, but you better come and see doctor on Monday"*.

There was no private doctor in Tennant Creek, only two, sometimes three, doctors attached to the Tennant Creek hospital. The medical superintendent at the hospital was Dr Laufer, a Scotsman. He had been there a year or so and previously had worked for several years in central African missions and associated hospitals before migrating to Australia. He confirmed I had hepatitis A, gave me a certificate for two weeks but said I could expect to be off work for longer. I was confined to barracks and had to come back in a week and see him again. He rejected my suggestion that I fly home to my parents and recuperate. *"They will probably put you in an infectious diseases hospital if you did that"* he remarked. The rest of the chaps at the station were not too happy. Apart from me being off sick, they had to all line up at the hospital for a jab, in the buttock, known for its painful effect and doubtful ability of preventing cross-infection.

Although I had improved significantly in the week between visits ... *"you don't drink, do you?"* ... *"why?"* ... *"it certainly helps your liver recover, but you are still a little too yellow around the eyes to let you travel yet"* ... *"come back and see me Thursday"* ... he said. It was just a matter of resting, and in any case I had little energy to do much else but sleep. The hotel was good and sent me down meals, it was just a matter of sitting around, resting and waiting.

I flew to Alice Springs on the Friday morning, had a few hours there, time to pack some warm clothes, then continued on to Melbourne by jet. I continued to take it easy and in a fortnight began to feel my old self again. My folks took me to Essendon to fly back to The Alice but we found the airport closed owing to fog. It was only months away to the opening of the new Tullamarine airport and although all the tarmac areas were virtually complete and useable the airport terminal facilities were still under construction. The Boeing 727, due to take me to Alice Springs, had been able to land at Tullamarine, so we were all bused across from Essendon to Tullamarine. We loaded using the rear built-in stairs and travelled on to Adelaide and The Alice, arriving at midnight, 90 minutes late, but I was able to say I was on one of the first flights out of Tullamarine.

I had the weekend in Alice Springs which gave me the opportunity to attend Pamela Beckmann's 21st birthday dinner party cum-engagement party to Keith Colebrook. Most of the party was from Hermannsburg, but I knew them all anyway. I also went to the football on Sunday and saw Melenka win their first game since being admitted to the league at the beginning of the previous season, kicking twice their previous highest score, causing quite a stir among football followers.

Just before I came down with hepatitis I had decided to stand for the first Alice Springs town council. However, Standing Order 103, in particular Clause (iv) prohibited me from making any public statement *"dealing with politics"*. It in effect prevented me from conducting a campaign and if elected, from speaking on any issue. I made a request to be exempted from this provision.

It was left to the A/Superintendent, Charlie Porter to respond *"I agree that it is creditable that a member should have an interest in civic affairs and I favour participation of members of the Police Force in community affairs. It not only brings the Policeman in close contact with his fellow citizens but also plays a big part in good public relations"*. But then he referred to my Oath of Office and the conditions under which I served. *"He must be prepared to serve in any part of the Northern Territory and to work such shifts as he is rostered to work, as well as being liable to recall to duty at a moment's notice in the case of an emergency"*. The main basis for his refusal lay in a policy of *"no special privileges"* to any member, continuing to emphasise *"all members of all sections or branches are treated equally"*. I was not only disappointed, but also annoyed with the response. I saw it as totally two-faced. In one sentence he said what I wanted to do and achieve was commendable, and in fact should be encouraged, then in the next he cut the ground from under my feet.

My response was that I agreed all members should be treated equally but made the suggestion that if the Standing Order was changed by deleting the words *"or dealing with politics"* then all members of the force would be given similar freedom of speech as other members of the community and at the same time the policy of equal privileges to all members of the force would be maintained.

I had my nomination form prepared and photos taken. The issue made the front page of the *"Centralian Advocate"* and the pages of the Adelaide *"Advertiser"* but there was no last minute change of heart from the Commissioner. On the flight from Alice Springs to Tennant Creek two members of the Legislative Council sat behind me – Tony Greatorex, the President of the Council, and Bernie Kilgariff. Both approached me and expressed their disappointment at the Commissioner's attitude, but it was out of their hands.

Of course the Commissioner could have made the change quite easily, just as easily as he could have transferred me out of the town the moment I nominated. In the finish 30 nominated for the eight councillor positions. When I looked through the list, I felt very confident that I could have beaten 25 of them. Still, I will never know. Six stood for the mayoral position, including the former Federal member for the Territory, Jock Nelson, who at the election, won the position comfortably.

First job back in Tennant Creek was to see the doctor. *"All you have now is a bit of Melbourne fat"* he remarked. I said I was surprised I had not lost any weight. *"I'd say you don't drink ... that is why you've recovered quickly, why you are now feeling so well, its the greatest thing in your favour ... and you won't get hepatitis again either"*. His last remark gave me the most comfort.

I only had another week or so in Tennant Creek, time to enjoy the weather, before a move back to Alice Springs, where the night chills of winter were fast approaching. I found that out quickly, going straight on to night shift. One thing about the cooler weather was a lowering in the number of drinkers about, those having to be fingerprinted during the shift, bailed, or fed in the morning. It was surprising how some nights, really mornings, there was incident after incident to attend to while another night there would be nothing at all. Well apart from Miss Pink that is. We had not been on shift long when a man came to the station to report he had been assaulted and robbed, right outside the Catholic church, on his way home from drinking at one of the late night restaurants-cum drinking holes. While he could give us a reasonable description of the offenders, they also left a good set of tracks on the sandy verge of the road outside the church. At dawn I collected the trackers, Larry and Alby Morris, from Amoonguna, and took them to the scene where they confirmed a scuffle had taken place, there appeared to be three involved, who had run off.

Of course their tracks didn't show up on the bitumen road at the Hartley Street and Wills Terrace corner site of the church, but they were quickly picked up "running" off the bitumen and into Anzac Oval Reserve, across to the oval fence which they jumped and on to the lush grass, again an untraceable surface. It was a matter of moving around the edge of the oval until they jumped the fence again, back on to the dirt surface and down into the sandy bed of the Todd River. As we crossed the river, they stopped and started to dig in the sand, pulling from it a wallet and some burnt papers. It appeared at this point the trio had stopped to see what they had scored, $80 in cash, then emptied out the wallet and set the papers on fire, covering it in sand. We continued on to the east side of the river, and on to Stuart Terrace. Again the tracks disappeared, the culprits smart enough to know the trackers would more than likely be able to follow them to this point. What they had forgotten was that the previous evening, the trio had walked to town along the dirt footpath of the East Side streets. The trackers quickly identified the same three sets of prints, and began to follow them backwards, from where they had come. As we moved along Giles Street, we came to a point where the three sets of prints walked off the bitumen and into the house from where the three sets of prints had walked the previous evening.

Just as we woke the household, the CIB arrived and took over the investigation. They later arrested three for assault and robbery, each later sentenced to two years imprisonment by the Supreme Court judge.

The incident again highlighted the value of the skills of the aboriginal police trackers attached to the force. Their keen eye never ceased to amaze me. They not only were the downfall of many offenders but they also were able to 'read' the ground and give a picture of what had happened at a crime scene. They could tell the number of people involved, through identifying the individual tracks and could usually tell if the tracks were of aboriginals or non-aboriginals. They could also tell the types of shoes the people were wearing, whether they were male or female, were wearing long trousers (the trouser cuff would mark as well as the heel of the foot or shoe) and whether the person was lame or had an unusual gait or was carrying something (the footprints would be more indented in the soil). They would stand and using a stick or twig point out the features, telling the story of a crime scene. This knowledge in the hands of an investigating officer during questioning put an offender in an uneasy position, wondering just how much you really knew about an offence.

———

Although there were no minerals around the township of Alice Springs itself, there were many past relics of mineral activity within reach of the town which had served as the service centre for either exploration or mining activity.

In the late 1870's gold was discovered at Arltunga, about 75 miles (120kms) north east of the town. In the early 1900's the population of the area was in its thousands, within years virtually nobody lived there. There were only the ruins of several stone buildings and the rusting hulk of boilers and associated mining equipment. The Central Australian Gem and Mineral Club decided, as part of the Alice Springs centenary celebrations, to stage a "Back to Arltunga" weekend on 18-21 June, 1971.

Two of us from Alice Springs, and Constable Eddie Josephs, the officer-in-charge at Harts Range, further north-east of Arltunga, were sent out for the weekend and set up camp at the site of the police station which had operated there when the gold field was active. The Arltunga police station is believed to be the second police station opened in the Northern Territory, in 1879 or 1880 and operated as a police station until 1944. It closed when the Harts Range station opened. The concrete slab floor of the station residence and its large stone chimney were still there, as was the stone single cell building, which overall, wasn't in bad condition. The door was still fixed, the roof was there but there was a hole in the stone wall. We set up our fire for cooking in the chimney and lay our swags out on the concrete slab, trying to make our-selves as comfortable as possible.

I'd never been to the area before. Usually, a four-wheel-drive was needed to get to Arltunga, that is, to get much beyond the Ross River Resort, but for the weekend the road had been graded and some of the creek crossings part-ly filled to allow more conventional vehicles to reach the site. The area was rugged. The goldfields where in a series of ranges and rocky valleys. The whole area had numerous dry creeks, cutting sharply through the road cross-ings. It had all the hall marks of a deserted mining area – the ruins, the grave sites and the pollution of ground water through cyanide use in the gold extraction process. Stories abounded of hardship as well stories of get-rich-quick miners who later settled in Stuart, the town that was to become Alice Springs when the railway arrived in 1929.

The organisers of the celebrations sold Miner's Rights for 50c as admis-sion to the goldfields area. As a memento I also took out a formal Miner's Right, also 50c (although the form still stated *Fee: Five Shillings*) from Eddie Josephs. Just as I had been at Maranboy, he was also authorised to issue Miner's Rights at his station at Harts Range.

The programme for the weekend included a mock Mining Warden's Court, working relics of a bellows forge and blacksmith's shop, horse trail rides, gold panning, rickshaw rides, whip cracking, a period costume Back to Arltunga Ball and folk dancing. There was also a post office selling a special endorsed envelope and the 6c Stuart's Desert Rose stamp, the mail carried by horseback from the goldfields to Alice Springs and postmarked.

One thing I remember most about the weekend was that it was bitterly cold, with clear sunny days meaning only one thing; cold clear nights and a heavy frost. I remember in the morning, pushing my hand from my swag to feel the frost on my pillow, right beside my head. There were no hot showers to rush off to, just get up, get the pot boiling and get some hot water for a quick wash. But what a magnificent spectacle it offered ... to lie in my swag, look to the sky and in the total darkness of night, see the vast mass of the Milky Way, the brightness of the Southern Cross, the pointer stars, or the var-ious formations of stars, so clear, so bright, in the clear winter night air. And in total silence. It was breathtaking.

I got back to town to find the fire brigade on strike and the station utility loaded with fire extinguishers as a "first-aid" fire vehicle until the main fire tender arrived. While the firemen would turn out to an actual fire, the police had to take the call and sound the siren. The town really had an excellent fire service with four or five full time firemen, who worked Monday to Friday. Auxiliary firemen, young local volunteer types were paid to spend the nights and weekends at the fire station, turning out to alarms and at other times backing up the full-time firemen. Fortunately, the strike, over pay, lasted only a couple of days and during that time we had no disasters.

Things generally continued pretty routine. For something-to-do on night shift, which now went from 1am to 9am, I decided to get out the only piece of technical equipment the police had in Alice Springs, the amphometer, a speed detection reader. We set it up, first on Gap Road, and next morning on Bloomfield Street, to catch airport workers as they sped out of town, late for work. The first morning we booked 10 in an hour, the next only three. The message soon got around.

I was soon to get into another regulations clash with the Commissioner. As I have mentioned earlier, the Standing Orders required all single officers to live in barracks. It also required them to physically be in the barracks between 2am and 6am except if on duty or absent from the police district with the permission of the divisional officer.

As the force expanded, many of the new married men joining were allocated newly built homes, with no more than a load of gravel for a driveway and a couple of truck loads of soil for the garden. With a great degree of pride, and in many cases, a bloody lot of hard work and personal expense, the fellows developed lawns and quite good gardens. It was a credit to them. However, when they went on leave, they could either see everything fall apart, or they could get someone to caretake the house. A lived-in house was more secure, the garden was maintained and the house usually kept spic and span for the return of the officer and his family. Several would like someone from within the force to caretake, leaving the single fellows at barracks as the contenders. I was asked by several members to caretake their house. When Sergeant Cossons planned to go on leave, he asked Terry O'Brien and I to move in. However, being a stickler for regulations and not wanting to lay himself open to criticism (especially as he was officer-in-charge of the station) he asked us to make a formal application for permission to stay out of barracks. Typically, the Divisional Inspector sat on the fence and shunted the request off to headquarters in Darwin.

It was thus no surprise when the Commissioner said "no". To us it was just another of his head-in-the-sand, nonsensical decisions which nearly everybody then set about to do everything they could to work around. While Terry and I didn't caretake Len Cosson's house, over the next few years we both looked after a number of member's houses while they were on leave.

It was also decisions like this that made some of us fight on about other matters we raised and felt 100% in the right about. An example was the provision in the Police Determination, our award, that provided $50-$100 to married officers as an allowance to defray uncompensated depreciation on furniture and possessions when the married officer was required to move house, usually on transfer. It was paid virtually automatically to married officers. However, when a provision for a $30 payment to single officers was written into the Determination, it had not been routinely paid.

I decided to make a claim, and submitted two in relation to my move to and from Tennant Creek on relieving duty. I did this after a disagreement about the use of my room at barracks by visitors while I was away at Tennant Creek. I was told that I couldn't expect my room to be kept for me in the Alice Springs barracks when I was on transfer to Tennant Creek relieving.

The initial refusal to pay the claims wasn't really a surprise, it had never been done before and the Inspector and the Commissioner couldn't see why they should start to pay it now. However, I was determined the Commissioner would pay the allowance. Finally, the Police Association decided to support my claim and force the issue. Their initial approaches were also rebuffed but they took the matter up with the Administrator who within days directed that the payments be made. I guess it was little wonder my application for inclusion in the Australia Police contingent to Cyprus, as part of a UN police peace keeping force, wasn't successful.

I returned to umpiring Australian Rules football, mainly reserve grade or under age games, but did one League game, making my first report, catching an incident behind play. The umpires hadn't had a good year at the tribunal but I felt confident, partly because of the clear-cut case I had and also because my work training would assist me in presenting the matter. As it transpired, the young fellow pleaded guilty and was suspended for two weeks. So with no football the following weekend due to Picnic Day and a bye for his team, he couldn't play again before the finals. My involvement in the football scene intensified when the League secretary, Graham Carpenter, an accountant in town, was transferred. He had to resign the secretaryship and I took on the job.

Later in the season, I also got to umpire some of the under age finals and finished my umpiring year with the reserves grade preliminary final, which I thought was a pretty good effort. However, the highlight of the season was my nomination for the H.A.C. Harrison Trophy, awarded annually to the person, on or off the field, considered to have contributed the most to Australian Rules football in Alice Springs during the year. There were four nominations. It was a real thrill to be announced the winner, have my name inscribed on a magnificent rose-bowl trophy I held for a year.

Although I didn't have to go to work at Harts Range over the Picnic Day weekend, it turned out a busy one in town. On the Monday afternoon a road train tanker decided to part company from the prime mover while negotiating what we called the 'big dipper' through the river crossing of the Charles River, four miles (6.4kms) into the hills just north of town. The tanks, with 8,000 gallons (36,400 litres) of kerosene and 8,000 gallons (36,400 litres) of super petrol speared into the rock-face edge of the road leading into the gully crossing of the river.

By some miracle the fuel did not explode or catch alight and most of it ran down to the dry creek bed and soaked into the sand. Only about 2,000 gallons (9,000 litres) of the petrol was saved. The closure of the main highway could not have come at a worse time as hundreds returned to town from weekend activities, in particular the Harts Range races. The highway, at this point, was really the only access to the town from the north. However, when we were satisfied the area was reasonably safe, we allowed traffic through slowly, stopping all vehicles to ensure there was no smoking. On reflection even this was risky; it would never have been allowed today.

Alice Springs had a series of major activities during the year, like the Bangtail Muster, organised by members of the Rotary Clubs and the sports by Apex, on the first Monday in May, the Show, now on the first Friday in July. The Rodeo came along later in mid August, organised by the Lions Club, and the Henley-on-Todd in early September, organised by the Rotary Clubs. The rodeo probably caused the most extra work. It was not just a matter of being present at the event over the weekend, but the rodeo attracted many stockmen, in particular aboriginal stockmen, from outlying cattle stations, missions and settlements and most of them were far more interested in a can of Fosters than the outcome of a bronco ride.

This year at the rodeo and around town in the evening there were 101 arrests, nearly all for drunkenness. There were 130 who faced court on Monday morning, all but a half-dozen being aboriginal. Each one had to be fingerprinted during the night shift, which meant the town was hardly patrolled despite being normally the busy night of the week not to mention the boost to the population. All the prisoners had to be fed as well, we had 115 breakfasts to serve two mornings, 70 another – porridge with milk and sugar, baked beans, sausages and bread, tea with milk and sugar. It all took time. With the weekend over, there were another 40 arrested on Monday evening. Many were the same ones as Saturday, released from court on Monday morning and back in the cells later in the day.

With the rodeo over for the year, we knew the warmer weather was on the way. We were quickly into summer uniform and the locals predicted a long hot summer with good rains.

Keith and Pam's wedding came along and I was asked to be groomsman. One of the other chaps in barracks, Gary O'Donohue, who had been in the same recruit school as Keith, was best man. Keith's mother and step-father travelled from Brisbane to attend. It was predicted to be a hot day, as it was 101F (38.5C) a couple of days before the wedding. We squirmed at the thought of being dressed in a full dinner suit but on the day, it was a mild 80F (27C) making it quite pleasant. The wedding was at the Lutheran Church and followed by a reception at the Mt Gillen Motel attended by about 60. It was the last reception to be held at the motel before it closed and was handed over to the Department of Health to be converted to a health centre for aboriginal women and children, in particular new born and babies, attached to the hospital but not part of the hospital.

At barracks we thought hard about what sort of prank we could play on Keith. Then some bright spark came up with a simple, effective and achievable plan. We got hold of his wedding shoes, and in the arch of the sole, using shoe whitener wrote HE over M on the left shoe and LP over E on the right shoe. At the church, when he kneeled to pray in front of the alter, Keith displayed to the congregation the words HELP ME. There was a real snigger around the church as people saw it. Keith's mother didn't know whether to laugh or cry. Perhaps just as well for us, she saw the funny side of the prank. Keith was not amused.

Although the football season was well over, the league president, Dean Newman, a former South Adelaide player, who had played, coached and still umpired in Alice Springs, had ideas for special celebrations for the 25th year of organised Australian Rules football in Alice Springs and the formation of the Central Australia Football League. First, he re-wrote the constitution of the league, transforming its administration to more of a board structure.

While club delegates still had a contribution and say, he had the foresight that to be successful in football administration, you needed a strong administrative panel of business thinking people who could get on with the job without the distraction of club interests.

He then wanted two South Australia National Football League (SANFL) clubs to come to Alice Springs during 1972 and play a game, if not for actual league points, then as a pre-season trial game. The SANFL agreed to this and sought expressions of interest from clubs wishing to make the visit, for a game in the latter part of March, 1972. This was going to cost $6,000 plus in airfares alone, so we needed to do some fund raising.

In an effort to get the support of the whole town, the league invited the who's-who of the town to meet for a drink and a nibble one November Sunday morning, in the downstairs function room of the Elkira Motel, to formally announce the grand plan. We were encouraged that more than $650 had been donated by people who could not come, along with two charity nights at the drive-in theatre, a set of golf sticks worth $340 to raffle, and other prizes. The morning went well, especially when we were able to win-over the editor of the local newspaper, Tony Malone, who had been sceptical of our plans and ideas.

I dubbed it "The Match of the Century" as we intensified our fund raising and organisation for the day. Next thing was a battle between TAA (now Qantas) and Ansett to fly the teams from Adelaide for the match. Peter Darley, captain of South Adelaide and former SANFL captain, was a sales representative for TAA and was soon in town with a bag of offers we could not resist. I went out and bought a typewriter, so I could prepare letters, stencils and other material. The organisation of the match was on in earnest.

Confirmation that SANFL clubs South Adelaide and Central Districts would come and play a match at Traeger Park on Saturday, 18 March. 1972, really cranked up arrangements. As a curtain raiser we invited long-standing rivals Mt Isa over to play. We would have liked a team from Darwin to have come down but the game was in the middle of their finals, so that was out of the question. We also arranged an Under 15 game, boys from the local high school, to start the day off.

Apart from the match itself, we set out to produce a souvenir issue of *"On the Ball"*, the football Budget, a term I could never get used to. In Melbourne we always called it the *Record* but for South Australians, and thus Alice Springs-ites, it was the *Budget*. The league president, Dean Newman, in particular put together the history of the league. He rounded up old photos and stories, I solicited adverts, it was a big job.

It's still the best record of the beginnings of organised Australian Rules football in Alice Springs ever put together.

In the midst of the preparations, we had the league's annual general meeting. I was re-elected secretary, I don't think there was anyone else silly enough to want to take on the job at the time. Overall, everything seemed to fall into place, even six inches of rain (150mm) and a flood through town a fortnight before, couldn't hold us back. However, the disappointment of the day was the attendance. Despite all the publicity, only about half the crowd we really hoped for turned up. Still, we saw three great games of Australian Rules, Mt Isa spoiling our day defeating Alice Springs by a solitary point in the final moments of the game, and as good a pre-season game as you could expect from two of Adelaide's League teams with the footballers of tomorrow showing their skills in the first game of the day.

Low number car registration plates were always of interest, that is to see who could get as low a number as possible. At least it was an interest to some people including myself. One afternoon I was just walking out of the District Office, where the motor registry operated, when Max Spurling, a chap I knew from the post office, walked in carrying two plates, number 167. *"What are you going to do with them?"* I asked. *"Oh, hand them in. The car has had it, it's just rusting away in the back yard. If I don't hand the plates in, they will be after me – would you like them?"* This was an opportunity too good to be true. We had a word with Bob Hamilton, the motor registry officer, who told us that after recent changes to the motor vehicle regulations, we could not exchange the plates between the two of us. However, it was allowable to exchange plates between the one owner, if both the vehicles were registered. The problem was, the vehicle wasn't registered. *"But ... knowing the situation ... if you ... I will co-operate"* Bob, quite out of character, assured us. So I went and paid for a Third Party Insurance policy, re-registered the car (I filled out the roadworthy certificate) we changed the ownership to my name, exchanged the plates, then cancelled the registration all in the one day. The insurance company gave me a full refund, the motor registry gave me a refund of all but the six weeks or so the old vehicle had been unregistered, and I had the old 167 plates on my car. When Bob Hamilton remarked *"I think you should order a new set of plates, the old ones are a bit knocked about"* I didn't argue with him and paid the $2 for a new set which arrived a week or two later, and we swapped them over. Yes, an eye or two turned as they noticed the low number plates on my car.

In the meantime, work was fairly routine. Miss Pink phoned and asked if I could call over, collect her revolver, give it a good clean and oil and return it the same day ... *"it is my only protection at night over here!"* she remarked. I reluctantly obliged.

An evening shift patrol turned a little more exciting when on patrol with Constable Bruce Long we drove past the Riverside Hotel to find the foyer of the hotel on fire. We immediately radioed for the fire brigade. The brigade seemed to take ages to get to the scene, although they really were there as quickly as could be expected. The blaze quickly took hold and we had to get people out of first floor rooms as well as clear the bars. The brigade quickly had a ladder to the first floor rooms. The hardest thing was getting some people to leave the "snake pit" bar.

A crowd quickly formed, especially when there was a call over the drive-in theatre system, for all off-duty firemen to report immediately for duty. I'm told half the theatre left and drove back to town to see what the excitement was. I was pleased with the postmortem of the event with favourable comment on how well the police were organised and handled things. The District Officer even spoke to me *"well, if you have no worries Dave, I don't have any either."* Later CIB arrested a chap and charged him with arson. It was alleged that earlier in the night he had been ejected from the hotel for gambling on the premises, and while being removed from the hotel, threatened to burn it down. He had been seen again in the foyer of the hotel a short time before it was discovered on fire. However when the Supreme Court trial came on the jury acquitted him.

The last day of high school for the year nearly turned to tragedy when a mid-morning storm caused the Todd River to flow. It came with a rush. The sudden torrent of water attracted not only townsfolk but many high school children who gathered to watch as they walked along the river bank, following the flow of the river.

Stephen Kelly, aged 13 years, was standing on some tree roots on a built-up section of the dry river bed, just on the south side of the causeway. Suddenly he realised the river had risen around his vantage point, and that he was trapped by the raging waters. His plight was quickly recognised by several bystanders including Graham Hunter, Don Jones, Bill Dobbin (a Commonwealth policeman) and another student Roger Bottrall.

I later had to collect a series of statements about the incident for a report to headquarters in response to a request that the rescue effort should be recognised. Graham Hunter got to young Kelly first, but before he could assist him back to the river bank, a floating log came by and trapped Hunter's legs to the tree where they were standing. By this stage the water was thigh deep. Young Roger Bottrall ran a rope from the footbridge downstream to where Kelly and Hunter were trapped, but as Kelly took the rope and began to be hauled back to safety, in the torrent of water, he lost his grip. As he shot through the water Don Jones grabbed him, held him, but as he attempted to reach higher ground, he too was washed off his feet, ending up against a semi submerged stump. But still he managed to hold on to young Kelly and was soon able to pass him on to others helping in the rescue. This left Graham Hunter to be rescued as the river continued to rage, but using a truck, ropes and sheer manpower, he was plucked from the river, shaken but safe.

There was hardly a "coming down of the Todd", particularly in the day time, that didn't provide the need for some rescue. Either people did not get out of the river bed as the river rose, or a vehicle would be swept off the causeway, the driver refusing to accept that the flow was too strong for a safe passage. It reached the point where we would rescue the people but leave the vehicle as a reminder to others to think twice before making the fool-hardy decision to try to cross.

Christmas came and went, it was 103F (39.4C) on Christmas Day but most people still had a traditional roast for Christmas lunch. I had Christmas lunch with Keith and Pam Colebrook who were being transferred to Darwin a week later. I made a few other visits and then worked from 5pm-1am, finishing the night arresting a chap for drunk driving, illegal use of a motor vehicle and driving without a licence. He got 18 months imprisonment and was disqualified from driving for five years for his trouble. It wasn't his first time.

New Year saw the introduction of compulsory seat belt laws in the Territory, legislation that was received with very mixed feelings. Many were determined that as they had never worn a seat belt before then they never would. However, like everywhere else, given a few weeks, there was general acceptance. One thing that was frustrating was that we as police had to ensure we were wearing seat belts all the time we were on patrol. As there were still no automatic retractors they became a hindrance when you had to unbuckle and untangle yourself to jump from the vehicle to intervene in a fight or footpath incident.

The shame of New Year's Eve was the desecration of the Flynn Memorial, five miles (8kms) west of Alice Springs, along the Hermannsburg Road. In the shadow of Mt Gillen, the magnificent boulder rock, originally brought from the Devils Marbles, south of Tennant Creek, sat on top of a stone cairn. While some of Flynn's ashes were said to be in the cairn, his ashes were also said to have been scattered over his beloved Mt Gillen. In later years, the ashes of his wife were interred in the cairn. There was a neat chain perimeter fence and a series of stone posts marking out the site of this small reserve. A young stately ghost gum stood near the entrance, set back from the road with a dusty gravel car park between the road and the reserve.

Sometime during the night, somebody sprayed the marble shaped boulder centrepiece of the memorial with red, green and yellow paints. The town was outraged. Within hours a $500 reward for information leading to "who dun it" had been offered. Five days later the CIB arrested four youths for the matter, filling the court house when they appeared

The next question was how to clean the Flynn Memorial. There was no shortage of ideas or helpers. Within a day it was cleaned, even if it had lost a little of its aged rustic look, the granite stone losing its former typically sandy red colour.

Nearly everyone in town had driven out to see the paint spattered memorial. When word spread that it had been cleaned there was a steady stream of sight-seers. Amongst them was a young man, his wife and two young children. They parked, walked up to the Memorial and as they looked over it a man said to be a part-aboriginal carrying a rifle walked out from the scrub beyond the cairn. The family ran to their car and got in but before they could drive off the man with the rifle walked up to the side window and at point-blank range, shot the husband in the head, then ran back into the bush. The injured man was dead on arrival at hospital.

Next morning aboriginal trackers traced the gunman from the memorial back to the outskirts of the town, finding the rifle abandoned along the way. At the time I was caretaking Bob Henfry's house and was out for the evening. When I got home I didn't turn on a light in the porch, just went straight to bed. Next morning I found a note asking me to report for duty, it had been left the night before. I went straight in and worked 11 hours that day, and worked every day for the following week, mainly on door to door inquiries, looking for a vital clue. At one house, the lady was sitting in her lounge, with a rifle she had never used, beside her.

Of course, Miss Pink drove the station mad, ringing about 50 times. I had to go over and put fresh ammunition in her revolver, repeatedly reassuring her that the offender wasn't in her area. Well, we hoped not anyway.

Despite months of intense inquiry, no one was ever arrested.

Night shift either passed without incident or was a shift of continual action. One of the worst nights came in mid February, 1972, with little more than an hour of the shift to go. While my two shift-mates were on a dawn patrol, the airport emergency phone rang. A Connair flight from Alice Springs to Ayers Rock, which had departed only minutes earlier with a pilot and six passengers had reported engine trouble and was endeavouring to return to the airport. I radioed the patrol car to head for the airport and I stayed on line. The news was getting grimmer. It was confirmed that smoke near the airport was from the plane in question. It was "down". I was immediately on the phone to the Inspector, the officer-in-charge, the OIC of CIB and the police photographer. It was virtually all hands on deck as I co-ordinated the police involvement for the first hour, until the end of shift.

From there things were fairly straight forward and the wreckage was quickly located. The plane had hit the ground at high speed, scattering wreckage for a hundred yards (metres) or so, smashing the bodies of those on board to pieces. It took one and a half days to get the bodies to the morgue. I personally knew five of the people on board, the pilot, a young man, his wife and their new baby and the manager of one of the Ayer's Rock motels. Tragically, too, the young woman was the daughter of the undertaker who faced the task of not only burying her, but also his son-in-law and grandchild.

Two mornings later, about 2.10am, my night shift patrol was heading out of The Gap when they came across two bodies on the roadway, the victims of a motor cycle accident. The Traffic section was called on duty to attend but later in the morning, I had the task of going to the home of the parents of the pillion passenger, a young girl, and telling them of their daughter's death. Breaking the news of death was a task I was becoming hardened to but it was a job I always hated.

I'd taken the precaution of starting five weeks leave a few days before "Match of the Century" to ensure I would be off duty not just the few days before the match but in particular, on match day itself. I used the rest of the time to take a 10 day trip to Fiji and spend some time with my folks.

My first day back at work was on May Day, the first Monday of May, in winter uniform, and on point duty for the Bangtail Muster parade. It was now five years since I first did point duty at the parade. It had certainly changed. To start with, the crowd estimate was 7,000, more than the entire population of the town five years earlier. Another change was the direction of the parade, instead of starting south of the town and heading to Anzac Oval, the parade started at Anzac Oval and moved to Traeger Park, a more secure venue to collect admission charges. On the floats, it was a year of flour bombs, and no better target were policemen on point duty. I successfully dodged most but suffered one direct hit.

Of course, night shift came around pretty quickly after my return and again it was to have its night of intense action. In the early hours of a Sunday morning a message from Papunya Senior Constable Basil "Bluey" Smith, the officer-in-charge of the recently opened police station at Papunya, was delivered to the station. It was a hurriedly written note to say the police station and residence had been set upon by rioters, after "Bluey" and Constable Mike Jenkinson, his off-sider at Papunya, had made arrests at the settlement picture night. The police office and residences were damaged and the families had taken refuge together in one of the two police houses. *"Send assistance"* the note pleaded. First job was getting the Inspector and the officer-in-charge out of bed before getting another 10 fellows on duty, including the officer-in-charge of the CIB. They were all set up with vehicles and away about 5am.

While two from barracks stayed on at Papunya for a week or so, the rest of the squad arrested 22 on about 100 charges, cases which went on for months.

The incident caused quite a ripple among members. It was all made worse when the Divisional Inspector instructed the families of the two Papunya officers to be brought to town and put them up in a motel. But then he couldn't give any indication who would pay for the accommodation. Feelings further deteriorated when the Commissioner indicated he wouldn't meet the cost, and the two members involved decided to use leave fare entitlements and fly their wives and children to southern capitals to be with family until things sorted themselves out.

I had become the chairman/secretary of the Alice Springs based members of the Police Association so ended up in the thick of it when nearly every member at Alice Springs, from the station sergeant down to the newest recruit, attended a special meeting of the Alice Springs branch of the association. Members were incensed not only with the Commissioner's attitude and response to date but with the whole equipment, security and communications situation for police, in particular those at remote stations.

At the first meeting of association members on the Thursday after the Papunya riot, the first motion proposed was one of no confidence in the Commissioner. However, as discussion continued, a more conciliatory approach, but no less heartfelt, prevailed with a unanimous decision of members expressing their disappointment in his decision. The association was asked to make a new approach for a clear statement from the Commissioner that he would immediately undertake to recompense members for the accommodation costs of their families, and reinstate the travel entitlements that members had used to fly their families south.

The meeting also called on the Commissioner to act immediately to ensure the issue of riot or hard-top helmets to all members, to provide an up-to-date fully-equipped armoury at the Alice Springs police station, that all future settlement police stations be planned and built on the basis of a five-man complement and also to immediately initiate investigations to up-grade the communications system to all isolated police stations, including the provision of radio-telephones, and for security fencing and lighting to be erected around the Papunya police compound.

The situation in Alice Springs was that the armoury consisted of two .303 rifles, two .22 rifles, 28 .38 revolvers and two riot (tear gas) guns. At Papunya there was no official issue of firearms as there wasn't a safe at the station. The officer in charge had been told no firearms would be issued to the station until the safe was delivered. How he was to get a rifle into the station safe hadn't been thought of. The truth was, the force relied on members' personal firearms, whether they were rifles or sidearm, as the back-bone of an armoury. At the same time there were modern firearms, like the new Lee Enfield SLR rifles, on issue in Darwin. Members felt they should also be available at Alice Springs, along with appropriate training in their use. The only on-going training in the use of firearms was when a few members, on their own initiative, might go to the pistol or rifle range and have a few shots.

Members also felt hard-hats should be available not just for riot use, but also when attending duties at a mine or building sites, at fires and the like. The Papunya police complex was unfenced and anyone could walk through the station or residence yards and have access to prisoners in the cells. It also came to light that when anyone walked out the back door of one of the residences, they were in clear view of the cells, with the wife and children of an officer already being abused by more than one drunkard. The major concern however was when the wives and children were left at the station while their husbands came to Alice Springs on police business. It was a situation members felt could no longer be accepted. The incident had confirmed their fears. They were not prepared to see their colleagues and families placed at risk in the way which had arisen at Papunya. The same sort of situation could quite easily happen again, if not at Papunya, then at other aboriginal community locations where police stations were being established. After all, the police stations were being established because of the increased lawlessness at the communities, not just for the sake of having a police station in a community.

While the Commissioner agreed next day to pay the accommodation costs incurred by the members, it was years before anything serious happened to improve security and facilities at bush stations.

⇒•◦•⇐

As the Queen's Birthday weekend approached, the CAFL got ready to make a trip to Mt Isa. I was appointed team manager. Mt Isa was a 750 miles (1,200kms) trip via Tennant Creek and the league hired a Pioneer bus for the trip – $900 for the return trip. The team members and official party of 30 in all paid $10 while other supporters could travel for $25 to help defray the cost of the bus. Nobody had a second thought about making the trip, leaving Friday evening, playing the game Sunday and travelling most of

Monday home again. I went to the trouble of making application to be rostered off duty for the days over the weekend and to leave the police district. Despite my report, all stamped with approval, and the roster being issued with the days off, it was all too good to be true. I no sooner had all my arrangements made than there was a sudden need to change the duty roster and I had to work two of the three days over the weekend. My trip was cancelled. It seemed to me there was an anti Australian Rules conspiracy. I'm quite sure if it had been a rugby trip, it would have been a different story. At least the league gave me the team jacket and carry bag printed in the league colours they had prepared for me.

I finally decided to join the Alice Springs Memorial Club, an institution of the town. I was one of only a few at the station who was not a member. Not only was it a drinking hole of the town, it had regular free family picture nights, games facilities and well priced counter meals, something I needed now we had lost our Mt Gillen Motel eating spot. It was only $20 or so to join 'the club' as everybody knew it, it was a good spot away from the hotel bars and honestly, away from many of the day-to-day work 'clients'. There was still the working-man's feel about the place and still the areas of the club where you could sit and have a relaxing drink, a lemon soda squash for me, a talk, a meal and then wander home.

Now that I had been in Alice Springs for a while, a story or two had appeared in the local paper at home giving me a mention like . . . *"Belgrave man in dramatic rescue ... David Pollock, son of Cr and Mrs Pollock of Belgrave, featured in a ... ".* All this no doubt helped prompt several holiday makers from the hills area to call at the station in Alice Springs to say hello. Some were bus drivers, like Jack Graham, others were Sir Gilbert and Lady Chandler, before he was knighted, and was still the Minister for Agriculture in Victoria; the daughters of Jack and Mary Rae, Judith and Noelene, who I had seen grow up; former Borough of Wonthaggi town clerk Neil Simmonds and his wife; Miss Gibson, a pre-school teacher who caught the same bus as I on the way to school from South Belgrave; Mr and Mrs Ed. Eldleston who ran South Belgrave Timber and Hardware; Mr and Mrs Terry (their son Lister and I went to primary school together at Lysterfield) and Jack Eudey from the Emerald Football Club. Another day I was walking past the Ansett office when John Fleming of Wonthaggi, the Holden dealer I'd bought a car from back in 1965, his wife and family stepped out, just arrived from Melbourne for a few days visit. Then a message from Uncle Bill, Bill Pollock, my father's young brother, at the time assistant director general, industrial relations with the PMG's department. He was going to be in town as he made an official visit to the Territory.

It was great to be able to pick him up at the airport, then after booking him into his motel, take him to the Old Telegraph Station and a few of the town sights before we went to dinner at Bob and Sally Henfry's. He remarked that it had been the first private home he had been to in the fortnight since leaving Melbourne on his northern trip which had taken him to Port Moresby in Papua-New Guinea and Darwin. He went on to become managing director of Telecom before he retired.

As the force expanded and the pressures were increasing on training (all recruits now went back to Darwin for a refresher course before their confirmation of appointment) a three week non-commissioned officers course was initiated.

John Lincoln, a fellow Sergeant Third Class, and I, were selected from Alice Springs to join seven others in Darwin. We flew up on the Sunday afternoon Fokker Friendship flight – four and a half hours with stops at Tennant Creek and Katherine. Before we left Alice Springs I mentioned to one of the ground staff I knew that I wouldn't mind having a look up front during the flight if he could mention that to the Captain. I was just putting on my seat belt when one of the hostesses came to me and said the Captain would like to see me. He pulled up the "jump seat", a third seat between the captain and the first officer, strapped me in and off we went. After reaching our cruise level, usually about 14,500 feet, I went back to the main cabin for a meal, then rejoined him for the landing at Tennant Creek. It was a great experience.

John and I both stayed in the new police barracks, for both of us quite a contrast in conditions to when we first joined the force. It was more than four years since I'd last been to Darwin, so to see the changes around the city itself was quite something. The new barracks were a couple of years old now, all single rooms, with built-in wardrobe, sink, hot and cold running water and a small refrigerator in each room-but it was still down the passage to the shower. The rooms had overhead fans and were heavily louvred to either promote a breeze or protect from the wind and rain. Still, it was the middle of the dry season, so rain was unlikely. It was mild at night for a good sleep but the days soon ran into the mid 80'sF (29C), making it warm to be getting about.

The main accommodation block was three-storeys. I was on the ground floor. Adjoining the block was a games room and an air-conditioned lecture

Simpsons Gap near Alice Springs

room along with offices. These days, with so many married recruits, the barracks only filled during recruit training courses, so while we were there, it was pretty quiet about the place. Although comfortable for the short time I would have in Darwin, I found the room fairly small. In fact it was too small to store my personal effects, swag and equipment I had gathered together over the time I'd been in the force.

We started the course with an exam, a couple of hours of theory and practice. We were told the course would cover man-management, problem solving, some law review, drill and parades, crowd control, a tear gas exercise, prosecuting and other exercises a Sergeant Third Class could be expected to be involved with. I was happy with the effort I made with the exam, fourth or fifth and only 5-6 marks below the top. It was a bit of a shock for a couple of the chaps, particularly those who hadn't done any further study after passing their Sergeant Third Class exam.

One afternoon was spent on the rifle range, first some use of a few old revolvers that were standard issue, then we each had 60 rounds with an Army type SLR .308 rifle, first firing from 100 yards (metres), then 200 yards (metres), then run 100 yards (metres) and shoot from 100 yards (metres), then advance and as the target appeared for three seconds, get two shots away. It was the first time I'd used such a rifle and was pleased as Punch with my tally. I was not the best but by no means the worst shot either.

Then we had some fun with some tear gas, again a first for me using the tear gas gun and grenades. To finish the afternoon off, they lobbed a tear gas grenade in the butts of the rifle range, and we each had to walk through it. No wonder it breaks up a mob!

The week was cut short by a public holiday for Darwin Show Day which gave me the opportunity to compare it with the Alice Springs show. I remarked that the only thing bigger about the Darwin Show was the crowd,. There were perhaps a few more side-shows and with the resources of Darwin, the government exhibits were better but the few general exhibits left the large exhibition sheds pretty bare.

The weekend also passed quicker when I was asked to help as a drink waiter at the wedding reception of one of the Alice Springs policewomen, Helen Kingsford to a Crown Law Prosecutor, Alasdair McGregor. They had met in Alice Springs while Alasdair had been in town for Supreme Court matters. Regulations then only allowed single women to be members of the force, so Helen had to resign to marry, and move to settle in Darwin.

Alasdair married wearing the Rob Roy tartan kilt. His best man, Spencer Lee, a young local chap of Chinese descent, also wore a kilt. A pretty big bloke for a Chinese, he was the first I'd ever seen in a kilt, probably the first time many in Darwin had seen a Chinese in a kilt. The reception was held at the Darwin Freemason's Hall, utilising the outdoor garden areas well as the hall for about the 90 present, on a very pleasant dry-season evening.

The course moved along well, there was not a lot of home-work, but there were a couple of assignments, like planning a search, done outside course hours. The pressure came on during the last three days, first a three-hour exam on man-management, then on the Thursday morning, a four-hour law paper, and on the Friday six practical exercises. For me the first was a Crime Scene, where I and two constables went to the scene of a reported rape, had to gather and preserve evidence etc. The second was a room search – two rooms of the barracks were said to be a flat occupied by a "baddie" played by a Detective Sergeant First Class. You had to search it, find the stolen goods – jewellery – then question and arrest the offender.

Next I had to prosecute a case before a dumb Magistrate who didn't know his powers with a constable who had forgotten the important parts of his evidence and a defendant who said it was all lies. Then I had to conduct a record of interview, the caution and questioning of a suspect followed by the interrogation of a person, played by the Inspector Crime Division about his possession of a vehicle you know is reported stolen interstate, then later, write down the conversation and compare it to the recorded actual conversation. For the day, I "arrested" the Inspector and two Sergeants First Class.

The Inspector Crime was Len Cossons, who had been the station sergeant in Alice Springs before his promotion and transfer back to Darwin. In the evening I met him and his wife at the newsagency. He told her she was talking to the dux of the day's work. I said I wasn't so sure about that *"Well, I'm told you got the highest marks, I hope I'm right"* So did I although I didn't let on to him that I knew I'd scored 23/25 for the record of interview, that I was the top mark for prosecuting and second top mark for the interrogation.

We were never officially told the results of all the exams. In fact, it was more than a year later before a short summary of our performance was sent to the Divisional Inspector. Sergeant First Class A. A. Grant, known to all of us as "Saus" Grant, though where he got that nick name from I'd never know, made individual assessments of the course participants. His comments on me read:

Sergeant Pollock showed sincere interest in all aspects of the course. He was fairly active in class discussions and his knowledge of the law was above average.

Sergeant Pollock has sufficient self confidence and this was evident during the practical exercise phase of the course. This phase placed N.C.O.'s under considerable pressure and the Sergeant's results were very good.

Sergeant Pollock showed sound common sense when dealing with practical problems during course discussions. He was willing to accept advice and criticism, when his reason was occasionally astray.

Sergeant Pollock has sufficient strength of character and ability to be an effective N.C.O.

Central Mt Stuart, geographical centre of Australia, and my car NT 167

"Rowing Eights" at the Henley-on-Todd" regatta in the bed of the dry Todd River

CHAPTER 15

Tennant Creek ... a near second home

"Well, back in The Alice and glad to be so too. I don't care what they say about the Darwin 'dry season' weather, I don't like the place, the general atmosphere is so different to here ..." I wrote in my first note home from the NCO's course.

After three weeks away it was straight back into night shift but with four on the shift now, one in the cell block all the time, there was no longer the real need for the Sergeant to take his turn at fingerprinting. It was August and the weather, particularly at night, was still mild to cold, down to 40F (4C) but the station building was heated which made it even more attractive to stay near the switchboard. One thing that had happened while I was away was two of the patrol vans, each with more than 90,000 miles (145,000kms) on the clock, had been replaced, so there was also an incentive to go on a town patrol, in a nice new van!

I was a little restless and thinking of something new to occupy my spare time. When a chap who had been a correspondent for the *Australasian POST* was leaving town, I spoke with him with the thought of continuing in his footsteps, under a nom de plume. I got my own personal PO box, so my mail didn't get put on the station mail board, I wrote to Mum and asked if she would mind if I used grandpa's name, John Vogler, as my nom de plume. She didn't think he would have minded at all.

I started to put a few story lines together ... a Customs officer in Alice Springs, more than a thousand mile from a sea port ... the mad-cap Henley-on-Todd where people raced along the dry river sand in bottomless boats, sea battles in four wheel drive motorised "vessels" and a competition trophy made from part of a trunk of an original 1870's telegraph pole, a stunning piece of territory cypress pine. It was disappointing advice that the *POST* decided not to continue its Centralian stories, so that idea went by the wayside.

However, I went out to the Old Telegraph Station on 18 August, 1972, where they were celebrating the 100th anniversary of the linking of the Overland Telegraph, which had actually been joined at Ironstone Ponds, nearly 500 miles (800kms) north of Alice Springs, when a party working from the north and one from the south met and joined the line to transmit the first morse code messages from Adelaide through to Darwin.

I noticed there were no media people at the celebrations, so I went and got some black-and-white film, took a few shots and put it on the afternoon flight to the Melbourne *Sun*. They later rang me, we put the story together and my photo featured in the metropolitan edition of the next day's paper. Later, I was delighted to get a $30 cheque in the mail.

A month or so later, when a Qantas flight was en route from Sydney to Singapore, and the hijack alarm had been accidentally activated, causing all sorts of pandemonium, some thinking the flight might land in Alice Springs to take on extra fuel to allow it to over-fly Singapore, the *Sun* rang the station and asked for me personally in an effort to get the hot news. However, with a black-out on the story, I had to act quite dumb.

The annual Henley-on-Todd was a fun afternoon and had become a significant tourist drawcard for the town, in particular for school parties, with the event being deliberately programmed to fit into the late August-early September school holidays. This year there were more than 100 bus loads of tourists in town, every caravan park was booked out and, there was not a spare bed in town as 7,500 people turned out to participate or watch the events.

It was now organised by the two Rotary Clubs in Alice Springs, the Alice Springs club and the Stuart-Alice Springs club. As well as the bottomless boat events and the greasy pole, there was an egg throwing – and catching event. Yes people actually threw an egg some distance and someone at the other end caught it without it breaking, and no, it wasn't hard boiled. There were still the rowing events, the boats were propelled along sets of up-graded rails laid in the sand by shovel wielding rowers along with clowns and anything of a nautical flavour to make a fun afternoon. The climax of the afternoon was still a sea battle now between three vessels, propelled by four-wheel-drives, and armed with a multitude of flour bombs, fire extinguishers and other water propelling devices – a battle between Rotary, Apex and Lions, a battle to the end where one of the vessels was overpowered by the crews of the other two, usually when the loser ran out of 'ammunition'.

Another football season was coming to an end. It had been a successful year with good games, good "gates" but an on-going row with the council over the League's share of the gate.

It was tradition for the SANFL to provide an umpire for the Grand Final and this year it was to be Max O'Connell, not only well known for his Australian Rules umpiring but also as a Test cricket umpire. Between the League president and myself, we kept him occupied, even if I was on night shift again.

It was also normal for the League secretary to be paid an honorarium, generally $150, as a token payment for the work done during the year. It had been a "full-on" year with the 25th anniversary programme and the general season. Although I had not been paid a fee the previous year the League was keen to pay me the $150 this year. As it would show-up in the League's accounts, I though it best I do the right thing, and submitted a report seeking permission to accept the $150 honorarium. It took a few weeks, but finally word came back "permission refused". I thought it was a petty, mean decision. Then that was Commissioner McLaren.

There was a very human touch to work at times, too frequently surrounding tragedy. An elderly Leeton, NSW, man had died in the aerial medical plane on transfer from Tennant Creek to Alice Springs following a road accident near Tennant Creek. This meant a member of his family had to come to Alice Springs and attend to formalities. A son flew up, I had to meet him, take him to the hospital mortuary for a formal identification, gather information needed for the death file, meet the undertaker to make arrangements for the transport of the body home and so on. It was gratifying to receive a personal letter:

Dear Sergeant Pollock

On behalf of my Mother, sisters and myself I would like to say thank you for the many kindnesses and assistance given to my brother Michael during his recent sad journey to Alice Springs . . .

It was a thoughtful gesture and it was a letter I kept.

I was back in demand for caretaking, looking after a series of homes while members were on leave. Some had the phone connected which was a help if needed at the station, but the main task was really to keep the lawns and gardens alive, especially when the summer came in with a vengeance in early October sending the mercury up to 100F (37.8C)

I knew that in mid-November I'd be going back to Tennant Creek for another three months, including Christmas, so I took the opportunity of a quick trip home on a four day break after yet another night shift – they seemed to come around every fourth or fifth week At least they had to give us a three week break between night shifts, otherwise, I think some of us would have been working it every second or third week.

A late October visit to the folks allowed me to bring back some of the southern spring flowers, including a big bunch of waratahs, and a tray of lovely fresh Silvan strawberries. They were something to give friends and have the pleasure of myself – a break from routine. The introduction of daylight saving in southern states and not in the Territory disrupted flight times, mail closing times and radio broadcast times, particularly the ABC.

In some ways, I left Alice Springs for Tennant Creek a day too early. My move was advanced a day, to Wednesday 15 November, 1972, so I could spend a little time with the sergeant going on leave. There was court the following week, and a few committal matters which needed a good briefing to help me prosecute them.

The Divisional Inspector, Tim Tisdell, was on a station inspection to the north and as I drove from The Alice to Tennant Creek I expected to pass him. When I arrived at Wauchope and had a cuppa with Don and Joan Burgess, they remarked that the Inspector hadn't called by.

As I came within radio range of Tennant Creek, about 25 miles (40kms) out of town, I heard the ABC news, and immediately knew why – an Ansett-ANA Fokker Friendship had been hijacked on landing at Alice Springs. One of my colleagues, Paul Sandeman was in a serious condition having been shot at least twice and the hijacker was shot in a volley of fire when coaxed into a position where Paul had first tried to shoot him. My good friend Ossie Watt had volunteered to be the pilot of a light plane which was going to fly the armed hijacker out to the desert to allow him to parachute from the plane. The hijacker died shortly after being admitted to hospital.

It had been a very serious incident, and considering the training, the equipment and facilities the chaps had at their disposal, they had done a great job. The fact was, they had virtually no training for such an incident. It was the first hijack in Australia involving a firearm. The best weapons available to the members were their own personal firearms, whether they were small arms or high powered rifles, a point members had strongly made after the Papunya incident earlier in the year.

Fortunately for Paul Sandeman, the town's surgeon, Dr John Hawkins, a keen amateur newsreel man, was at the scene, abandoning his camera for the real need, medical assistance, after the shootings. Dr Hawkins had a great reputation, he was a dedicated man, not just to his profession but to the people of Central Australia, a doctor and surgeon who everyone had the utmost faith in.

Later in the evening, the Ansett-ANA flight continued on through Tennant Creek. I was called out to take statements from a couple of chaps who had been on the plane throughout the ordeal, one being Fred Charleston, who ran the roadside inn at Frewena, 100 miles (160kms) or so along the Barkly Highway, out of Tennant Creek. Fred had been a constant applicant for a pistol licence which the police had consistently opposed, with the Registrar of Firearms, the Police Commissioner, finally refusing his most recent application. Apart from a good description of events, Fred's account of things was constantly interrupted by his remark *"if you blokes had given me that permit (Permit to Purchase a Revolver) ... I would have been bringing it back from Adelaide ... I would have had it in my brief case ... I would have shot the bastard ... I'd have fixed him up!"* He probably would have blown up the whole plane!

The incident again inflamed relations between the Commissioner, the Police Association and the local members of the Legislative Council. It was the final catalyst in the call for an inquiry into the conduct of the force. The Police Association took the unprecedented step of flying an association representative, Sergeant Neil Plumb, to Alice Springs to speak with members to gain an association perspective of the incident including claims of poor communications between the town and the airport and the need for members to use their private arms, rifles, in the incident.

In a later debate in the Legislative Council the blame for the poor facilities was placed at the feet of the Commissioner, with claims he wasn't in touch with the members of the force, in particular, conditions in Central Australia. The attacks on the Commissioner were so intense that the Police Association came out in his defence, claiming that it wasn't the Commissioner who had failed to provide facilities for members, rather, it was the Northern Territory Administration which had failed to respond and fund the needs of the force which had been brought to its attention by the Commissioner.

There was some truth in both claims. Members outside the immediate "Top End" held a genuine resentment that senior officers like the Commissioner, Superintendent and Chief Inspector spent far too little time visiting the wider police network while at the same time, the funding for police appeared to be kept to the barest essentials.

The Legislative Council motion for an inquiry into the police force was carried. It was months later that Brigadier McKinna, a former Commissioner of the South Australia Police Force, was appointed to conduct the inquiry. It wasn't until the next July that Brigadier McKinna made a tour of stations and spoke with any member who wanted to put any point to him regarding the conduct of the force. I was at Tennant Creek again relieving when he made his visit. I was fortunate to have half-an-hour or so with him, discussing some of the issues I felt strongly about.

These included single members accommodation and facilities, the living conditions of the single members in barracks in the condition that the Alice Springs barracks had been for years, the lack of recreational facilities, the refusal of the Commissioner to provide a television set for use at the barracks while it had been noted six television sets had been provided for prisoners at the Alice Springs gaol. I recalled a visit to the barracks two years earlier by an Assistant Administrator, Alan O'Brien, now secretary of the Department of the Northern Territory who had suggested a pool table would be an excellent recreational facility for the barracks, but when an official application was made, it was refused *"no funds"*. I stressed it was difficult for an N.C.O. – a Sergeant Third Class like myself – to live in the conditions provided, not the least when there was a blanket ban on allowing members to caretake residences, to be absent from barracks overnight. It also made life a little difficult for junior single members to live in a common barracks with their immediate supervisory officer.

I also raised the issues on non-allowance of members' participation in public affairs (which had prevented me from standing for local government), not allowing members to accept an honorarium from community based organisations and the poor police-public relations.

I left the major issues of poor equipment, armoury, communications and the need to relieve police of extraneous duties such as motor registry (in 1971-72 more than $35,000 was collected at Tennant Creek police station for motor registry functions, with at least one man being diverted to that work every week day) to the Police Association itself although these points were backed up along the line.

It was early 1974 before the McKinna report saw the light of day. Apart from his recommendations on the force structure, equipment needs and administration frustrations, he placed much of the blame on the Northern Territory Administration pointing out it had failed to respond to requests and submissions by the Commissioner. To me a central feature was his focus on the poor living conditions for single officers. The Brigadier commented . . .*"Advertisements promise free accommodation in order to entice recruits into the Force and while housing is reasonable for married members, the single men are getting a raw deal"*. I was fully vindicated in what I'd been saying for years.

Equipment did improve, police numbers increased, there was soon civilian clerical assistance for typing reports, moves were made to move the motor registry out of stations like Tennant Creek and Katherine but we still had the policies of Commissioner McLaren.

George Simpson, who had been my shift sergeant when I first arrived in Alice Springs back in April, 1966, was now a Sergeant First Class and recently appointed officer-in-charge at Tennant Creek. George was a fine fellow but erratic, and a real worrier. Many found him difficult to work with, but he and I had a good rapport and worked together well. I helped to act as a bridge between him and most of the staff at the station, now 10 in all, and that worked too. A two-man station had been opened at Warrabri Settlement, about 100 miles (160kms) south of Tennant Creek and 13 miles (21kms) east of the highway. This added to the court list.

Despite the distraction of the hijack, I was well briefed for court which passed without incident. We no sooner finished court than we had our own airport emergency. The Department of Health aircraft, a twin engine DeHaviland Dove, radioed that the "wheels down and locked into position" light wasn't on. So with police, fire brigade, ambulance and doctor on hand we anxiously watched the plane coming in to land. It touched down safely. A later inspection showed a wire broken, probably hit by a stone on take-off from a gravel run-way on its medical rounds.

Tennant Creek was growing with increased mining activity, in particular the development of a new mine at Warrego, about 35 miles (55kms) to the north west, and the building of a first stage copper smelter at the site. There was a drive-in theatre about to open, but the thing I missed from Alice Springs was the commercial radio station. The ABC's Territory regional service provided school broadcasts, *"Blue Hills"*, endless talk programmes but little music and no local input. In the meantime, television came to Alice Springs, a station with the call-sign ABAD-7, or as it was quickly dubbed "A BAD seven". The programmes were all pre-recorded in Adelaide, flown to Alice Springs and shown a week later than in Adelaide, all except the news. It was the night before's news! Later, a live broadcast of a voice over a plain blue screen with just the words "ABC News" was introduced to give both National, Territory and local news. It wasn't until the late 1970's that live news broadcasts were introduced with the building of a micro-wave link through the Territory, first from Queensland to Darwin via Tennant Creek and then south to Alice Springs.

The big change was to come on Saturday, 2 December, 1972, when Gough Whitlam led the ALP to victory in the Federal election. Although the Territory seat stayed in the hands of Sam Calder, the Country Liberal Party candidate, nationally, the ALP's "It's Time" campaign had taken Labor across the line. There were changes ahead. One was the decision to dispense with Imperial honours, and thus an appropriate recognition for bravery from the Queen, which would have gone to officers like Paul Sandeman and Ossie Watt for their bravery in the Alice Springs airport hijack, was never made.

With the busy holiday season approaching it seemed right for the pilots to go on strike. If it wasn't the pilots at this time of year, it was the post office or the air hostesses. It really threw things out in the Territory. Mails were late, interstate newspapers would be off-loaded in favour of higher priority freight while children at interstate boarding schools either just got home or had to wait on a few days until services resumed, then battle to get a seat. In Tennant Creek school was coming to the end for the year. The boss had three children at the Tennant Creek Area School, which went through to Form 4 or Year 10, whichever way you liked to put it. I was invited along to the speech night, with about 1,000 of the town turning our for quite a function, a chance to be seen in a different light and out of uniform.

Christmas came along quietly, Mum and Dad were great in again organising half a dozen or so punnets of lovely fresh strawberries to be flown up. The week before Christmas I was able to get down to Alice Springs and see a few friends, do some shopping and get my presents away in nice time. I worked Christmas Day, which was on a Monday, making it quite a long weekend. We made few arrests, only "musts", and tried to extend that Christmas spirit. But there were always the odd one or three who could never take a hint. Perhaps they really wanted a bed over the holiday season.

We had a bad patch on the roads with two boys seven and 13 year old, from Mt Isa, being killed on the Barkly Highway, 120 miles (190kms) east of town, a few days before Christmas. We worked hard to get all the paper work complete to allow the bodies to be taken back to Mt Isa and buried on Christmas eve. Then a week later another out-of-town fatality took the chaps on duty away from the town area. Some local louts were quick to try to take advantage of the situation, causing a fight at one of the local hotels. Soon there were nearly 100 people involved. Three of us from barracks were called on to attend but by the time we reached the hotel, all the action was over, only a couple of drunks to be found. It sort of supported the adage, never hurry to a brawl, then by the time you reach it, it will have sorted itself out and there will only be the scraps to pick up.

One thing I became interested in was mineral specimens. Hunting around I was able to find a few; one containing bismuth, a rare mineral which I believe is used in medicines; one containing gold, copper and bismuth and a couple of others that just looked pretty. I got to know a trainee geologist, at the Geo-Peko mess, and he not only helped me identify a few of the specimens, but also collected a couple to add to the collection. For the rest of my stay in Tennant Creek on subsequent visits and around Alice Springs I continued to collect some nice mineral specimens. Although I've always thought of putting them in a display case, it was pointless in barracks, and subsequently, I never have.

One drawback about Tennant Creek was the weather. In really dry conditions, the weather was a few degrees hotter than in Alice Springs, up around the 104-108F (40-42C) mark. But with some humidity, the temperature dropped, it became very muggy and the evaporative-type air-conditioners performance fell right away. Then a cyclone in the Gulf of Carpentaria crossed on to land forming a substantial rain depression passing across the Territory, north of Tennant Creek, giving us several inches of rain along with thunderbolts that knocked out the power supply and caused general inconvenience. Roads to the north and east soon closed, with constant enquiry at the station as to conditions. Even to the south, rains cut the link disrupting supplies, in particular perishable supplies of milk, fuel and the like.

The town had for some years now had a good regular water supply, from a bore field discovered south of the town, so rain, as a water supply, was no longer as important. As rain water tanks rusted out, they were taken away and not replaced. The town electricity supply came from the Peko and Warrego mine sites, although a new substantial power house for the growing town was being built on the southern outskirts. Peko and Warrego would be needing their power supply for their own expanding operations, including a new Gecko mine to the north west of the town on the road to the Warrego mine.

It was rare for the weather to interfere with commercial aircraft movements, but just the morning I was called on duty to do the bullion escort from the bank to the southbound plane, rain and low cloud prevented it from landing. After three instrument approaches, the pilot was not low enough to see the ground, so running short of fuel, went on, the bullion returning to the bank.

Mid-February and I returned to Alice Springs, now counting the days to my leave. It would be a frustrating four weeks, not knowing if rain would disrupt the rail, whether or not I'd be able to get away on the day I booked, whether, at the last minute I would have to abandon plans to rail/drive home and fly instead. What I planned to do was drive home, then a week or so later drive north, visiting friends at Finley, NSW, then Toowoomba, Qld., before attending a wedding in Warwick, Qld., of barracks mate Reg Henshaw. Then I planned to visit Brisbane, pick up my brother, John, and drive him, his wife and daughter back to Melbourne before flying off for an eight-day trip to Singapore and Malaysia on the very first Qantas Jetabout tour.

In the end it all worked out perfectly. The train ran to time, the road from Marree was in good condition and I was home in three days. A week or so later I headed up to Finley and spent a night with Pat and Ron Gray, family friends since my childhood days at Lysterfield. It must have been 20 years or so since the first time I'd been, with Mum and Dad, to visit them at Finley. Over the years, before I joined the force, and each leave home since, I'd been up to see them and their family, catch up with a few stories, spend a night out at a work camp where they were constructing irrigation works or whatever. This time, it was just overnight before I went on reaching Moree and staying the night.

In the evening I went for a walk and passed the local police station, noticing the plaque on the wall showed the building ... *"officially opened by Hon. Roger B. Nott ... 26 September, 1959"* ... a former local Member of Parliament, who later became the Administrator of the Northern Territory. As I read the plaque, one of the officers on duty came out, I guess inquisitive as to who was snooping around. We spoke, I introduced myself, and was immediately invited inside . . . *"We'll take you for a patrol down to our aboriginal camp ... "*. First we did a short patrol of the business district of the town, then headed for the aboriginal village. Not halfway there we caught up with a slow moving, wandering vehicle . . . *"Pull over driver!"* The officers spoke with him, then arrested him for driving under the influence of liquor, took him back to the station, charged him, put him in the cells and attended to formalities.

We headed for the aboriginal village a second time with a repeat performance, just a different driver! So we gave away the idea of a tour of the aboriginal village, I walked back to my motel and slept. The next night I spent in Toowoomba catching up with Glenn Beutel, the young trainee geologist I'd got to know in Tennant Creek before going on to Warwick, Brisbane and back to Melbourne.

At Ellery Gorge

The train trip back to The Alice was probably the best I experienced, only 40 minutes late. Dean and Pat Newman were at the station to meet me, with the keys of a house I was to caretake for the next three weeks, the home of a local insurance agent. As one member at barracks was quick to remark, *"you have moved into the private sector now"*.

The football season was with us again, Dean had done most of the early work, but there was the match day work to be done, which made it a long day – near eight hours at the football followed by an evening shift of eight hours. Still, I enjoyed it. It was May again and the Bangtail Muster. The tourists were starting to arrive for another busy season, the establishment at the station had further increased although the number of sergeants was still much the same.

There was always some variety in work, like the 90 minute visit to the town of the Crown Prince and Princess of Japan. They arrived at the airport, drove into town, up to Anzac Hill, spent a few minutes looking over the town, then drove back to the airport – 14 cars plus a bus in the convoy, the bus needed for the Japanese press team accompanying the tour. In true Japanese custom there was a supply of gifts for many who had assisted in the visit. As a traffic control sector commander I received a smart silver tie bar with chain with a gold rising sun mounted on the bar.

I continued to have visitors, Charlie Leggett, who had the Emerald dairy when my folks were in retail milk; Reg Butterworth and his wife, Reg was president of the Belgrave football club when I left Belgrave to come to the Territory in 1966, he was the one who wrote me a formal letter from the club wishing me all the best. Reg, a senior technician with Telecom, was about to return to Indonesia for six months on an Australian aid project, having already spent some time there in recent years in an earlier stage of the project. Another football connection, Dick Fenton, a farmer from Narre Warren North, supporter of the South Belgrave-Kalora Park football club when I was the under 16's boundary umpire 20 years ago, called. One of the difficulties about living in barracks was there was nowhere to take a visitor have a cuppa, sit down have a talk, but frequently, they were on a tight schedule, just wanted to say hello, and be able to go home to Mum and Dad and say *"we saw David in Alice Springs, he's well"*. That pleased them no end too. Uncle Bill was also passing through town, had half an hour at the airport on a flight through to Darwin, and rang to let me know, so it was good to get to see him too.

Then there was the routine work – a disturbance at one of the hotels – three aboriginal women fighting. By the time we arrived, they had most of their clothes ripped off, but still were in fine voice and prepared to struggle every inch of the way to the police van. Struggling women were a lot more difficult to arrest, to handle, and frequently were more violent resisting arrest than the men. This time one of the three managed to kick me, at least bare-footed, just above the groin, but still painful enough. Still, I had the last laugh, three hours overtime for court next morning, and she had three months imprisonment to think about it.

I was also quite pleased with another "clear-up" when four local louts decided to trash one of the hotel toilets – about $150-$200 damage, which was quite significant at the time. I was on a foot patrol and attended the complaint, then through someone I knew, I was given a solid tip-off. Within the hour we had the four suspects at the station for questioning. Only one of them, a part coloured guy, admitted anything while his three mates, all local and fairly well respected, denied all knowledge and went on their way. However, next morning I was able to get a little more information, passed it on to CIB, who went out, picked up the three and arrested them. On reflection, I believe I only got the original tip-off and the later information because of a special trust I had developed with people in the general community through my participation in local community affairs, like the football league.

This community contact was also not lost on life assurance companies who were on the lookout for local representatives, so in some ways, it should not have been a surprise to be approached by one of them to leave the force and join up. CML had a training programme as they called it, to let me continue to work in my job, but learn the ropes of life assurance, even build up a commission bank, before making the final move. It all sounded very attractive and at first I decided to at least follow through the initial stages of the programme. However, in the long run I decided not to pursue the offer.

Unseasonal heavy June rains, up to four inches in some places (nearly half the year's average) not only cooled the weather down but made it wet and muddy underfoot, a contrast to the normal dusty conditions. Fortunately, much of the rain was light soaking rain, so the run-off was not too dramatic. When the Todd River finally "came down" it only closed the causeway for a few hours. It was one of the rare occasions where football in Alice

Gold pour, Peko Mine, Tennant Creek

Springs was played in the rain. It made the Traeger Park surface perfect, no mud, but nice and soft for the football boot studs to give grip rather than bang against the normal dry hard surface.

At least the rains passed before the Alice Springs Show, letting most cattle exhibitors get their livestock to Traeger Park. The show also brought a lot of out-of-town visitors and provided the police with the most hectic weekend we had experienced – 56 arrests Thursday night, 112 on Show Day and another 50 on the Saturday. There were 201 for breakfast on the Sunday morning!

The arrests brought an immediate reaction from police headquarters in Darwin with the Superintendent being despatched to investigate why. In many ways, it was seen as an "after the horse had bolted" exercise, only undertaken because of the Legislative Council initiated inquiry into the police force.

It was off to Tennant Creek again for another six to eight weeks, but this time the barracks there were full. There was consternation as to where I would stay, especially when I said I was not interested in staying at one of the hotels. At the time there was no motel. I made the suggestion that the department approach the Geo-Peko Mess, a couple of hundred yards from the police complex, to see if they had a spare room. I knew they accommodated single teachers there. *"Yes, we will certainly be happy to have him here"* the mess manager told the boss when he rang to inquire.

I ended up with a room equal to or better than at barracks with meals provided in the all-up cost of $45 a fortnight. The Inspector was a little confused as to who was going to pay, but in the finish it was all quite simple; for the first 21 days I received $14.75 a day travelling allowance ($206.50) and would pay the cost. After 21 days, the department would pay the cost and I would get $1.50 a week travelling allowance.

The first day I was on duty at Tennant Creek I worked an evening shift. I was able to coincide my meal break with the mess meal time. As I walked in, in full uniform, there was a sudden silence, the mess manager rose from his seat and announced *"Chaps, Sergeant Pollock is going to be staying here with us at the mess for the next six weeks or so".* I'm sure I heard a couple of forks hit the crockery!

Apart from a couple of school teachers, the mess was a collection of 30 or more geologists, drillers and their off-siders. In recent months there had hardly been a weekend pass without one or more of the wilder natured characters of the mess ending up arrested down-town. Just as the mess manager was beginning to wonder how he could counter the problem, he received the phone call inquiring if they could accommodate me. This accounted for his immediate positive response. It worked. While I was there, and on a subsequent occasion, no one from the mess stepped out of line, not one ended up arrested drunk, disorderly or even cautioned.

One of the chaps at the mess was with the Australian National University which operated a seismic station about 25 miles (40kms) south-east of Tennant Creek, recording earthquakes, atomic blasts and the like. They needed to visit the station every day, the weekend visits being just a short trip to check everything was operating and note any activity. I went along one Sunday morning for the ride and he showed me over the station, all quite interesting and a local activity people only became aware of when news reports carried a story of a localised earth tremor or an atomic blast recorded at the station.

The Picnic Day weekend in Tennant Creek was time for the Goldrush Festival. It started seven years earlier to raise money to build a public swimming pool, now well established. The new fund-raising project was for a civic hall, estimated to cost $200,000. The Government promised $165,000 if the local community raised $35,000. On the first day of the appeal Peko Mines donated $5,000, and by the end of the festival they had near $17,000 in the kitty, a great effort for a district community of less than 4,000.

I wasn't a golfer, I still believe the game ruins a good walk, but over the long weekend it was the tradition to conduct the Northern Territory golf championships. This year they were held at the Tennant Creek course, complete with its sand 'greens', the same as in Alice Springs but some contrast to the lush Darwin or Katherine greens. I knew many of the good contingent of golfers from Alice Springs who had travelled up for the weekend so spent a bit of time at the course, and at the socials in the evening, taking a few photos which in turn I sent down to the Alice Springs paper, along with a report on the championship. It all helped break an otherwise quiet time around town.

I was also able to take a few photos one morning at the Peko gold pour – they poured about \$250,000-\$300,000 worth of gold the morning I was there. Using a metal die and a large hammer, I was also given the opportunity to actually number stamp some of the bars but was disappointed when they didn't give out any free samples!

The bridge over the Finke River south of Alice Springs was opened in1970. In 1972 water nearly topped the official opening monument; in 1974 it washed it away

CHAPTER 16

The last patrol

As much as I liked working in Tennant Creek, and didn't mind living there either, I was always happy to be back in Alice Springs. It had become my Territory home. It was nearly seven-and-a-half years since I had come to the town to work. In that time the town had more than doubled in population and its facilities had improved significantly. I knew the people and practically every nook and cranny of the town area along with a great deal of the surrounding district and its people, whether they were on cattle stations, tourist locations, missions or government aboriginal settlements.

The weather in early September, at least by day, was always a lot warmer than the winter months of only weeks before. We were back in summer uniform, at least for day shift, usually from the first Monday in September although it might be a fortnight later before night shift changed over. Even then the tunic coat was kept handy.

Coming back in the middle of a roster at least kept me away from night shift for a few more days, but it didn't stop the quick change overs, when working a 5pm-1am shift one day and starting again at 9am the next day. Thankfully, the Determination provided at least an eight hour break between shifts.

I worked a Friday evening and was in deep sleep at 6am when woken for a full alert at the airport. An air traffic controller up on the north west coast of Australia, Broome or Derby had walked out into his back yard for a 'call of nature' and heard, at high altitude, an aircraft moving south east, an aircraft he didn't believe should have been in that air space. He alerted authorities who feared that the plane could have been hijacked. Speculation was rife. One theory was that the plane was tracking for Alice Springs where in the morning darkness it could land, roll out a couple of armed personnel type vehicles, slip into town, take over the communications facilities, the police station, and hold the town to ransom. After all, there were no military personnel as such in Alice Springs, not even Army Reserves.

We were quickly armed, and raced to the airport. I was some sight, my gas mask, a tear gas launcher and a drum of tear gas grenades. There was no further sign of the aircraft and after a couple of hours, the alert was called off. As I drove back into town, I thought just how defenceless, how powerless we would have been to have combated any attack of the type speculated. I also thought just how feasible it would be; a couple of plane loads of equipment and personnel landing in the night, the town would be 'taken' while it slept. There was never any official explanation about the original sighting or of reports that an aircraft had been seen to approach Alice Springs and turn away. I think people liked to think of it as a bad dream.

The camel race held a couple of years earlier as part of the Alice Springs centenary celebrations had been adopted by the local Lions Club as a major fund raiser day with the establishment of the Camel Cup, a series of camel races on a course around part of Traeger Park oval. The main problem was that the low perimeter fence could hardly keep a racing camel within the confines of the oval, causing some near-misses with spectators, riders and camels alike. However, the uniqueness of the day drew thousands to the oval to watch, the day ending in a spectacular fireworks display, a rare event in The Centre. The camels certainly did nothing to help Traeger Park be fit for the Australian Rules football preliminary final the next day, but we managed.

Night shift as ever was just around the corner. Working the first week of a roster on night shift meant that I then had only three days to work in the next seven. So with a little organising, having the four off in a row after night shift, and working the Monday evening shift, it allowed me to make a flying trip back to Melbourne. The fact the trip coincided with the VFL Grand Final was in part coincidental, but I took full advantage of it.

The earlier rain and the warm spring conditions had the country side looking a picture. The lupin like maroonish red coloured 'wild hops' covered the whole side of the MacDonnell Ranges. Combined with the green grasses and other wild flowers pushing through, they made the place a picture. There was another resurgence of rabbits with some of the fellows at barracks, keen on a shot, going out a few miles (kilometres) and getting a feed of 'underground mutton'.

Prince Philip, Duke of Edinburgh, was making a visit to Central Australia with part of his visit being a two-night outdoor camp described as a bird watching expedition. The location of the camp was secret according to media reports. The Prince had developed a friendship with Tom Hare, executive officer of the Northern Territory Reserves Board. Tom himself was a keen naturalist and at his East Side home had aviaries with many rare and endangered species which were a focal point of many VIP visits to his home.

Constable Reg Henshaw and I were sent to Ellery's Hole, or as I knew it, Ellery Gorge, 60 miles (100km) west of Alice Springs, to establish a security post on the southern, general access, side of the gorge. The Prince and his party used another Gap, a little to the east of Ellery, to cross to the northern side of a range, and thus the northern side of the water filled Ellery Gorge, then moved on a few more miles to their camp site. The Divisional Inspector, his clerk, Constable Mike Jenkinson, and four army guys were also on the northern side of the gorge.

When we arrived at the gorge at about 4pm on the Saturday, there were the normal weekend campers at the very popular spot. We set up camp in a nice shady spot, not imposing on the campers already set up for the night, but where we could comfortably stay the couple of nights we would be there. We had our own (borrowed) BBQ stand and I had my small gas stove and gas lamp. When the Commissioner arrived, accompanied by Superintendent Hamilton of the Commonwealth Police, it really gave the game away to the civilian campers. You could hear the comments, *"we know where the Prince is"*. They had something to tell everyone when they went back to town next afternoon.

The gorge had a lot of water in it, perhaps more than a year or so earlier when I'd spent a couple of days at the spot in the search for a lad who had drowned in the chill water, protected from the sun by the ranges and the trees. It wasn't the most spectacular gorge of the area but it was a pleasant backdrop for a couple of days work, just keeping an eye open to see that nobody tried to cross the water into the area north of the gorge. There wasn't much to do other than write a couple of letters, read the papers and have a talk with the people camping at the gorge. After all, Reg and I knew most of them.

Mike Jenkinson, the Inspector's Clerk, was a little more adventurous. He had a float and paddled across to us to let us know what was happening on the camp side of the gorge – nothing! We had been told to be as inconspicuous as possible, so wore only casual clothes on Sunday. Then on Monday, when we again expected the Commissioner to visit us, we got back into uniform. We took the opportunity to take a few photos of each other, in uniform, at the gorge; Reg with his dog which he had brought along. Then after lunch, the Commissioner arrived, gave us our final instructions before he headed off to meet the party leaving the area. We followed the party back to town. It was really a working holiday, camped by a waterhole, about the 80F mark (26C), the nights down to about 55F (12.5C), good food, a good campfire and the swag. That was how life in the outback should be!

Things at the station were fairly routine, that is until a chap came to the counter and complained he had bought a snake which was said to be perfectly healthy and pregnant. He had now discovered it was neither and wanted to make a complaint that he'd been a victim of false pretence in the sale of the snake. I showed him the door but wrote up the complaint in the complaints and enquires journal just in case he returned and wanted to take the matter further. He didn't return, but next day when the media made its rounds for news, someone told the ABC the story. Next it was national news. Still, we didn't make any new enquiry; someone out there was sold a dud snake, I was just pleased he hadn't brought the snake to the station, dead or alive.

Through the Northern Territory ABC network news we also frequently heard of the violent electrical storms around Darwin, after all, the newsroom was in Darwin and I am sure some working there thought the Territory ended at the Berrimah cross roads, 12 miles (20kms) south of the city. In The Alice we could get heavy rain, but a fierce storm, and hail, was rare. However, it had to happen. For some days the weather had been building up, the temperatures rising with some humidity about. Then, just on dusk on a November afternoon a terrific electrical and hail storm ran along the MacDonnell Range and across town. In less than 10 minutes it caused hundreds of thousands of dollars damage, unroofed seven or eight blocks of flats, blew over many trees, including a tree in the yard of the barracks, a limb falling across the roof. This popped out the window of my room and hail belted in. Some was near the size of eggs, the largest I'd ever seen, in fact larger than anyone could remember. I ended up with several dents in my car bonnet from the hail; others driving around town sustained a lot more damage.

The whole town was blacked out with power not being restored to some areas for several hours. We were fortunate at the barracks, borrowing the Traffic Section emergency power unit, which they had to use at accident scenes. It was several days before the street lighting was restored.

About 15 of us were called on duty to sort out problems around the town. With no electricity for lighting, two of the hotels closed but the third stayed open until I told the licensee to close or I'd get a Justice of the Peace down and close him up. Everybody was in the dark, many half-drunk, some sitting in the street outside the hotel, drinking, throwing cans onto the road in front of Electricity Supply Unit and police cars. Apart from this irresponsible group, the rest of the town hopped in to help each other, all in a state of shock at the ferocity of the storm.

For us at barracks, the disappointment was that the tree didn't sufficiently damage the building to have it condemned. A team of workmen turned up, repaired a few struts in the roof, laid some new corrugated iron, fixed the windows and everything was "as new" again, as old as the building was.

I continued to receive, and accept, offers of house caretaking but with other sergeants on leave, it put added pressure on the roster, especially for those of us in a supervisory role. Our shifts sometimes meant we would work seven evening shifts straight, a day off, a day on a day off and then seven nights straight on night shift – working 15 out of 17 days, not to mention the call-outs for court that invariably followed evening shifts. But I never complained about overtime.

The storm in early November was a fore-runner to what was not only a hot and humid summer but also a very wet one. Before the end of November we had an evening of solid rain which brought the Todd River down closing the causeway for much of a day. Fortunately, it didn't rain before Christmas, so the train wasn't disrupted, all our supplies arrived for the festive season. Then the days after Christmas were very hot which could mean only one thing – thunderstorms, and sure enough they arrived, with solid rain, particularly on the northern side of the MacDonnell Range and in the catchment of the Charles and Todd Rivers (the Charles joining the Todd on the northern outskirts of the town). The Todd was flowing so strongly, and to such a height, that on the advice of engineers, we even closed the footbridge across the river. It was the first time I had seen that happen. Continuing wet periods over the first few months of 1974 saw the river ran continuously for the longest period on record – about eight months. Admittedly sometimes there was little more than a trickle across the main causeway and it would soak into the sand before it even reached The Gap, but there was still water across the road at the main causeway.

The new year arrived fairly quietly, the damp weather having a sobering effect on new year revellers. Uppermost in my thoughts was that there was only another fortnight's work before I went on leave again. In the past year, the Determination had again changed, and in addition to a nice pay rise (mind you we needed it to keep up with the Whitlam-Crean-Cairns induced inflation) we also were granted an additional week's leave from 1 January the previous year. So I had eight weeks leave to look forward to, rather than the six I had been planning on.

I arrived back in the middle of a power shortage. There was no street lighting, no power for air conditioning, hot water services, or display lighting with only two lights a house permitted plus power totally disconnected to some zones for two or four hours a day. Fuel supplies for the power generators had dwindled to a very low level but the ESU had been able to keep a minimal supply of power going until the first train in 9-10 weeks, carrying fuel, arrived in town a day or so after my return.

I was only in Alice Springs a couple of days before being sent off to Tennant Creek again. I had half expected the move so had decided I'd step down as secretary of the football league, remaining on the committee as the public officer, a statutory position for an incorporated association as the league was.

In Tennant Creek the power situation was even worse with the whole town losing power between 9am-11am, 2pm-4.30pm and 6.30pm-8pm. There were the same restrictions on air conditioning, lights in a house and the street lighting was off. While the road from Alice Springs to Tennant Creek was open, there were a number of causeways where water was still running across the road. However, the road on to Darwin was closed to all traffic at Threeways, with up to 8 feet (2.1m) of water over the road at the Newcastle Waters causeway, for a distance of a mile (1.6km) or more.

While I was the only member in the barracks, the first night I arrived there were actually 18 people – four police families – billeted at the barracks, unable to return to Darwin from leave because of the road closure. They had been at Elliott for up to a fortnight waiting for the waters across the highway to go down, but there was no immediate sign of movement. It just kept on raining. One family had been "on the road" for two months. However, the department finally showed compassion and put them all on a flight out of Tennant Creek, leaving their cars and vans in the yard at the police complex.

The police had to man a 24-hour road block on the highway at Threeways, 15 miles (24kms) north of Tennant Creek, at the junction of the Barkly Highway, to ensure traffic didn't attempt to travel north. Most of this duty was done on overtime, made comfortable by being able to sit in a big, new air conditioned Shell roadhouse (they had their own emergency power) with a good view of any traffic that might approach. People knew the road was closed and on the several shifts that I worked at the road block, nobody tried to pass illegally. Sitting inside, particularly at night, also kept the mosquitos at bay. They were really bad after all the rains, to the degree that the Health Department was fogging the town at night to keep them under some control.

In the first fortnight I was in Tennant Creek, between road-block duty, call-outs during the night and court, I had more than 40 hours overtime.

With the trains starting to run again from Port Augusta to Alice Springs, supplies were finally getting through. Fuel arrived to relieve the power situation, as well as replenish food supplies. The shelves of the supermarkets were getting pretty bare. It was down to only marmalade or fig jam, no perishable stocks, apart from a little air-freighted in. The Ghan train's timetable was so disrupted by the slow travel on the flood-affected sections the railways had a unique way of getting around the problem – they adjusted the timetable so that the train *"will not run late any more"*. Sometimes you wondered if we would be better going back to the camels.

It was only a fortnight or so before further rain in the southern part of the Territory and northern South Australia put the train out of action for another 10 days, so there was no fresh milk over Easter, although supplies to Tennant Creek, with the opening of roads east, were now being arranged from Townsville.

For Easter I was sent off to Renner Springs for the annual race meeting, driving up the 100 miles (160kms) on Good Friday and home Tuesday morning. The officers from Elliott and Anthony Lagoon were also there. Once again, the roadside inn provided us with one of the cabins for accommodation and "office". There were the usual races on the Saturday and Monday, the rodeo, parachuting and a fishing contest, held in the big lagoons between the roadhouse and the racecourse, on the Sunday and a dance each night, a ball the final evening.

It was a quiet weekend except during the rodeo a young fellow was seriously hurt during the buckjumping. Helped by St John Ambulance people, he was taken to a light plane, from one of the cattle stations attending the races, and flown to Tennant Creek in 30 minutes rather than the two-hours plus journey by road. The road trip would be slow because of the many wash-aways, detours and even water still across the road in a dozen places. Sadly, he died during the night.

The buckjumping was very spectacular, the horses were big and bucked the best I'd ever seen. The bullock riding was equally spectacular. Of course, the animals were in prime condition after several weeks of great seasonal conditions. The horses would be little short of brumbies, rounded up for the occasion.

I was still the only one in barracks, so the call outs continued. One was from Threeways where an off-duty officer, Paul McKeiver and his wife were having an evening out when a couple of fellows, urged on by a mate, decided to do a strip and walk naked, ("streaked") along the bar. He took offence and decided to arrest them. Then their mate stepped in and assaulted him. He called for assistance. I took a van out, Paul and I had quite a struggle to get two of them into the van. We brought them back to the station, booked them in, then went back out and rounded up the third fellow.

On the Monday morning they faced court – Ian Tuxworth JP and Bob Boys JP on the Bench. The trio pleaded guilty to all charges and ended up fined a total of $467. To add to their indignity, the Justices refused them time to pay, so we escorted them to their rooms at the mine, collected their bank passbooks and had the fines paid before they returned to the mine to find themselves out of a job. They left town on the next day's plane.

It was only a month later that I was assaulted again ... this time I was off duty, up the main street, talking to people I knew when a young fellow walked out of the hotel and started to urinate on the footpath. When I identified myself and suggested he stop, go back to the hotel toilet, he just gave me a half-smart look and continued to urinate. So I arrested him on the standard charge of offensive behaviour. He stacked on quite a turn and I ended up a little the worse for wear before assistance arrived. My nice new hand knitted jumper was torn at a seam, I had a blood nose, a black eye and a couple of bruises but had the last laugh – three hours overtime at court next morning. His need to spend a penny cost him $200, including $100 for assaulting me.

All the work at Tennant Creek wasn't just around drunks at the pub or someone causing trouble arising from too much to drink or a noisy dog. The town had its occasional break-enter-and-steal or burglary but with some intense enquiry, contacts, and the help of police trackers, we had a pretty good 'clear-up' rate. It was surprising how often people would leave their employment at one of the mines, do a "job" in town and then try to do a runner from the Territory. The six-hour plus drive to the border, with a police station virtually on the border pulled up many trying to reach the haven of Queensland. They knew that it was unlikely we would try to extradite them back to the Territory. What they didn't know was that, as inoffensive an image the police force might have had, we had a great network, a great team of fellows with real bush initiatives that brought many an offender unstuck.

It wasn't always robbery, frequently it surrounded valueless cheques or it might be someone wanted interstate who got the feeling we were closing in on him.

The Territory force was made up of a great number of "boys from the bush", country born and bred guys, who had that special knack. This combined with the deep thinking city chaps, helped form that team making it hard for many a criminal to get past. One thing about Chief Inspector Bowie, when he was recruiting, was that he was prepared to take on the chap who might not fit in to a State force, but had the initiative that would make him a good Northern Territory officer. A classic case I always recall was Terry O'Brien, an ex-NSW prison officer, recruited from a forestry prison. Terry had a middle finger missing from one hand and in all probability wouldn't have been considered for recruitment by a State force. He was a great worker, great police officer, whether in uniform or in plain clothes, for the Territory. The disappointments in recruitment tended to be those recruited while members of other State forces ... *"back in Victoria we did it ... ."* some, too many, could not acknowledge they were no longer in Victoria, they were in the Territory, where things were different.

One of the last call-outs during my stay at barracks came with a near simultaneous report of a hit-run accident and a stolen vehicle. It still surprises me how some people can't see how police immediately see through these reports, and with a few inquiries find that the car was never stolen, the owner was the actual driver in the accident, who dumps the car and then reports it stolen. It just makes a lot of extra work, and ends up lightening the pocket just that much more. In this case the young fellow ended up fined $200 for dangerous driving, $50 for failing to stop after an accident, $100 for making a false report to police and walking for the next two years.

In the finish, I was looking forward to going back to Alice Springs, especially when the Divisional Inspector told me I could return to Alice Springs on the Queen's Birthday Saturday and have the Sunday off to attend the Alice Springs-Mt Isa football match before getting back into stride. I should have known this was too good to be true. Not only at the last minute was I sent back to Alice Springs on the Friday, I was then sent back 175 miles (280kms) to Barrow Creek for their annual race meeting,

Nobles Nob open cut mine, Tennant Creek

The Devils Marbles

again races on the Saturday and Monday with a gymkhana on the Sunday. Officers from Harts Range and Ti Tree were there for the weekend too while the chaps at Warrabri also visited during the day, so there wasn't a shortage of police. I am convinced I was sent there because the boss knew that as a non-drinker, I would be sober 24 hours a day; if there was an incident, there would be a senior police officer there able to make rational decisions. Not that the chaps attending drank on duty; we were all considered off-duty in the evening and some of the chaps did enjoy a drink or two, it was hard to resist the "shout" of a few local station people who you helped during the year; this was their annual get-together.

Again at Barrow Creek, accommodation and meals were provided at the hotel, although I had to sleep in my swag on the back verandah. With a dance at the hotel and a band playing to 2.15am, there wasn't a lot of sleep, perhaps a penalty for being sober!

While I had thought it rough being assaulted a couple of times during my last stay at Tennant Creek, one of my barracks mates, Col. Hardman, also originally from the Belgrave Heights, (he had gone to school with my brother, I had gone to high school at Upwey with his sister), was out at a new station established at Yuendumu. He came to town for court having been assaulted five times over the weekend and his off-sider at the station three times. At one stage they had been held at gunpoint, by a fellow with a .22 rifle, which they didn't know was unloaded. It was a frightening experience.

The culprit was sentenced to only a month's imprisonment.

While there was an occasional fight in a local hotel back bar, they were uncommon in the working class bars of the hotels. It was quite a shock when a Friday evening incident at the Hotel Alice Springs public bar turned into a stabbing, the victim, Eric Erlandson, being a virtual innocent bystander, stabbed with a broken glass and dying before be could be taken to hospital.

Eric was captain of one of the local cricket clubs, a former A grade footballer and now coached a reserve grade football team. He had a wife and nine children. He was not a bad sort of bloke and liked his drop of beer with the boys after work. I didn't know him well, but through my connections with football and other interests in town I was asked to attend a meeting called to set up an appeal for his family. First I was asked to be chairman or secretary but ended up as treasurer of the appeal committee.

Over the next few weeks we raised more than $5,000 and helped his wife and children re-establish themselves, although the loss of her husband, and father, could never be remedied.

The disappointment of not being allowed to stand for the Alice Springs Town Council elections three years ago still rankled with me. Although I had been deeply involved with the Australian Rules football scene in the time in between, on the surface, I had kept clear of politics, although a couple of months earlier, at Tennant Creek, I had spent a couple of hours at the Peko polling booth handing our how-to-vote tickets for the Country-Liberal candidate at the Federal election, where out of uniform, I wasn't recognised.

A promise of the returned Whitlam Labor government was to give the Territory a fully elected Legislative Assembly, to replace the present part-elected Legislative Council, so when the boundaries for the new 19 elec-torates were announced, my interest in politics was also renewed.

In the Central Australia area, where there had been two seats in the Legislative Council, one town based and one rural based, there were now going to be four Legislative Assembly seats, two town based and two rural based. One of the rural based seats, named as Macdonnell, was the area vir-tually east and west of Alice Springs to the Queensland and Western Australia borders and south to the South Australia border, a district of more than 100,000 square miles (260,000sq. kms), bigger than Victoria. It includ-ed the farm area just outside The Gap at Alice Springs, Ayers Rock, and all the cattle stations in the Finke and Kulgera police districts I had worked at back in 1968-69. The Santa Teresa Catholic Mission, the Lutheran Finke River Mission at Hermannsburg, and the government aboriginal settlements at Jay Creek, Areyonga, Haasts Bluff, Papunya and Docker River also fell in the electorate. It was a vast area but was only the third largest electorate in the Territory. The other Alice Springs based rural electorate incorporated the Racecourse residential area to the north of the town and the Yuendumu aboriginal community and an area east and west to the state borders and north to where it met the Barkly or Victoria River electorates.

Bernie Kilgariff, who presently represented Alice Springs in the Legislative Council announced he would be seeking Country Liberal Party (CLP) endorsement for the Assembly Alice Springs electorate while Tony Greatorex, the current President of the Legislative Council, and represent-ing Stuart, the rural electorate, announced he would be retiring. When the

CLP advertised for people interested in gaining pre-selection, I began to make a few enquiries. I formally joined the party and in turn attended the local branch meeting called to consider endorsements.

In the finish there were four interested in the four seats – Bernie Kilgariff wanted endorsement for Alice Springs, an automatic decision. Roger Vale, the secretary of the local branch of the party, was seeking endorsement for Stuart while Jim Robertson, a local law clerk, was keen on endorsement for the town electorate of Gillen, where he lived. That left me with Macdonnell.

The electorate had a population of 2,500-3,000, with less than 1,500 on the electoral role. The majority of electors were aboriginal but I believed, having worked virtually all the area over my years based in Alice Springs, I could attract sufficient of their vote to gain election.

My agreement to accept endorsement was conditional that my eligibility to return to the force, if I failed to be elected, was guaranteed. I was employed as a Northern Territory public servant – only the police, prisons and fire brigade were employed under this Ordinance, the rest of the Territory's public servants employed under the Commonwealth Public Service Act.

Bernie Kilgariff undertook to have that issue clarified, asking a Question during the last sitting of the Legislative Council. I also approached the Divisional Inspector and told him what was happening and sought his assurances on the issue. The situation was that I couldn't nominate while a servant of the Crown. I had to resign, then if unsuccessful at the election, under the provisions of the Public Service Ordinance, I would have the right to return to the force as if nothing had happened. The Ordinance was quite clear as far as the Legislative Council was concerned but the change to a Legislative Assembly left a doubt in some minds. However, when the questions were asked, the government made it clear, any public servant, Territory or Commonwealth, who resigned to stand for election, would be protected.

The final endorsement, and announcement, came on 20 August, 1974. I was in Tennant Creek for a couple of days for court matters left over from the last time I'd relieved which made it difficult to gauge reactions. My endorsement took most people, including those I worked with, by surprise.

After the announcement that the election would be held on Saturday, 19 October, 1974, I formally gave notice of my resignation to be effective at the close of business, Friday, 20 September, got my nomination together and lodged it on the Monday after my resignation took effect. Nominations closed on Friday, 27 September. In the finish there were three candidates – Malcolm Wolf, originally endorsed by the ALP but then deciding to stand as an Independent, and a late ALP endorsement, a part aboriginal, Bruce Breadon.

It was a hectic three weeks to the poll with few of the media and even party officials, not giving me much of a chance. But on election night it was clear I had won, and with the counting of postal and other votes later in the week, I was elected the first Member for Macdonnell with an absolute majority.

The Country Liberal Party won 17 of the 19 Assembly seats, the remaining two going to Independents, one too stubborn to join the CLP, the other to the left, some saying so far that she was out of sight. The ALP was deeply scarred, following on results in Queensland, the ALP left with only 11 members, the ACT Legislative Assembly left in the hands of conservative forces and even the Broken Hill Barrier Labor Council being defeated in local government elections.

———✦———

I had moved out of barracks just before I resigned, to caretake another officer's house. However, I didn't clean out my room or hand in my accoutrements and warrant card until after the election.

As the Assembly settled into its work, I was elected to the first Territory Executive as the Executive Member for Social Affairs and so began a new adventure. The week or so before Christmas I was invited to the police Christmas party at the barracks. As the fellows stood around having a drink and a bite to eat, Sergeant First Class Gary Burgdorf, now in charge at Alice Springs, who I had relieved as a Constable at Larrimah and as a Sergeant Third Class at Tennant Creek stepped forward and called the gathering to order. He called me forward too. After a few appreciated words made on behalf of the members at the station, he presented me with a green alabaster base and pen with a small Northern Territory police badge mounted on one corner.

It has sat on my work desk every day since as a constant reminder of the adventure Douglas Lockwood spoke of in that article I had read years before; of the men and women of both the force and the Territory I worked with, but above all, the eight-and-a-half years I spent outback in uniform.